D0096762

Contents

PART I: THE ENVIRONMENT

PART II: THE LIBRARY MEDIA PROGRAM

List of Figures

Preface

The American Association of School Librarian's (AASL) approval and publication of *Standards for the 21st Century Learner* necessitated a revision of this guide and textbook for school library media specialists to reflect the substantial changes in national standards for information literacy instruction at the K–12 level.

These new standards offer dimensions of information literacy far beyond those of previous national guidelines. AASL's 1998 standards for information literacy emphasized student competencies in the information search process. While *Standards for the 21st Century Learner* continues to define competencies (i.e., skills and understandings), these new standards emphasize additionally dispositions of the learner along with a delineation of responsibilities in working with information and self-assessment strategies. These additional dimensions acknowledge the complexity of information literacy.

For example, students accomplish nothing if they learn skills but lack the curiosity to apply those skills to gain new information. Similarly, by adding emphasis to self-assessment, these new standards emphasize the importance of learners becoming independent, self-reliant information seekers who can determine for themselves their success or shortcomings in information work. These added dimensions call for an environment that examines information literacy in a more holistic way—looking at real-world application of the competencies. AASL's new standards demand that we consider not only what we teach in information literacy but also the context within which such instruction is situated and the context within which these competencies will be applied.

Creating opportunities for authentic inquiry—students posing their own questions generated by their curiosity—is a challenge raised by these new standards. For too long, student inquiry has been an externalized process, but these new standards present the prospect for supporting students' ownership of their inquiry as we pay attention to not only their competence but also their dispositions, their responsibilities, and their self-assessment.

This revised second edition of *Enhancing Teaching and Learning: A Leadership Guide for School Library Media Specialists* has been updated to incorporate the new standards. Its overall purpose—to help school library media professionals effect change in their program by integrating it into the school's overall instructional plan—remains unchanged. Leadership requires a delicate balance between being simultaneously proactive and responsive. On the one hand, the library media professional has an agenda for developing information literacy, advocating for reading, and facilitating effective uses of information technologies. Advancement of this agenda demands leadership. On the other hand, this agenda can only be effectively accomplished when it is integrated into the curriculum, and such integration requires collaboration between the library media professional and the teaching staff. The result of the interaction between the library media program and the other components of the students' school experience is synergy—the effect is greater than the sum of the parts. When the library media program is integrated with curriculum and involved with parents and the community each of these interactions serves to increase its impact on students. However, when the parts work in isolation, the potential for their effectiveness is diminished.

All professions are inclined to become "egocentric." In medicine, the family physician sees his or her role as central to patient care, while the surgeon sees himself or herself taking the lead in case decisions. In education, a school administrator is often perceived as the pivotal instructional leader of the school. Language arts and reading teachers are often seen as central to student success because reading and writing are essential for success in all curricular areas. The school library media program is easily perceived as central to education because of its relationship with all curricular areas and all grade levels in the school, its association with school administration, and its ties to the community. Yet, it is important to maintain respect for the expertise of classroom teachers, the position of school administrators, and the beliefs and values of the community at large. Striking the balance between collaboration and leadership is a key to successful implementation of an effective library media program. My hope is that *Enhancing Teaching and Learning: A Leadership Guide for School Library Media Specialists,* Second Edition Revised, helps you find the appropriate balance. Finding that middle point means that the library media program is at once affected by and affects its surroundings.

During my 13 years as a district-level library media and technology coordinator, I observed a variety of implementations of the fundamental principles of effective school librarianship. No two schools in that district had identical library media programs, yet each was effective in meeting local needs. There is not just one right way to carry out a successful library media program. Certainly the library media profession has nonnegotiable elements: there must be an information literacy curriculum, teachers and library media specialists must collaborate to integrate information literacy into the curriculum, there must be support for a collection of resources that meets the needs of students and teachers, facilities must accommodate a variety of simultaneous activities, and students must have access to the resources of the library media center. The library media specialist must advocate for these principles. Yet the implementation of these principles in any given school must be adapted to suit the local school culture; what works in a multiage, continuous-progress setting may not fit a more traditional school, and within parameters certain adaptations must be made. Where to draw the line of acceptability is the key decision for library media professionals.

The revised second edition of *Enhancing Teaching and Learning* reflects changes—professional, theoretical, legal, and political—in the library media field and in education. As you read, you will encounter coverage that explores the new standards, the impact of No Child Left Behind legislation, the substantial influence of the Web, the educational needs of millennials (those born since 1983), changing reading habits, and more. Each chapter offers a scenario for discussion, which will help you and your colleagues explore the complexity of schools and schooling. Finally, statistics and data have been updated to reflect current trends and findings.

This book is divided into two parts: Part I, "The Environment," addresses the components of the school environment—the students, the curriculum and instruction, the principal, the school district, and the community. I devote a separate chapter to each of these five components in order to show how the library media program can interact with these elements to enhance learning. In the first chapter, "Students," questions to be considered include: What conditions of students' lives affect their learning? How does the library media specialist's role in working with children differ from that of the teacher? What motivates students to be learners? Chapter 2, "Curriculum and Instruction," considers how these aspects of education are changing and how the library media program can help improve learning. Chapter 3, "The Principal," offers insight into the work of school leaders and strategies for working effectively with school administrators. Beyond the school itself is the school district, which influences many decisions within the school and is discussed in Chapter 4, "The School District." Chapter 5, "The Community," focuses on the school's external relationships with the community of parents, other service agencies, and local business.

Part II, "The Library Media Program," provides specific tactics for establishing the library media program as an active player in teaching and learning. Chapter 6, "Collaborative Planning," proposes planning with teachers for instruction as one way the library media specialist can become a part of instruction. Because scheduling is a mechanism for organizing the library media program within the school day, Chapter 7, "Scheduling Library Media Activities," presents various models and their benefits. Chapter 8, "Collection," discusses the development and maintenance of materials with an emphasis on their relationship to curriculum. Chapter 9, "Literacy," explains both aliteracy and illiteracy and answers important questions, including what the role of the library media program is in reducing both. Chapter 10, "Technology," looks at the place of technology in the library media program and its pervasive role in the school. The information literacy curriculum is addressed in Chapter 11. Chapter 12, "Assessment of Student Work," addresses instructional assessment, with particular attention paid to evaluating students' development of information literacy. In addition, this chapter offers a discussion of testing and its relationship to the library media program. Chapter 13, "Program Evaluation," emphasizes data collection and analysis in the school library media program. Finally, Chapter 14, "Leadership," focuses attention on the unique role of the library media specialist who leads from the middle and uses influence more than power to assert the perspectives of the library media profession into the greater school context.

Each chapter ends with two features. First, a list of suggested action strategies related to three program elements: Learning and Teaching, Information Access, and Program Management. These strategies are intended to help apply principles and concepts of the chapter. The second is a scenario for discussion, which will help you and your colleagues explore the complexity of schools and schooling.

I wrote *Enhancing Teaching and Learning: A Leadership Guide for School Library Media Specialists*, Second Edition Revised, to help library media specialists implement their programs collaboratively. In addition, I urge you to use this material in your discussions with administrators, parents, board members, and other interest groups and school leaders. Our role in the education of children remains as important and challenging as ever.

Acknowledgments

This book grew out of years of experience and study, both of which were influenced and aided by several people. Two important mentors for me have been David Loertscher and Al Azinger. David gave me a vision for school library media programs and Al taught me how to lead. The library media specialists in the Iowa City Community School District invested energy and talent to bring that vision to life in schools where they have made important differences in teaching and learning.

This project required that someone believe that I had something to offer the profession. Virginia Mathews was persistent in her encouragement and advice as I wrote the first edition. June Gross brainstormed with me, read versions of chapters, and gave me advice. She helped ensure that each edition of the book reflected excellence in school library media practice. Jennifer Sprague created the index. Dean Dennis Damon Moore gave me the gift of time. Charles Harmon supported the work beginning to end. My family tolerated the imposition on their time for me to complete this work. Finally, I appreciate Ann Carlson Weeks who read this edition to help ensure that it represents current issues for the profession.

In this book is a quotation from Robert Reich: "Rarely do Big Ideas emerge any longer from the solitary labor of genius." This book, like all other work I have done in my life, is the product of collaboration with others. The synergy that comes from many people sharing ideas and working together is what produced this book, and that is its topic as well.

PART I:

The Environment

Chapter 1

Students

This chapter:

- describes conditions of youth attending American schools and how those conditions affect their learning
- discusses the ever-growing demands for meeting the needs of students with special needs
- describes the nature of motivation and its effect on learning
- relates the library media program to the needs of students
- identifies action strategies for working with students

Denise: ambitious . . . hard-working . . . hoping to become an engineer . . . eager to please her teachers . . .
Jana: pretty . . . popular . . . chatty . . . wants to be liked . . .
Kate: angry . . . outspoken . . . hostile . . .
Michael: quiet . . . shy . . . tense . . . anxious . . .
John: bright . . . inquisitive . . . success-oriented . . .
Peter . . . Tom . . . Angelique . . . Joel . . . Manuel . . . Kerri . . . Andrew . . .

A chapter about students is an appropriate beginning for a book about the library media program. While the library media center has many constituencies—teachers, parents, and the community at large—its primary goal is to help students become effective users of information. To accomplish this goal, the library media program must be sensitive to young people's cognitive and affective needs.

The relationship between adults and youth can be fragile. Power and authority, levels of self-confidence, and implied and explicit expectations complicate the relationship. An adult's unintended cue can direct a less-than-confident student away from the library media center. Young people's assumptions about authority figures or their desire for independence can prevent them from seeking help. Many students see the library media specialist as different from the teacher—sometimes less threatening. However, some may find the library media specialist more intimidating because they have relatively few interactions. Each interaction with a student determines whether that student will want to return to the library media center. The situation is analogous to an encounter with a salesperson in a retail store in which the quality of interaction will determine whether the customer will return. Effective "customer relations" requires understanding and appreciating the nature of the customer. This chapter focuses on the most important library media program "customers"—the students.

Students entering school library media centers seek help and resources for a variety of reasons, and each student brings a different degree of confidence. Typically, students arrive hoping that they will find what they need and have access to friendly, knowledgeable, and sincere help. The library media specialist is in a unique position for building relationships with students. Teachers set expectations for student performance. Library media specialists help students meet those expectations. Library media specialists enjoy a special partnership with students. Those students who feel disenfranchised from the school culture may benefit particularly from the special nature of that relationship. The library media specialist shares the goal of getting the assignment done or finding the answer as compared to the teacher's role of giving the assignment or asking the question. The library media specialist has a special opportunity to facilitate learning.

CONDITIONS OF AMERICAN YOUTH

The conditions of American young people vary dramatically. In affluent families, children have their own computers, cell phones, PDAs, and other devices. Other students have none of these resources. In each school, considering students' economic and family conditions is a first step toward being responsive to their needs. It is also helpful to understand the conditions of young people in the nation; this knowledge helps educators relate the condition of local youth to others. Schools tend to be insular, but in many situations, students are transient.

In 2006, the American federal poverty level for a family of four was $20,650 according to the National Center for Children in Poverty (www.nccp.org) (Chau, Douglas-Hall, and Koball 2006). Based on that figure, 17 percent of American children lived in impoverished families in 2007, and 39 percent of American children lived in low-income families; the National Center for Children in Poverty defines low-income families as those in which the parents earn less than double the federal poverty level, which is $41,300. National Center for Education Statistics (www.nces.ed.gov) *Fast Facts* reports a 2005 high school dropout rate of 9.4 percent nationally; however, these rates vary significantly by racial group—6 percent for whites, 10.4 percent for blacks, and 22.4 percent for Hispanics (National Center for Education Statistics 2007b). These data reveal that poverty and racial factors create significant differences in degrees of success among students. While library media specialists, like all educators, have concerns about young people, some of these realities extend beyond the library media program. Still, library media specialists can be factors in encouraging a student to stay in school. For example, the library media center may be a refuge for a student with a special interest in technology who is otherwise unmotivated in school. Sometimes, a media center can be a haven for someone who feels socially alienated elsewhere in the school.

Fast Facts from the National Center for Education Statistics (NCES) reports that 11 percent of students in public schools were receiving English language learning (ELL) services in 2003–2004 (National Center for Education Statistics 2007b). Immigrant children newly arriving in the United States do not all face the same issues. Some face language barriers, some face poverty, and others are affected emotionally or psychologically by their life experiences. For a large proportion of them, English language acquisition is an immediate challenge. Their potential to acquire English language skills depends on a variety of factors, such as age, length of time in this country, socioeconomic status, parental education, and residence location (Rong and Preissle 1998). Some of these students arrive here having been firsthand witnesses to horrors of war and inhumanity; these children's learning challenges are intensified by the emotional complications their experiences may have created. Some have left family behind and may no longer have an adequate social network to support them. These added emotional and social circumstances make even more difficult their attempts to learn a new language and learn in a new language. The library media specialist again may be in a particularly strong position to offer consolation and support to these students. Studies suggest that literacy in the native language enhances language learning (Goldenberg 1990; Hudelson 1987). Maintaining literacy in native languages has implications for library media center collections.

Data in the *NCES Condition of Education* indicate that students with disabilities represented 13.8 percent of public school enrollment in 2005–2006 (NCES, 2007a). The landmark Individuals with Disabilities Education Act (IDEA) Amendments of 1997 stipulates that students with disabilities are entitled to participation and progress within the general education curriculum (Yell and Shriner, 1997). A renewed emphasis on individual learners emerges from IDEA initiatives. With this comes a call for alternative media for both accessing information and communicating information (Hitchcock, Meyer, Rose, and Jackson 2002). These alternatives create an essential role for library media specialists to provide resources and to recommend and teach a variety of communication tools (for example, KidPix, Keynote or PowerPoint, Inspiration) and to make available assistive software and hardware for improving visual or auditory access to information. Physical access is an important consideration in the library media center. Examples include work stations and space between shelving ranges that accommodate wheelchairs, adjustments of screen displays to accommodate visual needs, and provision of audiobooks. School library media specialists can help special needs students become more confident and independent by helping them develop skills in accessing information in the library media center. Cooperation with public libraries provides an opportunity to acquaint these students with a resource that will be valuable to them beyond their school years (Murray 2000).

The library media program can improve access and help increase opportunities for learning by considering level of difficulty and ethnic representation in collection development, by teaching information skills, and by responding to the impact of out-of-school influences.

IMPROVING ACCESS

In 2005, 40 percent of children in kindergarten through eighth grade participated in nonparental after-school care arrangements; half of these were school- or center-based programs (National Center for Education Statistics 2005). The same NCES data set indicates that the amount of time students spent in such programs in 2005 averaged 7.5 hours per week. The library media center ought to be accessible to children whenever they are at the school. This may require library media specialists to give up some control of the facility. Providing some training to after-school program staff and having them operate the center before and after school can extend access if library staff contracts would otherwise limit access. If there is no existing before- and after-school program, the library media specialist might advocate extending the library media center hours to accommodate children who have essentially no safe place to go after school (U.S. Department of Education and U.S. Department of Justice 2000).

While it is tempting to say, "But that is not my responsibility," there is a need for a safe and productive way for children to use the hours from the end of the school day until the time when parents come home from work. Library media center resources offer opportunities for making those hours safe and productive. Collaboration with other community agencies, especially the public library, may pave the way for homework help or arts activities in the library media center as well. The library media center can no longer be seen as a facility that operates for children only from 8:30 a.m. to 3:00 p.m. and then withdraws concern for their learning. Many library media specialists make resources available after school. NCES data from 2003 indicated that 68 percent of students use computers at home (National Center for Education Statistics 2006). This leaves more than 30 percent of student still dependent on school computers—a factor to be carefully considered in establishing hours of access for students, especially before and after school.

School library media centers need to forge close alliances with local public libraries. Bringing public library staff to school library media facilities for "rush hours" may be one creative solution, or adjusting the work hours of school library media staff to include early morning, late afternoon, or early evening hours may be solutions. Neighborhood centers or other facilities where students can do homework also offer means to provide access to information resources with the cooperation of the school library media program. Cooperative grant seeking may be a path to added resources to meet these needs.

The needs of secondary school students call for careful policymaking for both school hours and after-school hours. Extended hours increase access for some secondary school students. However, according to the Bureau of Labor Statistics, 31.4 percent of high school students were working during the 2006 school year (Bureau of Labor Statistics 2007). Open access to the library media center during the school day may be the only opportunity for these students since their jobs may fill their after-school hours. After-school time is also heavily booked for students involved in extracurricular activities—music, drama, and athletics, for example.

Access to the library media center is a two-way concern. While the library media center must have an open-access policy, teachers must also have a policy of open access, that is, they must allow students to leave their classrooms and their study halls to go to the library media center. Although it is common for high school teachers to allow students some time in class to work on assignments, it is sometimes difficult for students to move to the library media center to access resources they might need. Concerns for safety and orderliness in the halls and accountability for students' whereabouts can conflict with providing school-day open access. Solutions to that conflict require the systemic thinking of teachers, administrators, and the library media specialist. Library media specialists encourage school policies that facilitate open access. As secondary schools investigate block scheduling or initiatives to expand the length of class periods, eliminate study halls, and make other modifications in the schedule, library media specialists must be alert and assertive in protecting student access to the library media center.

Block scheduling has an impact on access for secondary students. Block scheduling involves stretching the length of classes to 90 minutes or longer each day, and reducing the number of classes meeting each day. This longer block of time can increase access, as teachers organize the longer time period into several activities, one of which may be accessing the library media center (Baker and Turner 1996). Schools have reported a major increase in library media center use with block scheduling (Galt 1996). Using the block-scheduled class time, students who may not previously have had access to the library media center have access when time is booked for their classes.

Access to the library media center is one way to help alleviate concerns about equity among students in terms of use of computers. A study titled *Internet and American Life* (Madden 2003) indicates that Internet adoption has increased in all demographic groups, but there are still pronounced gaps in Internet use along several demographic lines. Minorities, especially non-English-speaking, are less connected than whites; those with modest income and less education are less wired than those with college educations; and rural Americans lag behind suburban and urban Americans in the online population (Madden 2003). These differences in access at home underscore the role of the school—and especially the school library media center—as a force for equity.

The advantage students enjoy when they have access to a computer at home is evident to all teachers who collect homework and who observe students' level of sophistication in using electronic information resources. In an information-based environment—and that is what school is—skill in using the computer as an information and communication tool is highly advantageous.

MILLENNIALS

The students populating high schools today are members of the generation dubbed "Millennials" by Neil Howe and William Strauss (2000). These authors have been profiling generations for a couple of decades, and the portrayal of the Millennials is one of optimism and great promise. This generation has benefited from careful attentiveness by their parents. According to Howe and Strauss, seven in ten parents of elementary school students consider it "extremely important" for them to get their kids to do their homework, and four in ten have spoken to their kids' teachers more than five times during the school year (p. 147). Attributes like confident, sheltered, pressured, achieving, and team-oriented fit the profile of the Millennials. One indicator of the high-achieving characteristic of this generation is their high school course selection:

> Compared to Gen Xers in the late '80s, today's Millennials seniors are nearly three times as likely to take calculus, twice as likely to take all three major sciences (biology, chemistry, physics) and are taking twice as many Advanced Placement tests. (p. 164)

In a 2001 interview, Strauss described Millennials as "very serious students relative to what came before." He goes on to state:

> They are used to competing against their peers, even to the point of stress. They will appreciate being challenged and not look at that as a burden. They will want to get something out of college as a lifelong experience more than a cash value element. . . . They will listen when faculties tell them that we need to have a core curriculum because this is something that develops you into a fuller person. . . .

They tend to take more of the long view, which reflects their optimism. (Lowery 2001, p. 9)

Howe and Strauss (2000) portray this as a generation that trusts authority more than recent generations. If this characterization is accurate, the
value of libraries and information literacy should not be a difficult "sell."
Library media specialists may find that this generation of students will
exhibit interest in developing lifelong learning skills that will help them
succeed. Their academic ambition is likely to bring them to the library
media center. It will be important to adopt positive assumptions about
these students and create programming that feeds their academic appe-
tites—book discussions, book talks, guest speakers (including authors),
and opportunities for problem solving come to mind as possibilities that
may suit this age group.

COLLECTION DEVELOPMENT TO MEET STUDENT NEEDS

Some clearly identifiable conditions call for consideration in collection
development. The percentage of children of immigrants in school systems across the country rose from 6.3 percent in 1970 to nearly 20 percent in 1997 (Ruiz de Velasco and Fix 2000). Not surprisingly, the growth
in immigrant populations in schools has been accompanied by a rise in
the size of the limited-English-proficiency population in schools to an
estimated 5 percent of the total student population (Ruiz de Velasco and
Fix 2000). While political climates change, and the current wave suggests interest in establishing English as the language of the nation, schools
continue to have children arriving at their doors speaking Spanish, Chinese, Japanese, Vietnamese, Russian, and a score of other languages.
Still, the majority of these students are Spanish-speaking (Ruiz de Velasco
and Fix 2000). Providing materials that help these children develop their
skills in English is an important contribution of the library media program. Also important is providing materials in formats and styles that
facilitate English-as-a-second-language students' learning content across
all curricular areas. Marketing the library media center to these students
is a critical part of advocacy. Electronic resources that offer voice as well
as text may be particularly helpful to their language development.
    The need for materials that fit the cognitive and affective realities of
students is keen. Materials that include not only text but also graphics,
charts, and tables are essential for conveying information. Some stu-

dents may need electronic resources with sound and motion to augment textual information. According to the *Nation's Report Card*, nearly 33 percent of fourth graders and 26 percent of eighth graders scored below the basic level on the 2007 NAEP reading test (National Center for Education Statistics 2007c). This measurement underscores the need for materials at various levels of difficulty. Attention to readability of materials may be especially important at the middle school and high school levels.

Materials also need to show sensitivity to students' lives. In 2006, about 67 percent of American children lived with two parents according to the federal government's child statistics (www.childstats.gov). According to those same data, approximately 28 percent of all U.S. children lived with only one parent in 2006. Children from single-parent families often have added stresses related to family conflict and the disruption and deprivations associated with living with a single parent (Federal Interagency Forum on Child and Family Statistics 2007).

In the final analysis it is difficult to generalize about the young people attending school in the United States today. The diversity may be greater than ever in terms of income, access to information, language and literacy, home and family culture, and aspirations. That very diversity suggests that the library media program may be more important than ever for schools trying to meet the range of challenges that this generation of young people face.

MEDIA INFLUENCE

The societal concern about the "information age" has stimulated renewed interest in the library media curriculum; increasingly, there is respect for the importance of developing skills in accessing, interpreting, and evaluating information. Information literacy is taking its place in school curricula in the company of problem solving, critical thinking, and decision making.

The Internet opens today's students to a range of experiences that includes such activities as online games, participation in social networks like MySpace or Facebook, online chats, virtual worlds, YouTube, and other Web-based applications. The research is nascent in determining the effects that time spent in these environments has on performance in school. Speculation might center on questions like the following:

- What activities are displaced by the time spent in online games, virtual worlds, and social networks? Does the trade-off favorably or unfavorably affect academic performance?
- What is the prevalence of Internet addiction and how does it affect other activities—social and academic—in the lives of addicts?
- Does the instant feedback of synchronous activities on the Web affect students' patience or persistence in research work?
- How are communication patterns and skills—especially writing— affected by the prominence of chat, e-mail, and other informal communication modes?
- What are the effects of virtual worlds and online interactive games on problem-solving skills and habits?
- What are the social impacts of extended time spent online?

These and other questions arise and will require careful consideration for their effects on students' engagement in the school learning environment. How schools adapt and ask students to adapt will require extended discussion. Library media specialists are in the heat of such discussions as they provide Internet access and observe students in the less structured environment of the library media center.

Some research is emerging, particularly related to online gaming. Engagement in games that feature aggression does appear to lead to increased aggression in individuals, and academic achievement may be negatively related to overall time spent playing video games (Anderson and Dill 2000).

Another pervasive source of information and entertainment is television. According to a study conducted by Knowledge Networks/SRI, 61 percent of children have a television in their bedrooms (Yin 2004). Young people spend an average of 6.5 hours per day with all media, including computers, video games, radio, and CD players (Roberts, Foehr, Rideout, and Brodie 1999). In at least two ways, time spent with potentially intellectually "empty" media can be detrimental: it is time not spent doing something more intellectual (like reading), and the content within these media may involve violence or misinformation or content that may be inherently detrimental. In a review of the research on the relationship between television viewing and academic achievement over a 25-year period, Thompson and Austin (2003) surmised that:

- Moderate levels of viewing are better than high levels or no viewing at all.

- The type of programming is more critical than the intrinsic qualities of the medium itself, i.e., informational versus noninformational.
- High informational viewing generally correlates positively with achievement, while low informational viewing correlates negatively.
- Once IQ, SES, and other mediating factors are accounted for, the relationship between television viewing and academic achievement weakens.
- It is not clear at this time whether negative television viewing causes or is caused by low levels of achievement.

The crux of the issue may be what programming children watch and how it is used to advance learning. Television has valuable programming to offer. Concerns are often raised about how inappropriate televised material affects young people. Heintz (1994) described an interesting study of teenagers having "massive" exposure (three hours per night for five consecutive nights) to prime-time, sexually oriented programming. Such viewing was found to influence the moral judgment of 13- and 14-year-olds. Specifically, the teens who had been exposed to such programming in the experiment rated a series of sexual indiscretions and improprieties as "less bad" and described the victim as "less wronged" than did teens who had not seen the programs (Heintz 1994). The power of the medium is evident, but it needs to be channeled into productive uses, especially for youthful audiences. Overall, research findings indicate a positive correlation between television violence and aggressive behavior (Smith 1996).

While parents can use television for teaching, research clearly indicates that few parents involve themselves in their children's consumption of media. A 1999 study found that 49 percent of families have no rules about television use and that parents of children ages 8 to 18 were watching television with their kids only 5 percent of their viewing time (Roberts, Foehr, Rideout and Brodie 1999). Similarly, Warren (2003) found that parents of young children—ages one to five—were less likely to co-view television programming with this young age group than with older children at ages when children may most need the cognitive assistance adult co-viewers could provide in distinguishing fact and fantasy and in deciphering television's symbol systems (e.g., scene transitions, distinguishing programming from commercials, etc.). Warren asserts that adult mediation can guide children's attention to relevant information and enhance higher cognition such as understanding story structure. An apparent lack of parental intervention signals the need for schools to develop students' skills as critical, thoughtful consumers of television. Advocacy for media literacy curricula is evident in such organizations as the Center for Media Literacy (www.medialit.org), a nonprofit educational organization that provides leadership, public education, professional development, and educational resources to support media literacy education as a framework for accessing, analyzing, evaluating, and creating media content. In most communities, instruction for media literacy exists only due to the energy and initiative of a single teacher, not because of a coordinated, community-wide programmatic plan of implementation. Library media specialists can be advocates for media literacy education. Developing critical viewing skills is parallel to developing critical reading skills; in this media age, such skills need to be taught with equal or greater emphasis. Examples of outcomes of media literacy curricula might include increasing knowledge of the strategies used in advertising, raising awareness of the ways that violence is shown in the media, or raising consciousness of the portrayal of women and/or people of color (Scharrar 2002). These potential outcomes reinforce the critical thinking of the information literacy curriculum.

In summary, many environmental conditions affect students. Educators cannot simply throw up their hands in dismay and say, "I can't fix all that is wrong with society." Granted, the library media center cannot resolve all the difficulties in young people's lives, but some actions may improve students' opportunities to succeed. The hard task is determining what can be done within the school to address equity, attention, or involvement in learning. Advocacy and sensitivity are dispositions for an effective school library media specialist to create a student-friendly environment, acquire materials that match students' needs and interests, and attempt to increase opportunities for all students. Many factors have significant influence on students' disposition toward school and learning. They intensify the need for educators to focus attention on motivating students to want to be learners. Understanding theory of motivation in the context of the lives of today's students is exceedingly important in creating in all students a readiness to learn.

MOTIVATION FOR LEARNING

Motivation Theory

Recent work in motivation has focused on the teacher as a caring classroom leader. This line of research has particular relevance for the library media program in which creating a caring environment can cause students to want to avail themselves of the offerings of the center and to take advantage of the human resources available to them there. Wentzel (2002) examined student motivation in relation to teacher caregiving. Of the dimensions of caregiving she studied, high expectations with adequate support seemed to produce increased academic motivation and negative, harsh feedback reduced motivation. Wentzel (2002) also asserts the positive effect on student motivation of modeling interest in academic pursuits; modeling curiosity comes naturally to the library media specialist. Similarly, Stipek (2006) has researched relationships between teachers and students and found that students actually function more effectively when they feel respected and valued. She asserts, "the key to raising achievement is connecting students with teachers who support them not just as learners, but also as people" (Stipek 2006, p. 47). She suggests that supportive environments encourage students to take risks that lead to increased learning—undertaking more challenging problems, persisting with difficult problems, and asking questions. Willis (2007) summarized findings from brain research as it relates to student learning; she emphasized in particular the affective aspects and summarized by stating that it is essential to find the right balance of activity that promotes moderate challenge and stimulates students' authentic curiosity. These studies of the affective dimensions of motivation offer opportunities for library media specialists. Developing supportive relationships with students should be easy when library media programs are aimed at helping students succeed. Also, library media centers offer opportunities for nurturing young people's interests "not just as learners, but also as people." Attention to the ways in which affective dimensions can increase motivation to learn will enhance the relationship between students and the library media program—and can have a favorable effect on student motivation to learn.

A classic work in motivation is Maslow's (1971) hierarchy. He theorized that human needs fall into a hierarchy and that the higher needs arise only after lower needs have been met. At the lowest level are physical and organizational needs, that is, the basic needs for security and survival. Above these basic needs are social needs, the need for esteem and for a sense of belonging. As social needs are met, intellectual needs, such as the need for knowledge and understanding, emerge. Above these are the aesthetic needs met by the appreciation for life's order, beauty, and balance. At the top of Maslow's hierarchy is self-actualization. He described the self-actualized person as one motivated by needs to be open, to love others and self, to act ethically, and to express autonomy and curiosity.

Students need approval, affiliation, and achievement. Some students are approval-dependent; they conform because they need the assurance from others that their performance is at an acceptable standard. Other students have less need for approval and are motivated by their own need for achievement or affiliation. A corollary to the achievement need is the need to avoid failure. Motive will affect the risks one is willing to take; for example, often students who are driven by a fear of failure will be less willing to take risks, to try new strategies or tasks. Similarly, students high in the need for affiliation perform in ways that they perceive to be respected by their peers.

Individuals who generally attribute their successes and failures to their own behavior are said to have an internal locus of control, while those who generally attribute their success and failure to luck, task difficulty, or some action of others are said to have an external locus of control. Self-concept as a learner also appears to affect a student's achievement motivation. The student with an internal locus of control for success and a positive self-concept as a learner ("I can succeed because I have the ability and I can exert the effort") has a better chance for high achievement than the student with an external locus of control ("I can't succeed because the teacher doesn't like me").

In his contentious book *A Nation of Victims: The Decay of the American Character* Charles Sykes (1992) posits that as a society we have adopted a stance of externalizing control, making martyrs of ourselves, and accepting no responsibility for any of our culture's social, political, or economic woes. If his perspective on culture is accurate, a larger societal milieu is challenging schools as they try to help students see that they are responsible for their own achievement.

Motivation Strategies

Intrinsic motivation refers to the perception that one engages in an activity because it is rewarding. Extrinsic motivation, on the other hand, is the perception that one engages in an activity for some external reward. The research literature contains more than 100 studies that conclude that extrinsic rewards are often ineffective, and in fact can be detrimental in the long run. In one typical experiment, Lepper, Greene, and Nisbett (1973) observed three- to five-year-old preschool children coloring with felt-tip markers. The researchers observed that the children enjoyed playing with the markers. Next they asked the children to draw with the markers. The researchers promised some children a "Good Player Award" for drawing pictures. Other children drew pictures without the promise of a reward. Two weeks later, the researchers returned and observed the children's inclination to draw with the markers. Those children who had been promised a reward spent only half as much time drawing as they had originally. Those who did not receive rewards showed no decline in interest. Many studies follow this pattern with similar outcomes—ultimately a decline in motivation to do the task is associated with external rewards.

The literature identifies three types of reward contingencies (Dickinson 1989). Task-contingent rewards recognize participation; in the preschool coloring activity, for example, the children were rewarded just for participating in the task. Performance-contingent rewards are provided only when the student completes a task. In such studies, rewarded students were less inclined to perform the task later than were the students who had not been paid (Deci 1971). Every parent who has paid a son or daughter for sidewalk shoveling knows how likely it is that sidewalk shoveling will be done voluntarily in the future. Success-contingent rewards are given for good performance. Dickinson (1989) maintains that extrinsic rewards can be effective when they are contingent upon successful performance and when the standard for success is attainable. Chance (1992) offers some suggestions for judicious use of rewards, and urges that educators remain aware that extrinsic rewards can have adverse effects on student motivation:

- When possible, avoid using rewards as incentives. For example, don't say, "If you do X, I'll give you Y." Instead, ask the student to perform a task and then provide the reward for having completed it.
- Remember that what is an effective reward for one student may not work for another. Effective rewards are things that students seek—positive feedback, praise, approval, recognition; they relate to the needs of each student.

- Reward success and set standards so that success is within the student's reach. To accommodate differences among students, reward improvement or progress.

DeCharms (1968) designed a program to change motivation in children from external to internal with favorable results in their achievement. The students learned their own strengths and weaknesses, chose realistic goals, and assessed their own progress toward their goals. The program stressed personal responsibility. DeCharms reported that children in the study improved in both their achievement motivation and their actual achievement. In a follow-up study, he found that the improvements had persisted and indicated that the participants showed evidence of being likely to graduate from high school (DeCharms 1970). Educators want students to believe that they have some internal control over their own prospects for success. What teachers and other school adults say and do influences the attribution patterns that students develop and ultimately influences their achievement (Bal-Tar, Raviv, and Bal-Tar 1982). One important aspect of DeCharms's work was the effort to help students assess their own strengths; within the body of research on intrinsic and extrinsic motivation, many studies emphasize the difference that self-concept makes in motivation. Children with a high self-concept tend to attribute their success to their own ability and they are less dependent on extrinsic motivation—they are self-rewarding (Ames 1978).

Kohn has studied motivation extensively. He states that internalization of motivation is crucial to developing enduring habits and behaviors. To that end, he declares that extrinsic reward and punishment systems are counterproductive (Kohn 1993). In an interview he states:

> In general, the more kids are induced to do something for a reward, whether tangible or verbal, the more you see a diminution of interest the next time they do it. That can be explained partly by the fact that praise, like other rewards, is ultimately an instrument of control, but also by the fact that if I praise or reward a student for doing something, the message the child infers is, "This must be something I wouldn't want to do; otherwise, they wouldn't have to bribe me to do it." (Brandt 1995, p. 15)

Kohn recommends, instead, three ways to motivate students. First he suggests that the work must interest students. He poses this question: "Has the child been given something to do worth learning?" His second recommendation has to do with the school community. Do students feel part of a safe environment in which they feel free to ask for help? Finally, he raises the issue of choice. He urges teachers to give students opportunities to choose what they will do, how, and with whom.

The Library Media Program and Motivation

Harvey Silver and his colleagues take a similar position on motivation. They have identified four human needs, which hearken back to Maslow: success (the need for mastery), curiosity (the need for understanding), originality (the need for self-expression), and relationships (the need for involvement with others) (Strong, Silver, and Robinson 1995). *The AASL Standards for 21st Century Learners* (American Association of School Librarians 2007) propose a standard that the information literate student will pursue personal and aesthetic growth. Under this standard are close parallels to the needs identified by Silver:

- Read, view, and listen for pleasure and personal growth (curiosity)
- Use creative and artistic formats to express personal learning (originality)
- Organize personal knowledge in a way that can be called upon easily (success)
- Use social networks and information tools to gather and share information (relationships)

Strong, Silver, and Robinson (1995) describe motivation strategies for helping students address each of these needs. To respond to the need for mastery, students need to have the criteria for success clearly articulated—what does successful performance look like? Student success is enhanced when the teacher models successful performance and labels the parts of that successful performance. For example, when asking students to take notes on what they have read, by modeling the note-taking process for them and thinking aloud during the demonstration, the library media specialist can show them what the process looks like when executed well.

One strategy related to curiosity is to provide incomplete or contradictory information that compels the student to explore information resources. Another way to pique curiosity is to suggest topics for research that relate to students' personal lives. Giving students a choice in deciding what they will investigate also supports curiosity.

ENHANCEMENT IN ACTION:
THE LEARNING LAB

A high school social studies teacher uses the library media center as a "learning laboratory" for his American studies classes. Students work as teams on a three-week project in which they spend every class period in the library media center. Each team has responsibility for studying a dimension of American life (for example, sports, politics, prohibition, entertainment, transportation, economics, religion) in the 1920s. Their goal is to investigate and work as if each team were a department of a magazine staff. The final product will be a magazine that brings together the work of all teams. This unit motivates students. The library media center has created a collection that will respond to these students' needs; they will be successful in their search for information. They have access to the necessary hardware and software for Web desktop publishing to create the end product. The library media staff provides the support to students as they work in this "learning lab" atmosphere. Curiosity is the key to this project; the students generate their own information questions—they have control over their work. The end product allows for originality as students design the magazine; in this case students use Apple's Pages for the final project. They count on one another. The time the project takes allows group members to develop meaningful relationships and identify the substantive contributions that each member can make.

The need for self-expression calls for students to have a variety of media available for projects and activities in response to assignments. Developing multimedia, designing print publications, or producing dramatic productions are examples of ways to build creativity into student work that will increase their motivation with appeal to their desire to be original. Another strategy to respond to the need for creativity is to expand the audience for student work—use cable television to send student work out into the local community, use the World Wide Web as a publication forum, or identify interest groups or other classes within the school as audiences for student work.

Finally, to respond to students' need for relationships or social interaction, cooperative learning strategies and group projects with accountability shared among all members of the group are ways to cultivate student interest. The library media program can be a valuable asset to the teacher and everyone else in the school who is seeking to cultivate motivation through success, curiosity, originality, and relationships. As a "learning laboratory," the center becomes the ideal space to support curiosity with its resources, to encourage relationships with its ambiance, and to support creativity with its multimedia.

It is not unusual for teachers to assign group tasks, but teachers too often expect groups to come together outside class time and work independently. Given the complex lives of today's students, group work requires providing some designated group work time. By making this project a "learning lab" activity in which students work in the library media center, teachers can help all group members be participants and realize that the appropriate support in resources and technical assistance are available for everyone to succeed.

Among researchers in the library media profession, Ruth Small (1999) has shown the most interest in motivation as it relates to the library media program in general and to teaching information literacy in particular. She has used the "ARCS model" developed by Keller (1983) as a theoretical model for her own investigations. The ARCS model profiles four components of motivation:

[A] gaining and sustaining **attention** by stimulating curiosity and interests

[R] establishing the **relevance** (i.e., importance or value) of the learning

[C] building learners' **confidence** in their ability to succeed at the task

[S] generating feelings of **satisfaction** as learners experience the consequences of their work

In a 1999 study, Small explored the motivational strategies used by library media specialists during information literacy instruction. She found, in summary, that library media specialists used attention-focusing strategies heavily along with extrinsic motivators. She suggested that a possible explanation for this tendency might be that library media specialists interact less frequently with a given group of students and may therefore need to work at gaining and sustaining their interest. She also speculated that the content of their instruction, information literacy, may be perceived as less interesting for students. Small's research generates interesting questions about instruction in the library media center. Raising awareness of the ARCS model itself may cause library media specialists to attend to all four components of motivation and incorporate relevance and confidence into instruction sessions. Relevance will be particularly natural if instruction in the library indeed has relevance to classroom work that students face. Indeed, this component of motivation provides justification for flexible scheduling of classes in the center and point-of-need instruction. Similarly, the intrinsic rewards of developing information literacy competencies are most likely to become evident to learners in point-of-need instruction situations.

When adequately motivated, students take responsibility for their own learning. To deliver an effective library media program, it is important to consider the larger context of the students' experiences and background—their prior learning, family and economic advantages or disadvantages, and their personal traits and skills. In addition, it is important to position what is taught in the library media program into the larger context of the students' universe.

ACTION STRATEGIES

Learning and Teaching

- Enlist at-risk students with the aptitude for technology as student aides.
- Encourage teachers to allow students to complete assignments using alternative media (for example, a computer-based multimedia production or art media) rather than the formal written paper.
- Beyond providing access, teach students how to use electronic resources. For example, offer voluntary "short courses" outside of the school day focusing on specific technology applications, or coordinate with teachers to teach electronic resources for specific assignments during class time.
- Support teachers who engage their students in creative work—promote the center as a "learning laboratory."
- Consider strategies that motivate students to learn information literacy skills and concepts that will help them succeed throughout their academic undertakings.

Information Access

- Provide materials at various levels of difficulty to meet assignment demands, especially in core courses.
- Cooperate with such agencies as neighborhood centers to seek funding for online access to school and public library resources.
- Provide leisure reading, especially magazines, on topics of high interest—if necessary, seek local business funding to support subscriptions.
- Provide access to the World Wide Web with bookmarks for topics that match local students' interests. In this way, students begin to explore how to locate and evaluate information about topics of personal interest to them.
- Maintain open hours in the library media center before and after school for students. This schedule may require adjusting work hours or seeking after-school volunteers.
- Market materials at various levels of difficulty to teachers so that students with special learning needs can access information with less frustration.

Program Management

- In secondary schools with block scheduling, encourage class use of the library media center. Arrange the facility to accommodate multiple activities and groups.
- Emphasize the importance of relevance as a motivational consideration for instruction in the library media center. Encourage teachers and administrators to schedule instruction accordingly.

SCENARIO FOR DISCUSSION

Some students who attend an elementary school are living at a neighborhood shelter until their families find housing. The shelter is crowded and little space is allocated for families. It proves difficult for many students to take care of their books or return them on time. Books often are lost. Often students' families leave without notice, taking their books with them. Many overwhelming family issues present obstacles. The library media specialist wants to support students in developing an interest in reading, and he wants to help them develop responsibility for taking materials home, returning materials on time, and returning materials before moving. He is also committed to the value of helping them develop basic literacy skills of daily reading at home. He wants these children to have opportunities equal to those of the more privileged children in the school. How can he do it?

REFERENCES

American Association of School Librarians (2007). *Standards for the 21st Century Learner.* Chicago: American Library Association. Available: www.ala.org/aasl/standards.

Ames, C. (1978). "Children's Achievement Attributions and Self-Reinforcement: Effects of Self-Concept and Competitive Reward Structure." *Journal of Educational Psychology 70* (3): 345–355.

Anderson, C. A. and K. E. Dill (2000). "Video Games and Aggressive Thoughts, Feelings, and Behavior in the Laboratory and in Life." *Journal of Personality and Social Psychology 78* (4): 772–790.

Baker, R. and W. Turner (1996). "Block Scheduling: Impact on Library Media Programs." *Florida Media Quarterly 21* (2): 10.

Bal-Tar, D., A. Raviv, and Y. Bal-Tar (1982). "Consistency of Pupils' Attributions Regarding Success and Failure." *Journal of Educational Psychology 74* (1): 104–110.

Brandt, R. (1995). "Punished by Rewards? A Conversation with Alfie Kohn." *Educational Leadership 53* (1): 13–16.

Bureau of Labor Statistics (2007). "College Enrollment and Work Activity of 2006 High School Graduates." Retrieved March 3, 2008, from www.bls.gov/news.release/hsgec.nr0.htm.

Chance, P. (1992). "The Rewards of Learning." *Phi Delta Kappan 73* (3): 200–207.

Chau, M., A. Douglas-Hall, and H. Koball (2006). *Low Income Children in the United States: National and State Trend Data, 1995-2005.* New York: National Center for Children in Poverty. Retrieved February 5, 2008, from www.nccp.org/publications/pdf/text_681.pdf.

DeCharms, R. (1968). *Personal Causation: The Internal Effective Determinants of Behavior.* New York: Academic Press.

DeCharms, R. (1970). "Motivation Changes in Low-Income Black Children." Paper presented at the American Educational Research Association, March 2–6, Minneapolis, Minnesota.

Deci, E. (1971). "Effects of Externally Mediated Rewards on Intrinsic Motivation." *Journal of Personality and Social Psychology 18* (1): 105–115.

Dickinson, A. (1989). "The Detrimental Effects of Extrinsic Reinforcement on 'Intrinsic Motivation.'" *The Behavior Analyst 12* (1): 1–15.

Federal Interagency Forum on Child and Family Statistics (2007). *America's Children: Key National Indicators of Well-Being, 2007.* Washington, DC: U.S. Government Printing Office. Available: www.childstats.gov/pdf/ac2007/ac_07.pdf.

Galt, J. et al. (1996). "Block Scheduling: Comments from Inside the Media Center." *Florida Media Quarterly 21* (2): 12–13.

Goldenberg, C. (1990). "Beginning Literacy Instruction for Spanish Speaking Children." *Language Arts 67* (7): 590–598.

Heintz, K. (1994). "Smarter Than We Think—Kids' Passivity, and the Media." *Media Studies Journal 8:* 205–219.

Hitchcock, C., A. Meyer, D. Rose, and R. Jackson (2002). "Providing Access to the General Curriculum; Universal Design for Learning." *Teaching Exceptional Children 15* (2): 8–17.

Howe, N. and W. Strauss (2000). *Millennials Rising; The Next Great Generation.* New York: Vintage Books.

Hudelson, S. (1987). "The Role of Native Language Literacy in the Education of Language Minority Children." *Language Arts 64* (8): 827–841.

Keller, J. M. (1983). "Motivational Design of Instruction." In C. M. Reigeluth, ed., *Instructional Design Theories and Models: An Overview of Their Current Status* (pp. 383–434). Hillside, NJ: Erlbaum.

Kohn, A. (1993). *Punished by Rewards.* Boston: Houghton Mifflin.

Lepper, M. R., D. Greene, and R. E. Nisbett (1973). "Undermining Children's Intrinsic Interest: A Test of the 'Overjustification Hypothesis'." *Journal of Personality and Social Psychology 28:* 129–137.

Lowery, J. W. (2001). "The Millenials Come to Campus." *About Campus 6* (3): 6–12.

Madden, M. (2003). "America's Online Pursuits: The Changing Picture of Who's Online and What They Do." *Internet & American Life.* Pew Research Center. Retrieved February 12, 2008, from www.pewinternet.org/pdfs/PIP_Online_Pursuits_Final.PDF.

Maslow, A. H. (1971). *The Farther Reaches of Human Nature.* New York: Viking Press.

Murray, J. (2000). "How School Librarians Can Contribute to the Personal Growth of Students with Disabilities." *Orana 36* (2): 5–11.

National Center for Educational Statistics (2005). *After-School Activities: 2005.* Retrieved March 3 from http://nces.ed.gov/pubs2006/afterschool/tables/table_4.asp.

National Center for Educational Statistics (2006). "Libraries and Educational Technology." *Digest of the National Center for Educational Statistics.* Retrieved February 10, 2008, from http://nces.ed.gov/programs/digest/d05/ch_7.asp.

National Center for Educational Statistics (2007a). *The Condition of Education.* Retrieved April 28, 2008, from http://nces.ed.gov/programs/coe/2007/section1/indicator07.asp.

National Center for Educational Statistics (2007b). *Fast Facts.* Retrieved February 7, 2008, from http://nces.ed.gov/fastfacts/display.asp?id=96.

National Center for Educational Statistics (2007c). *The Nation's Report Card.* Retrieved February 10, 2008, from http://nationsreportcard.gov/reading_2007/r0003.asp.

Roberts, D. F., U. G. Foehr, V. J. Rideout, and M. Brodie (1999, November). *Kids and Media at the New Millennium.* Menlo Park, CA: Kaiser Family Foundation Report.

Rong, X. L. and J. Preissle (1998). *Educating Immigrant Students: What We Need to Know to Meet the Challenges.* Thousand Oaks, CA: Corwin.

Ruiz de Velasco, J. and M. Fix (2000). *Overlooked and Underserved: Immigrant Children in the U.S. Secondary Schools.* Washington, DC: Urban Institute.

Scharrar, E. (2002). "Making a Case for Media Literacy in the Curriculum: Outcomes and Assessment." *Journal of Adolescent & Adult Literacy 46* (4): 254–358.

Small, R. V. (1999). "An Exploration of Motivational Strategies Used by Library Media Specialists During Library and Information Skills Instruction." *School Library Media Research 2.* Retrieved October 5, 2003, from www.ala.org/ala/aasl/aaslpubsandjournals/slmrb/schoollibrary.htm.

Smith, M. (1996). "Television Violence and Behavior: A Research Summary." *Emergency Librarian 24:* 34–36.

Stipek, D. (2006). "Relationships Matter." *Educational Leadership 64* (1): 46–49.

Strong, R., H. Silver, and A. Robinson (1995). "What Do Students Want (And What Really Motivates Them)?" *Educational Leadership 53* (1): 8–12.

Sykes, C. (1992). *A Nation of Victims: The Decay of the American Character.* New York: St. Martin's Press.

Thompson, F. T. and W. P. Austin (2003). "Television Viewing and Academic Achievement Revisited." *Education 124* (1): 194–202.

U.S. Department of Education and U.S. Department of Justice. (2000). *Working for Children and Families: Safe and Smart Afterschool Programs.* Washington, DC: U.S. Government Printing Office.

Warren, R. (2003). "Parental Mediation of Preschool Children's Television Viewing." *Journal of Broadcasting & Electronic Media 47* (3): 847–863.

Wentzel, K. R. (2002). "Are Effective Teachers Like Good Parents? Teaching Styles and Student Adjustment in Early Adolescence." *Child Development 73* (1): 287–301.

Willis, J. (2007). "Preserve the Child in Every Learner." *Kappa Delta Pi Record 44* (1): 33–37.

Yell, M. and J. Shriner (1997). "The IDEA Amendments of 1997: Implications for Special and General Education Teachers, Administrators, and Teacher Trainers." *Focus on Exceptional Children 30* (1): 1–19.

Yin, S. (2004, February) "Kiddy Clickers." *American Demographics 26* (1): 13.

Chapter 2

Curriculum and Instruction

This chapter:

- describes major influences on curriculum and instruction
- identifies how the library media specialist fits into the curriculum development process
- identifies action strategies for working within the context of curriculum

CURRICULUM

Curriculum can be defined as the substance of the experiences teachers intend for students to have in school—the content and the experiences of interacting with that content. Changes in curriculum and instruction occur gradually in some schools and dramatically in others. Curriculum changes affect both instructional content and processes. A number of influences on curriculum have particular relevance for the library media program because they either change the nature of assistance teachers and students seek, change the ways in which the library media program interacts with classroom instruction, or affect what students need to know. Examples of curriculum and instruction phenomena that have particular impact on library media programs include the emergence of the cognitive theory of constructivism, emphasis on critical thinking skills, increased emphasis on accountability as a result of No Child Left Behind legislation (Public Law 107-110 "No Child Left Behind Act of 2001," January 8, 2002), acknowledgment of learning's social nature, expanded availability of the Internet in schools and homes, and recognition of a variety of learning styles.

Constructivism

Stoddart (1992) describes the theory of constructivism as follows:

> We believe that learners construct meaning through personal and social experiences; they develop theories about how the world works. We believe they already possess knowledge and beliefs about the content to be learned, so the teaching-learning process involves not simply adding facts or skills but rather developing a new and often very different conceptual perspective through which they understand subject matter. Learning often means changing beliefs, and show-and-tell methods are rarely sufficient to accomplish this. (p. 26)

Constructivism pervades content areas; for example, mathematics and science educators particularly tend to be committed to constructivism where students work with manipulatives and perform hands-on experiments to create their own understanding of numeracy and scientific phenomena.

In a library media center, how do students approach a meaningful information process task? They pose a question, locate information, extract relevant information, and **construct** a meaningful response to the posed question. Information processing is a constructive task, **if** students begin with posing a researchable question. For example, if students are challenged to envision what the major social issues of the twenty-first century will be, they might begin by collecting demographic data such as population projections for the next 50 years. Using these data, they begin to relate population projections to other projections, e.g., land-use trends. Similarly, they might investigate scientific advancements in medicine, transportation, or energy. Once these data are collected and discussed, students can begin to **construct** a picture of the future and envision social problems that may result from these physical, social, and scientific trends. On a much simpler scale, young children can construct their own understanding of community by investigating examples of communities around the world and developing some generalizations about what those various communities have in common. They then construct for themselves the concept of community. Such constructive tasks are substantially different from writing a report about a country or a historical event in which students report what they find but do not create meaning. It is meaning-making that occurs in a constructivist learning environment. Library media specialists must be creative in codesigning with teachers such learning experiences so that they challenge students to construct meaning as they solve problems or make decisions. This process requires teaching the necessary skills to locate, analyze, evaluate, and synthesize information.

A tension exists between teaching to content standards and adhering to constructivist principles of learning. It is analogous to the tension between teaching factual content and teaching learning processes. Those favoring the concern for factual learning support the idea that there is a canon of learning that should constitute the K–12 curriculum. Furthermore, this sector tends to believe that students can and should be tested on the canon in a high-stakes testing system in which school funding, student progression from grade to grade, and/or teacher pay or advancement are examples of the stakes at issue. Sometimes, the commitment to the canon or the pressure of high stakes leads to rote learning of factual information as the most feasible way for students to acquire the knowledge expected of them. Embracing constructivism does not deny that there is fundamental knowledge that students ought to gain. As Brooks and Brooks (1999) assert, "State and local curriculums address *what* students learn. Constructivism, as an approach to education, addresses *how* students learn" (p. 23).

Constructivism supports the engagement of students in inquiry, and that engagement in inquiry creates the need for information that brings students to the library media center. In their inquiry, students ask themselves, "What do I already know? What questions do I have? How do I find out? What did I learn?" (Kuhlthau, in Donham, Bishop, Kuhlthau, and Oberg 2001, p. 1). Through this process, students are active participants in their learning rather than passive recipients of knowledge. The end result can be the same factual content as a more didactic approach to learning, but constructivists contend that the potential for deeper understanding is greater when students are active learners constructing meaning by integrating prior knowledge with new information. Furthermore, they suggest this inquiry approach holds potential for learning beyond the limits of content that might have been prescribed in a more didactic model. Moreover, students develop the skills and dispositions to learn independently beyond school.

Critical Thinking Skills

Ennis (1987) defined critical thinking as "reasonable reflective thinking that is focused on deciding what to believe or do" (p. 10). In today's world of self-publishing and wide distribution of information without the benefit of editorial or peer-review processes accompanied by the profitable marketing of information, critical thinking may be more important than at any previous time. While there is frequent talk of the information explosion, it is important to emphasize that much of the "information" available comes from special interests who present only what will serve their intentions well. Ivie (2001) suggests a model for teaching critical thinking skills that incorporates these stages:

- Posing a central question. The central or essential question is based on a concept or principle, e.g., what is the nature of free speech? In short it is a "big idea" question.
- Describing positions. The student must think about the various positions that might be held, e.g., (1) free speech means unlimited rights to say anything, (2) free speech means having the right to say anything that does not transgress the rights of others, or (3) free speech means the right to speak without violating limitations of obscenity or tyranny.
- Establishing reasoning or evidence. The student must research and set out the reasoning and evidence to support each position, using research literature, logical argument, extended examples, etc.
- Examining assumptions. All argument is based on assumptions. Students need to ferret out the assumptions underlying each position.
- Suggesting a metaphor. Examining each position and assigning a metaphor to each.

Reflective thought occurs as the student moves through the stages of thinking that Ivie (2001) describes in his model. Each stage in his model requires the student to look back at his or her thinking and examine ideas. The *AASL Standards for the 21st Century Learner* call for students to inquire, think critically, and gain knowledge (American Association of School Librarians 2007). Ivie's model provides one way to structure students' critical thinking. While it may not fit all teaching domains, it provides a powerful tool especially in social studies and reading contexts.

National education associations have published standards to describe instructional content and processes. For example, in the national social studies standards, exemplary programs are described in various dimensions (National Council for the Social Studies Task Force on Standards for Teaching and Learning in the Social Studies 1994). One dimension focuses on encouraging students to apply specific thinking skills:

- acquiring, organizing, interpreting, and communicating information;
- processing data in order to investigate questions, develop knowledge, and draw conclusions;
- generating and assessing alternative approaches to problems and making decisions that are both well informed and justified according to democratic principles; and,
- interacting with others in empathetic and responsible ways.

These thinking skills in the social studies standards align well with the information literacy standards of the library media program. Furthermore, Ivie's (2001) critical thinking model aligns well with these thinking skills and provides a concrete model for teaching them.

The pervasive Web provides a readily available forum for self-publication. While visitors to Web sites can sometimes attain useful information, the openness of this venue for publication demands astute critical examination. Naiveté about information is not limited to students. Often, teachers and parents assume that all information is equal in accuracy and authority. This digital information environment demands careful scrutiny and a disposition of skepticism. Library media specialists play an important role in teaching students to be critical information consumers and in advising teachers and parents as well. By helping teachers set standards for what sources of information are acceptable for student work, by advising parents about criteria for evaluating the authority of Web sites, and by teaching students to look for evidence of authority in their information sources, the library media specialist can help establish high standards for quality of information.

No Child Left Behind

Perhaps one of the most influential pieces of federal legislation to affect schools in recent times is the No Child Left Behind (NCLB) Act of 2001.

The act, which is scheduled for enforcement until 2014, contains four basic principles:

- increased accountability;
- increased local flexibility in use of federal education funds;
- emphasis on research-supported teaching methods; and
- expanded options for parents.

This legislation has had particular impact on curriculum because of its first principle—increased accountability. This provision calls for states to establish standards and standards-based assessments in reading, mathematics, science, and English language proficiency. This assertive call for standardized testing to document progress has come to dictate curriculum. With potential sanctions such as transfer of students and their funding, the pressure for students to succeed on these high-stakes tests has provoked teaching to the tests. Subsequently, this test-driven approach to curriculum has led educators toward a canon of factual learning in K-12 education. This emphasis on testable content has lessened the emphasis on process learning that is difficult to objectively test, e.g., information literacy, critical thinking skills, or creative arts. This redirection of curriculum contradicts an important aspect of the futures of our students. Many sources speak to the rapid rate of change today, the enormity of new knowledge generation, and the speed of technological development. Wurman (2001) is among many authors who describe the explosion and rate of change. Such rapid change infers that the importance of learning how to be a learner may be the most important lessons for schooling—yet NCLB presses educators to exclude process learning for the sake of content learning.

Such an emphasis has created significant challenges for school library media specialists, whose intention is to develop in students those skills, understandings, and dispositions to be independent learners when they leave school. Yet, the content emphasis of NCLB education has extracted time and resources from library media programs in favor of more textbook-based learning. Library media specialists have a difficult advocacy role to play in this context—a role that requires the development of argument in favor of teaching students how to be learners and how to become information literate in preparation for a changing world that will require continuous learning. Even without NCLB, the importance of helping all constituents—parents, community, teachers, administrators—understand the importance of the processes of independent learning and the role of information literacy in that context presents an advocacy challenge for every school library media specialist.

Robert Linn of the University of Colorado has been engaged in testing and assessment in education since 1965 (Bracey 2000). Bracey quotes him on the efficacy of standardized tests:

> As someone who has spent his entire career doing research, writing, and thinking about educational testing and assessment issues, I would like to conclude by summarizing a compelling case showing that the major uses of tests for student and school accountability during the last 50 years have improved education and student learning in dramatic ways. Unfortunately, that is not my conclusion. Instead, I am led to conclude that in most cases the instruments and technology have not been up to the demands that have been placed on them by high-stakes accountability. Assessment systems that are useful monitors lose much of their dependability and credibility for that purpose when high stakes are attached to them. The unintended negative effects of the high-stakes accountability uses often outweigh the intended positive effects. (p. 137)

Linn cites one of testing's elder statesmen, William Coffman, on the problem of standards: "Holding common standards for all pupils can only encourage a narrowing of educational experiences for most pupils, doom many to failure, and limit the development of many worthy talents" (Bracey 2000, p. 137).

Striving to make the required "adequate yearly progress" (AYP) has forced schools to be more concerned about teaching students to perform well on the tests than teaching what might be appropriate to develop skills and dispositions as lifelong learners. In addition, the legislation mandates "adequate yearly progress" by students in special education programs. Meeting the expectations of the legislation has increased diversion of resources to special education to improve these students' performance. The stakes are high in this legislation. Consequences for failing to meet the expected adequate yearly progress threaten to:

- defer programmatic funds or reduce administrative funds;
- institute and implement a new curriculum;
- replace personnel;
- remove particular schools from the district and establish alternative governance;

- appoint a trustee in place of the superintendent and school board;
- abolish or restructure a school district; and/or
- authorize students to transfer to a higher-performing school and provide transportation.

These sanctions place substantial pressure on school districts to see that students perform well on tests to demonstrate their yearly progress. The seriousness of the stakes encourages schools to align curriculum closely with the tests mandated by their respective states. In such a context, library media specialists have a challenge to affirm the importance of teaching not only content but also processes that will result in students learning to learn and in learning to think critically.

The advocacy posture in favor of not allowing content-learning to edge out information literacy and critical thinking includes arguments related to testing as well as arguments related to preparing students for a world of dramatic change where new knowledge is generated rapidly, and knowing how to access, evaluate, and use it will be a survival skill set.

The Pervasive World Wide Web

By fall 2005, nearly 100 percent of public schools in the United States had access to the Internet, compared with 35 percent in 1994 (National Center for Educational Statistics 2007b). *The NCES Digest of Educational Statistics for 2006* indicates that nearly 70 percent of students have at-home access to computers (National Center for Educational Statistics 2007a) and the majority of those have at-home Internet access. The Internet's influence on curriculum and instruction is pervasive. Where textbooks once held the position of authority for classroom information, now the Web offers readily available sources of information, and textbooks offer Web sites to accompany their print publications.

Such ready access to the Web offers possibilities for inquiry-driven curricula, but the test-anxiety created by NCLB may limit how readily teachers avail their classes of this opportunity. Nevertheless, in many classrooms, the Web influences how teachers expect their students to acquire information, how they communicate with one another about the content of their curriculum, and how they publish their findings.

The wide availability of the Web also raises concern about adding to the curriculum not only technical skills to navigate efficiently but also the ethics of Internet use. Topics such as plagiarism, intellectual property, evaluation of Web-delivered information, copyright, need to find a place in the curriculum and be taught explicitly if students are to really understand the nature of being responsible citizens on the Web (Kruger 2003). These are not concepts likely to appear on high-stakes tests, but they are important in developing good citizenship in the information-rich world dominated by the Web. Library media specialists have responsibility for being both advocates and experts in the area of information ethics.

Another dimension of the Internet is its social and cognitive influence. Students at younger and younger ages spend increasing amounts of time socializing via electronic channels—cell phones, online chat, social networks, and online gaming. Student engagement with these technologies has an array of influences on their approaches to learning and their expectations for a learning environment. Johnson (2006) asserts that the Internet influences cognitive processes. She states:

> During Internet use, language centers of the brain are active, particularly in online communication. Meta-cognitive abilities are required for a variety of online activities including playing games . . . Internet games as well as synchronous communication increase cognitive processing speed. Internet games require simultaneous processing; online communications requires successive processing. Internet games make extreme demands on visual and metacognition skills." (p. 3045)

These patterns of mental activity seem likely to influence the ways in which students process information and interact socially offline as well. For example, if gaming and online synchronous communication are indeed associated with increased cognitive speed, then the expectation for rapid response in interfacing with academic online resources is likely—along with consequent impatience. Style of discourse online is likely to influence written communication in academic environments, and more intentional instruction regarding style of discourse for both reading and writing seems increasingly appropriate. The extended time spent in a visually stimulating screen environment may manifest itself in preferences for visual stimuli. Continued research as these technically engaged students mature is likely to provide insights that affect modes of instruction for the future.

Learning Styles

While there are several models describing learning styles, the work of Dr. Anthony Gregorc (1982) is classic. He characterized four psychological learning styles that can be summarized briefly:

Concrete sequential learners are typically practical and prefer instruction that is ordered, practical, detailed, exact, and that includes clear directions. They prefer an orderly, quiet environment; they like to know the specifications for successful work, and they like to apply ideas in a practical hands-on way.

Concrete random learners are typically inquisitive and independent and prefer instruction that offers options, is open-ended, and might include experimentation, problem-solving, and creating products. They are self-directed and have a high degree of curiosity.

Abstract sequential learners are typically intellectual and prefer the abstract world of thoughts and symbols, reading, working alone, and doing independent research. They think in a structured way, they are analytical, and they work best when they have references and expert sources close at hand.

Abstract random learners are typically sensitive and subjective and prefer instruction that might include multimedia, thematic approaches, role-play, and peer group work. They like personal attention and support and they prefer a noncompetitive atmosphere.

Other researchers have devised their own theories and models of various learning styles. Prominent among them is David Kolb who suggests that learning style is a result of heredity, experience, and environment to produce four basic learning modes: concrete experience, reflective observation, abstract conceptualization, and active experimentation (Dunn and DeBello 1981). While not exactly identical to Gregorc, the similarity is evident. Not all learning style researchers agree with Kolb's notion of inheritance; for example, Dunn considers learning style a result of experiences and environment. Likewise, while Dunn recommends that students should always be taught through their strengths, Kolb suggests that awareness of learning styles should encourage teachers to develop instructional experiences to enhance not only individual strengths but also less dominant orientations.

Research indicates that students whose learning styles are accommodated would be expected to achieve 75 percent of a standard deviation higher than students whose learning style has not been accommodated (Dunn and Griggs 1995). A study of a middle school class studying the Holocaust provides additional support for attending to learning styles in the classroom (Farkas 2003). In this study two control groups were taught using "traditional methods" of lecture, group discussion, and visual resources; two experimental groups were taught employing methods matched to their learning style classifications resulting from a learning style inventory. Results showed higher final scores in achievement, attitude, and empathy among the experimental groups; these results support Dunn's notion of improving performance by matching learning style and teaching strategy. It may be impractical, or maybe impossible, to tailor all learning experiences to match each child's learning style, yet library media specialists can raise awareness of the variations among children and suggest alternatives for teaching and learning so that various styles are accommodated. An obvious example is alternative media for students to use in presenting their work; the library media specialist can offer support and teach students to use video, multimedia, still photography, desktop publishing, and other presentation media. Likewise, the library media specialist can work toward making information resources available in various formats as well.

Related to—but distinct from—learning styles research is the work of Howard Gardner in the area of intelligence. In his work, Gardner suggests that for too long educators have defined intelligence only in terms of verbal or mathematical aptitude. He suggests that while these are two kinds of intelligence, there are at least six more, namely musical, spatial, bodily kinesthetic, interpersonal, intrapersonal, and naturalist (Gardner, accessed 2008). Unlike learning style, intelligence refers to a biological and psychological potential that is capable of being realized to a greater or lesser extent as a result of the experiential, cultural, and motivational factors affecting a person (Gardner 1995). This suggests that educators have significant influence over how well the potential is met as they design educational experiences. Attention to all intelligences is a responsibility that teachers and library media specialists can share. Individuals are never endowed solely with one intelligence. Rather, Gardner's theory suggests that people blend their various intelligences (Gardner 1983). Sensitivity to Gardner's theory as well as the concept of learning styles will help library media specialists working in collaboration with teachers to design instructional experiences that accommodate and take advantage of the various styles and intelligences within any given class.

Social Nature of Learning

With the adoption of workplace teams, business and industry have focused the nation's attention on the importance of cooperation among workers. Likewise, educators recognize that students must learn to work together, to accept group roles and responsibilities, and to learn to organize themselves to accomplish tasks as a team. The library media specialist fosters this team approach by making the library media center a group-work place. The center's physical arrangement, the ambiance, and the tolerance for productive noise can contribute to learning as a social activity. The library media specialist can collaborate with teachers to design tasks that lend themselves to teamwork. This means providing students with open-ended questions rather than convergent tasks where students are simply seeking a "right" answer. Cooperative work among groups of students improves when teachers facilitate group cohesiveness, clear role expectations, and accountability (Furtwengler 1992).

Talking—a social activity—can have a substantial influence on learning. Consider for yourself the effect that talking about an idea or a problem can have. Talking forces us to articulate our thoughts with enough clarity for others to understand. In the process of communication, ideas become more clearly formed for ourselves as well. Talking about ideas with someone else affords the opportunity to have ideas affirmed or challenged so that they can be refined. Talking substantively with others invites elaboration or expansion of our ideas. As students work in the library media center, it is worth taking time to allow them to work in pairs or triads to share ideas; raise questions; seek clarification, redirection, or affirmation; and perhaps gain confidence. As they do so they will find language that may help them in their search for information, and they are likely to have a more clear sense of purpose. When both the library media specialist and the teacher work as facilitators, these social processes can be monitored and improved.

THE LIBRARY MEDIA SPECIALIST'S EXPERTISE

Teachers have obvious roles in curriculum and instruction. Perhaps more subtle is the role of library media specialists. However, library media specialists can bring important assets to enhance the curriculum because of their unique perspective and skill set.

Uniqueness

The unique perspective of the library media specialist can contribute to curriculum. A library media specialist knows the curriculum content and the teaching strategies in each classroom. The principal and the guidance counselor are also in touch with each teacher. However, their relationships to classrooms usually focus on managerial issues or individual students' personal concerns. The library media specialist's connection with each teacher tends to focus on what is being taught, with what, and how. Such a relationship may place the library media specialist into the position of knowing more than any other professional in the building about the total curriculum. Such knowledge can then be valuable for curriculum articulation.

The library media specialist also has special expertise in both information and instructional technology. Parents and administrators pressure teachers to incorporate technology into their classrooms. For some, this is naturally easy. But for many, technology is intimidating or at least bothersome. Library media specialists guide decisions about meaningful technology use so that children's experiences with technology help them reach high cognitive levels. The library media specialist can also provide teacher in-service on new technologies, can team-teach in order to reduce teacher anxiety, and can provide facilities and assist students.

Knowledge Base

It is easy for educators to be naive about the expertise of library media specialists. In the history of American education, the field is relatively young. Schools are still populated by many teachers who did not have experience with school library media specialists as they attended school themselves. Colleges of education tend not to teach about collaboration with school library media specialists. Many people who teach expect that their work will be relatively isolated. Unfortunately, many teachers do not even know that in many states, library media specialists must also be trained as teachers. So, library media professionals typically have the educational background of teachers. What more do they bring to the table? Some key examples of specialized knowledge include:

- information technologies and strategies for using them powerfully and efficiently;
- learning resources in the form of trade books, software, Web sites;

- design and production skills in a variety of media formats;
- planning and management skills and knowledge;
- curriculum and instructional design;
- information ethics;
- computer systems; and
- program management.

This set of knowledge and competency is added value that library media specialists bring to the curriculum-planning table.

Coaching

Library media specialists must apply the questioning skills they learned as reference interviewers to their consulting work with teachers. A reference librarian seeks as much information as necessary in order to provide the client with exactly the needed information. The reference questioning strategy proceeds from identifying the topic, to refining the question, analyzing the question to formulate a search strategy, and evaluating the information found to establish that it meets the client's need. A good reference interview accomplishes two objectives: the first "intended" objective is that the librarian understands and subsequently meets the actual information need of the client; the second, perhaps not intentional, is to clarify for the client what it is he or she is actually seeking. Working with teachers, library media specialists apply similar strategies, with similar results. The questioning strategy of the library media specialist is similar to the strategy of cognitive coaching (Costa and Garmston 1994).

In a case study of the library media specialist's consulting role, coaching was identified as one important way for the library media specialist to work with teachers (Donham van Deusen 1996). In one example from this case, a teacher approached the library media specialist about teaching students to look for magazine articles. Through the reference interview, the library media specialist pursued what the teacher really wanted children to learn. Her questioning revealed that the teacher wanted to improve children's skill in reading nonfiction. The library media specialist offered to locate articles so that the children spent their time on the reading skills that the teacher wanted to address. She and the teacher team-taught strategies for extracting information from articles. Interaction with the library media specialist caused the teacher to refocus the lesson from using an index to strategies for reading nonfiction.

The coaching model emphasizes the importance of reflection on teaching and learning. The coach uses questioning to help the teacher process information that will lead to decisions or future teaching. The model is not an expert providing direction to the teacher, but rather a colleague encouraging another's thought and reflection. Although in this case the library media specialist had opinions about what to teach, rather than declare her position she raised relevant questions so that the decision was collaborative. Those questions followed a pattern that proceeded from "What is your lesson about?" (describing) to "What exactly will the students be doing?" (translating) to "What will be the order of activities in the unit?" (sequencing) to "How will you know that students have been successful?" (operationalizing criteria). These are similar to the questions identified in Costa's coaching model (Costa and Garmston 1994). By posing these questions, the library media specialist encourages teachers to think through plans, clarify them for themselves, and communicate them to the library media specialist who can then assist in implementing the teaching.

CONCLUSION

Participation in curriculum involves not only being a part of the planning process but also being part of the implementation. Each example described in this chapter has some common features. Most important, in each case, the library media specialist is working with teachers—not working in isolation. Also, in each case, the expertise that the library media specialist offers is different from the classroom teacher's—it is the expertise of a specialist. Finally, in each case, the library media specialist is taking initiative—not merely responding to a specific request by providing materials.

The worst-case scenario is for the library media specialist to be included in curriculum planning meetings but to fail to contribute in unique and useful ways. Being on committees is not enough. The challenge is to improve instruction. The question for every library media specialist after every curriculum-planning meeting, and after every interchange about curriculum must be: in what ways did my contribution improve the content and delivery of the curriculum?

ACTION STRATEGIES

Learning and Teaching

- Demonstrate interest in what teachers are teaching:
  1. Share interesting curriculum-oriented articles with staff either one on one or at staff meetings.
  2. Join, encourage, or initiate study groups on cross-disciplinary study topics such as multiage grouping, student performance assessment, block scheduling, or instructional technology.
  3. Attend parent information meetings in your school when teachers are describing curriculum or discussing curricular issues.
  4. Become familiar with state and national standards in content areas.
- Maintain current awareness of new software and hardware:
  1. Embrace the role of technology advocate and facilitator.
  2. Help teachers set criteria for selecting appropriate ways to use technology so that technology is used as a tool for higher-order thinking—analysis, synthesis, and evaluation—rather than for simple recall.
  3. Offer teacher in-services on instructional technology uses.
  4. Encourage software preview; do "buddy" software previews with teachers.
  5. Offer to team-teach with new technologies the first time a teacher tries something new, to reduce the anxiety about the technology.
- Develop a written information skills process curriculum:
  1. Share the curriculum with all teachers.
  2. Together with teachers identify the units into which the information skills process curriculum will be infused.
  3. Ensure that no part of the curriculum is addressed only once; students need many opportunities to practice applying information strategies.

Information Access

- Participate in curriculum development projects. Expect the principal to make you a part of the team, and say so:
  1. Provide literature searches in the topics of interest.
  2. Locate instructional materials to consider.

3. Design activities for students sensitive to various learning styles and intelligences.
4. Exploit your knowledge of children's or young adult literature to help teachers identify specific titles to develop truly thematic, not topical, literature units.
5. Design student projects to be used in assessment.
6. Design lessons to infuse information skills into the content.
7. Provide information about what is taught at other grade levels or in other disciplines.

Program Management

- Maintain current awareness of trends in the content areas:
  1. Read (or at least skim) articles (i.e., not just materials reviews) in journals from curriculum areas, such as:
     Social Education
     Social Studies
     English Journal
     Language Arts
     Phi Delta Kappan
     The Reading Teacher
     Science Teacher
     Teaching Children Mathematics
     Mathematics Teaching in the Middle School
     Educational Leadership
  2. Attend a professional conference outside the library media area.
  3. Purchase and become familiar with national standards and guidelines from various disciplines.
- Participate in long-range curriculum planning and evaluation.

SCENARIO FOR DISCUSSION

A middle school faculty is reviewing its policy on homework. The next two faculty meetings will be devoted to this topic as faculty members consider these questions:

- How much homework should students be given?
- What is the parents' role in homework? Should there be homework-free nights to support family time?

- What kind of homework should we give students and what assumptions should we make about access to resources for doing homework?
- What is the role of the library media specialist in the discussion of these issues?

REFERENCES

American Association of School Librarians (2007). *Standards for the 21st Century Learner*. Chicago: American Library Association. Available: www.ala.org/aasl/standards.

Bracey, G. (2000). "The 10th Bracey Report On the Condition of Public Education." *Phi Delta Kappan 82* (2): 133–144.

Brooks, M. G. and J. G. Brooks (1999). "The Courage to be Constructivism." *Educational Leadership 57* (3): 18–24.

Costa A. and R. Garmston (1994). *Cognitive Coaching: A Foundation for Renaissance Schools*. Norwood, MA: Christopher-Gordon.

Donham, J., K. Bishop, C. C. Kuhlthau, and D. Oberg (2001). *Inquiry-Based Learning: Lessons from Library Power*. Worthington, OH: Linworth Publishing.

Donham van Deusen, J. (1996). "The School Library Media Specialist as a Member of the Teaching Team: 'Insider' and 'Outsider,'" *Journal of Curriculum and Instruction 11* (3): 229–248.

Dunn, R. and T. DeBello (1981). "Learning Style Researchers Define Differences Differently." *Educational Leadership 38* (5): 372–375.

Dunn, R. and S. A. Griggs (1995). "A Meta-Analytical Validation of the Dunn and Dunn Learning Style Model." *Journal of Educational Research 88* (6): 353–361.

Ennis, R. H. (1987). "A Taxonomy of Critical Thinking Dispositions and Abilities." In J. B. Baron and R. J. Sternberg, eds., *Teaching Thinking Skills: Theory and Practice* (pp. 9–26). New York: W. H. Freeman.

Farkas, R. D. (2003). "Effects of Traditional Versus Learning-Styles Instructional Methods on Middle School Students," *Journal of Educational Research 97* (1): 42–51.

Furtwengler, C. B. (1992). "How to Observe Cooperative Learning Classrooms." *Educational Leadership 49* (7): 59–62.

Gardner, H. (1983). *Frames of Mind: The Theory of Multiple Intelligences*. New York: Basic Books.

Gardner, H. (1995). "Reflections on Multiple Intelligences." *Phi Delta Kappan 77* (3): 200–207.

Gardner, H. *Howard Gardner FAQ*. Accessed February 10, 2008, at www.howardgardner.com/FAQ/faq.htm.

Gregorc A. F. (1982) *An Adult's Guide to Style*. Maynard MA: Gabriel Systems.

Ivie, S. D. (2001). "Metaphor: A Model for Teaching Critical Thinking." *Contemporary Education 72* (1): 18–22.

Johnson, G. (2006, June 1). *A Theoretical Framework for Organizing the Effect of the Internet on Cognitive Development*. Online Submission (ERIC Document Reproduction Service No. ED493998). Published in *ED-MEDIA Proceedings* (2006), pp. 3041-3048. Retrieved April 26, 2008, from ERIC database.

Kruger, R. (2003). "Discussing Cyber Ethics with Students Is Critical." *Social Studies 94* (4): 188–189.

National Center for Educational Statistics (2007a). "List of Tables by Chapter." *Digest of Education Statistics, 2006.* Washington, DC: NCES. Available: http://nces.ed.gov/programs/digest/d06/tables_1.asp.

National Center for Educational Statistics (2007b). *Fast Facts.* Retrieved January 27, 2008, at http://nces.ed.gov/fastfacts.

National Council for the Social Studies Task Force on Standards for Teaching and Learning in the Social Studies (1994). "A Vision of Powerful Teaching and Learning in the Social Studies: Building Social Understanding and Civic Efficacy." In *Expectations of Excellence: Curriculum Standards for Social Studies* (pp. 155–177). Washington, DC: National Council for the Social Studies.

Stoddart, T. (1992). "Commentary: Fostering Coherence Between Constructivism on Campus and Conventional Practice in Schools." *The Holmes Group Forum 6* (2): 26–28.

Wurman, R. S. (2001). *Information Anxiety 2.* Indianapolis, IN: Que.

Chapter 3

The Principal

This chapter:

- outlines standards for school administrators
- describes the role of the principal as leader and manager
- relates the principal's role to the library media specialist's role
- describes the impact of the principal on the library media program
- describes the effect of shared decision making
- identifies action strategies for working with the principal

STANDARDS FOR SCHOOL PRINCIPALS

Just as school library media professionals are guided by the expectations set forth in *Information Power*, so principals are guided by expectations set forth by their professional organizations (American Association of School Librarians and Association for Educational Communications and Technology 1998). For example, the Interstate School Leaders Licensure Consortium has set forth six standards for school administrators (Council of Chief State School Officers 1996). They state:

A school administrator is an educational leader who promotes the success of all students by:

- facilitating the development, articulation, implementation, and stewardship of a vision of learning that is shared and supported by the school community

- advocating, nurturing, and sustaining a school culture and instructional program conducive to student learning and staff professional growth
- ensuring management of the organization, operations, and resources for a safe, efficient, and effective learning environment
- collaborating with families and community members, responding to diverse community interests and needs and mobilizing community resources
- acting with integrity and fairness and in an ethical manner
- understanding, responding to, and influencing the larger political, social, economic, legal, and cultural context

According to the Council of Chief State School Officers, most states have either adopted or adapted their standards and are in different stages of implementing the standards in reforming educational leadership within their state. While these standards were developed before passage of the No Child Left Behind (NCLB) Act of 2001, they continue to serve as a set of guidelines for licensure across state lines and offer a yardstick for educational leadership. The Council of Chief State School Officers continues to support these guidelines, but will review them in light of the demands of NCLB. These standards reveal that the library media specialist and the principal have much in common. In fact, many of these standards for school administrators have direct relevance for the work of the library media specialist as well as the principal. In the language of the stage, in some areas the library media specialist may perform in a supporting role and in some areas he or she may costar. For example, the first standard involves the articulation and implementation of a vision of learning that is shared by the school community. The roles for the library media specialist are immediately evident. As "costar" he or she can help shape the vision so that it incorporates the notion of learning to learn that is so fundamental to information literacy. Then, in a supporting role the library media specialist must advocate within the school community for "buy-in." Similarly, each of the other standards suggests roles for the library media specialist to work cooperatively with school administrators. A library media specialist will do well to determine how the library media program can support and enhance the work of the principal as defined by these standards.

In similar fashion, the National Association of Elementary School Principals has published a set of standards for elementary school administrators (National Association of Elementary School Principals 2001).

These standards are substantially similar to the Interstate School Leaders Licensure Consortium standards, but they are worthy of review for library media specialists at the elementary school level. These standards encourage principals to be leaders of learning rather than managers of facilities. They focus on six priorities:

- making student and adult learning the priority
- setting high expectations for performance
- gearing content and instruction to standards
- creating a culture of continuous learning for adults
- using multiple sources of data to assess learning
- activating the community's support for school success

How do principals meet these standards? Blase and Blase (2002) provided a partial answer by asking teachers to describe the behaviors of principals who had a positive influence on student learning. Two broad themes emerged: talking with teachers and promoting professional development. These themes were expressed in specific behaviors, such as making suggestions, giving feedback, modeling effective instruction, soliciting opinions, supporting collaboration, providing professional development opportunities, and giving praise for effective teaching. Two of these teacher priorities have particular relevance for the library media specialist: supporting collaboration and providing professional development. Library media specialists who can help a principal envision their potential role in these two priorities are likely to see their programs thrive.

PRINCIPAL AS LEADER AND MANAGER

The school principal experiences a constant tension between two distinct expectations: to be a leader and to be a manager. A considerable body of research confirms this role ambiguity (Manasse 1985). More recently, the tension has grown so strong that Kennedy (2001) recommended schools hire two principals—an instructional leader and a building manager. She cites a recommendation from Pierce (2000):

> The principal teacher, with "a well-established teaching history rooted in strong instructional practice," would supervise teachers, provide them with feedback, and engage them in reflective prac-

tice. The principal teacher also would be responsible for student achievement, curriculum, instructional technology, and the hiring and firing of teachers. The principal administrator would be responsible for plant management, transportation, food and custodial services, secretaries, scheduling, data collection, and parent involvement. This person would be accountable to and supportive of the principal teacher. (p. 60)

Staff members, the parents, and their superintendents often disagree about the principal's role expectations. As instructional leader, the principal sets a vision for the school and engages in the design of the instructional program. As school manager, the principal attends to the organization, climate, schedule, and administration so that the organization will run smoothly. While these two roles are not necessarily in conflict with one another, either one takes substantial time, knowledge, and skill. These roles might be seen as opposite ends of a continuum, and each principal will function at some point along that continuum at any given time.

Leithwood (1994) describes behaviors of principals as leaders. Guiding the school in developing and communicating a vision is perhaps the most prominent activity of a leading principal. By helping teachers, parents, and students perceive and maintain that vision, the principal provides a backdrop for decision making. Setting expectations is another aspect of leadership. School leadership also involves providing intellectual stimulation by encouraging staff to try new practices and to share ideas with colleagues and by modeling good professional practice.

What does the principal do as manager? Establishing a climate conducive to learning is a crucial responsibility of the principal. Creating clear and consistent school rules and policies tends to improve the general disciplinary climate of the school and contributes to improved staff and student morale (Bryk, Lee, and Smith 1989). The managerial role also includes the administration of resources: budget, time, and staff. Leadership and management responsibilities are both important for an effective school.

Library media specialists face a similar dilemma in determining how best to use time. There is a tension between the operational demands and the educational demands of the library media center. And, just as the balance between leader and manager is a key to success for the principal, so is the balance between two competing sets of priorities for the library media specialist. Parallel lists of leader and manager tasks for

FIGURE 3.1 Comparison of Dual Roles	
Principal	**Library Media Specialist**
Leader	**Leader**
Goal setting	Goal setting
Modeling	Teaching
Decision making	Collaborating with teachers
Coaching	Providing staff development
Interacting with parents about school vision	Communicating with teachers, administrators, and parents about the library media program
Monitoring programs	Monitoring programs
Manager	**Manager**
Scheduling	Scheduling
Supervising	Supervising
Purchasing	Purchasing
Maintaining the physical plant	Maintaining the facility
Writing policies	Writing policies
Responding to parental concerns	Troubleshooting

both the principal and library media specialist are shown in Figure 3.1.

By acknowledging that the principal and the library media specialist struggle with the same tension between roles, the library media specialist can empathize with that situation and can enter into dialogue, conscious of whether the topic at hand deals with management or leadership, with the principal.

The principal is a decision maker, whether the decisions are related to instructional leadership or to school management. The decisions principals make as managers are influenced by their activity as leaders. The vision for the school can lead the principal to commit resources to further that vision. If a principal envisions a school characterized by teamwork, then such a vision will undoubtedly influence decisions about hiring; it might also influence decisions about scheduling or purchasing materials. In other words, principals make decisions within a framework that grows out of their leadership values and beliefs.

Leithwood (1994) describes a problem-solving model that characterizes the influences on decision making in leaders. The model identifies mental activity that can be classified as follows:

- *Problem interpretation*: What is the nature of the problem?
- *Goals*: What relatively immediate purposes need to be met in response to the problem?
- *Constraints*: What barriers or obstacles must be overcome?
- *Solution processes:* What does the leader do to solve the problem?
- *Principles/values:* What long-term purposes, operating principles, values, and assumptions guide the leader's thinking?
- *Affect*: What are the leader's feelings, mood, and sense of self-confidence?

Awareness of this problem-solving model provides an important perspective for the library media specialist. By anticipating each aspect of the problem-solving process, the library media specialist can be prepared to take to the principal not only problems, but also potential solutions. Also, the library media specialist can anticipate what information will help the principal progress through the problem-solving process more efficiently. For example, realizing that constraints will enter into the solution, the library media specialist needs to be ready with solutions for overcoming them.

Manasse (1985) summarizes several portrayals of the principal's workday as fragmented days composed of as many as 400 short unplanned verbal interactions regarding 50 to over 100 separate events. Consider a stream of events that includes dealing with a potential child-abuse situation, a clogged toilet, a teacher in need of more mathematics textbooks, a parent seeking advice about homeschooling his child, a student sent in with chewing tobacco in his pocket—all unrelated events requiring prompt attention. This is the school principal's day. Manasse

---

**ENHANCEMENT IN ACTION:
SCHOOL AND COMMUNITY**

Assume that a principal has a vision for the school to be perceived as a central feature of the community it serves. Likely goals would be involving parents in the school, increasing communication about the goals of the school, and making the community feel at home in the school. The library media specialist wants students to increase their use of information technologies. By fitting the library media goal into the community vision of the principal, an alliance occurs that helps to further both goals. The library media specialist suggests to the principal offering evening classes for parents to teach them about Internet resources useful for their children. For example, at the high school level, a session on Web resources for college selection, or at the elementary level, a session on resources useful for curriculum-related topics. A variety of "community nights" in the school's library media center target various populations (such as grandparents, parents of young children, or persons considering purchase of a new computer), depending on local demographics.

---

also alludes to studies indicating that secondary principals have been found to spend relatively more of their time in scheduled meetings than do elementary principals. Still, the bombardment of unrelated problems is a reality for all principals.

RELATING THE PRINCIPAL'S ROLE TO THE SCHOOL LIBRARY MEDIA PROGRAM

In a study by Yetter (1994), one finding was that crucial to the success of a library media program is the library media specialist's leadership ability, including the capacity to envision a resource-based process and connect it to the principal's agenda. By recognizing the nature of the principal's work, the library media specialist can learn to interact with the principal to marry their goals. Consider first the principal as leader. What is the principal's vision for the school and how does the library media program facilitate bringing that vision into reality?

In the example related in the "Enhancement in Action" shaded box, the library media specialist has used the vision of the principal to engender community support for a component of the library media program. By fitting the library media program's agenda to that of the principal, the library media specialist communicates important messages. Hartzell (2003) aptly describes this strategy as WIFM—what's in it for me? By thinking about what the principal is aiming to accomplish, the savvy library media specialist can advance the library media program as well. In the school library media profession, it is common to read of the loneliness of the library media specialist as one of a kind in the school. This same aloneness characterizes the principal. The two are a natural team since both must be concerned with all teachers and students in the school. Both share an across-grade-levels and across-disciplines view of the school. But to make the alliance work, it is important for the library media specialist to see the principal's vision as the guiding light for the school. While language like "The library media center is the hub of the school" is common in advocacy literature, the reality is that the library media program is a comprehensive support system but it is not the driving force of the school's educational agenda. That driving force is the school's mission statement. So, the library media specialist does well to align his or her program explicitly with the school's mission.

Another message sent when the library media specialist aligns the library media program with the principal's vision is that the library media program itself is part of the implementation of the vision. Making the role of the library media program explicit and highly visible is crucial to gaining support for successful library media programming. In the shaded box example, opening up the library media center to the community may garner support from the community for technology expenditures. More important, however, it can engender parental support for the instructional work that the library media program represents in teaching students to be effective users of electronic information resources. When the parents support the school's instructional efforts, the ultimate winners are the students.

The principal also makes decisions as a manager, and the library media specialist hopes these decisions will benefit the library media program. Again, it is important to consider how the concerns for the library media program can align with the management concerns of the principal. Emphasizing these common concerns can help the library media specialist take a more active role in the decision-making process.

ENHANCEMENT IN ACTION:
TALKING ABOUT THE BUDGET

Budget is often a point of contention for the library media specialist and the principal. A conventional approach to budget by library media specialists is to examine the collection, determine what the needs are, and approach the principal for dollars to meet those needs. The needs analysis may be done via a collection map in which the library media specialist assesses the age and quality of materials by category or topic, compares those findings to the demands made on the collection via a curriculum map, and then determines a dollar amount needed to resolve the discrepancy between an existing and ideal collection of materials. The development of collection maps is indeed important; however, these data must be related to the principal so as to fall within his or her context for decision making. Consider the context of the decision making by looking at Leithwood's (1994) problem-solving model.

Why are budget talks often problematic? The principal's perception of budget allocation is likely to be different from the library media specialist's. The principal perceives budgeting as addressing many competing demands and apportioning limited resources. The library media specialist, on the other hand, sees budgeting as allocating resources to meet expressed needs. It is again likely that the principal's vision for the school will drive budget allocation. So, identifying the place of the library media program in the school vision is important in addressing budget issues. If a part of the principal's vision for the school is an integrated curriculum, then the presentation of library media collection needs should be aligned with that vision. The collection map should highlight the relationship between the status of the collection and the demands of curriculum priorities in the school. How will the enhancement of the collection help teachers move toward integrating mathematics and science instruction, for example? What specific types of materials will be purchased to further this goal? Who will participate in the decision about what to buy? Will teachers who are adopting integrated curriculum participate in decision making? Can the library media program be a catalyst for integration? The principal will likely be concerned with constraints as well. Often, money is allocated to teachers on a classroom-by-classroom or departmental basis so that individual teachers can buy items exclusively for their classrooms or departments. If the library media specialist wants the principal to increase the collection budget, the money has to be taken from some other source. Classroom and departmental allocations might be that source, if the library media specialist and the principal can work together to assure teachers of their continued participation in purchasing—but purchasing for a central collection rather than for an exclusive collection.

Strategizing how to overcome obstacles is part of the decision-making process; the library media specialist must be ready to cooperate with the principal in overcoming obstacles. The principal follows some internal assumptions, principles, and values in making decisions. By careful observation, the library media specialist can learn what those values are and can consider them in requests. And, finally, the affective concerns of mood and assuredness on the part of the principal are important concerns of the library media specialist seeking decisions.

Besides considering the decision-making process of the principal, the library media specialist must also keep in mind the nature of the principal's day. The characterization of the day as a bombardment of as many as 400 separate interactions stands as a reminder that getting the undivided attention of the principal for extended development of ideas requires some advance notice and planning. Sensitivity to the nature of the principal's work can help the library media specialist work as a teammate rather than as one more interruption.

Considering the time constraints of the principal, the library media specialist does well to provide critical information efficiently. Monthly reporting on the use of the library media center and its resources is one solution. Good management calls for data-based decisions, and only the library media specialist has the data to portray the activity in the library media center. Conventional statistical data—for example, circulation statistics or facilities usage counts, as shown in Figure 3.2—are useful.

Even more helpful, however, are reports that succinctly describe the activity of the library media program to demonstrate its relationship to classroom teaching. The report in Figure 3.3 is an example of such a descriptive report. It shows what classes in the library media program required direct teaching by the library media specialist. A brief description of the activities shows the curriculum connection. The information

---

FIGURE 3.2
Monthly Statistics Report to Principal

High School Library Media Center
February Statistics

Books and print materials circulated	3,189
Nonprint materials circulated	75
Total circulation	3,264

Center use	Computer lab	Library media center
Classes schedule	268	204
From classes	3,210	3,710
Study hall/open hour	1,560	6,575
Total	4,770	10,285
Student/day average	251	541.1

Daily use of LMC and computer lab

Total classes scheduled	472
Average classes per day in 7 available periods per day	24.8

---

skills column lists the skill areas taught. The levels of instructional support provide a taxonomy of collaboration between the teacher and the library media specialist. This single page conveys considerable information about the nature, as well as the amount, of teaching and learning activity occurring in the library media program.

While a principal may simply file this document away, if the library media specialist then meets even annually with the principal to review the needs for resources or staffing or space, the data are available and can be used effectively and efficiently to help characterize the nature of the needs. Also, in the face of any question from parent, central office administrator, or teacher, the principal has available documentation to characterize the library media program.

IMPACT OF THE PRINCIPAL ON THE SCHOOL LIBRARY MEDIA PROGRAM

Both the leadership and management roles of the principal govern the potential for the success of the library media program. At the leadership end of the continuum, it is important for the principal to understand the library media program's potential to advance the vision and mission of the school. Yet studies suggest that principals frequently have little knowledge of that potential. Wilson, Blake, and Lyders (1993) surveyed 1,000 principals and 1,000 library media specialists to measure their level of expertise about library media programming. In that study, over 68 percent of the principals responding felt that they were not adequately trained in the area of school library media programming, and over 78 percent indicated that they should have more training. In a 1996 survey of NCATE programs that offer principal licensure, only 18 percent included information about school library media in coursework (Wilson and MacNeil 1998). This naivete is cause for concern. It seems difficult to imagine that a principal can effectively hire personnel for a library media program without an understanding of the program's role and relationship to the overall school program. Likewise, performance evaluation of library media specialists cannot be effective without fundamental knowledge about library media programming. The intent of evaluation is improvement of professional practice, yet such guidance cannot occur without awareness of what constitutes effective practice.

There is a continuing tendency to use a teacher model for performance appraisal of library media specialists (Bryant 2002). While the teaching role of the library media specialist is indeed important, it is only part of the position. For example, organizing resources for ready access—whether those resources sit on a shelf or a server—is a significant aspect of the library media professional's work. Similarly, collaborating with teachers for instructional planning and collection development is a crucial aspect of the position. These and other library media specialist responsibilities do not typically appear on the standard teacher appraisal template. Principals have significant impact on the library media program through the performance appraisal process, wherein they set expectations that indicate value for the variety of components in the library media role. They would do well to ensure that the local school district endorses specialized performance appraisal criteria for library media specialists. A Web search for "media specialist evaluation form"

FIGURE 3.3
Instructional Support Monthly Data Summary

This report summarizes support to teachers in preparation for classes. It stresses those areas where the media program enables resource-based teaching and the areas of the information skills curriculum addressed.

Key to levels of instructional support:
1. Gathering materials in response to teacher requests
2. Working with students on a small-group or individual basis during a teacher-planned activity
3. Teaching classes in support of a teacher-planned activity
4. Sharing equal responsibility with the teacher for planning and delivering instruction

Keys to areas of information skills curriculum:
1. Task definition
2. Information-seeking strategies
3. Location and access
4. Use of information
5. Creation and communication
6. Evaluation and self-assessment

Date	Teacher	Periods	Level	Activities	Info. Skills
April 1, 2	Cochran	1, 2	2	English 11 research papers	3, 4
April 1, 3, 5	Smith	4, 5	4	English 9 Shakespeare and his times	2, 3, 4, 5
April 1	Garden	5, 6, 7	2	Adv. Biology Honors research	3
April 1, 4	Roshek	1, 2, 3, 5, 6	2	European History research	3
April 2, 3, 4, 5, 8, 9, 10, 11, 12, 15	Warner	7	3	Futures Careers research	3, 4, 5
April 4, 5, 8	Cooper	3	3	Environmental Analysis research	3, 4
April 4, 5, 8	Phipps	1, 3, 6	3	US Lit Biographies	2, 3
April 5,10,12,15,17	Brown	3,4,6,7	2	Humanities decades research	3
April 15	Brack	1, 5, 7	4	US Lit decades research	3, 4, 5

FIGURE 3.3 (Cont.)

Date	Teacher			Description	
April 15	Finken	1, 3, 4	3	China/Japan fiction book selection	3
April 16, 17, 18, 19	Finken	6, 7	3	Global Studies change agent research	2, 3, 4
April 17, 18	Brothers	5	3	Personal history collages	3
April 18, 19, 22	Phipps	1, 3, 6	2	US Lit research	3
April 19	Castor	1, 3, 6, 7	3	English 10 research	3
April 22, 23	Brown	3, 4, 6, 7	2	Humanities	3
April 23, 24, 25, 26	Brown	2	3	English 10 Honors research	3, 4, 5
April 24	Roshek	1, 2, 3, 5, 6	2	European History research post–WW II	3, 4
April 24, 25	Mitchell	4	2	English 10 research	3
April 24, 25, 26	Becker	7	2	Panel discussion research	3, 4
April 24, 25	Finken	6, 7	3	Global Studies change agent research	3, 4
April 26, 29, 30	Cohn	6	2	Panel discussion research	3, 4
April 29, 30	Phipps	1, 3, 6	2	US Lit research	3, 4

yields a variety of forms and formats tailored to the expectations for a library media specialist.

Perhaps the greatest impact the principal can have is on integrating the library media program into the school program. A study of the occurrence of consulting between library media specialists and classroom teachers revealed the influence of the principal's expectations (Donham van Deusen and Tallman 1994). In that study, library media specialists reported whether they perceived that their principals held expectations for them to collaborate with teachers. Library media specialists who perceived that their principals expected them to collaborate with classroom teachers reported significantly more instances of consultative work with teachers than those whose principals were not perceived as holding that expectation. In the same study, library media specialists reported the occurrences of their teaching information skills *in association with* classroom instruction. Again, the principal's expectation that such collaboration occur made a significant positive difference in the amount of consultation done by the library media specialist. Likewise, Campbell (1994) found that support from the principal is essential for library media programs to succeed, regardless of the professional level of the library media specialist.

PARTICIPATIVE DECISION MAKING

While principals play a major role in shaping school decisions, the movement toward participative decision making affects the ways in which principals lead. The participative management movement is founded on certain assumptions. One assumption is that when those who are affected by a decision share ownership of the decision, their commitment is greater. Another assumption is that better decisions result from the collaboration—a benefit of diverse interests and perspectives. Another expectation is that participation in decision making will serve to unify the participants so that they cooperate. Vroom and Yetton (1973) delineate four degrees of participation in managerial decision making:

1. Autocratic decision making: The principal makes the decision alone.
2. Information sharing: The principal obtains information from subordinates but makes the decision alone.
3. Consultative decision making: The principal shares the problem

with a subordinate and then makes a decision that may or may not reflect the subordinate's influence.

4. Democratic decision making: The principal shares the problem with subordinate(s) and together they analyze the problem and arrive at a solution.

A study by Somech (2002) indicated that any given principal engages in various degrees of participative management. Perhaps more important, this study found that autocratic decision making was relatively rare among principals; instead principals often tended to function at the consultative decision-making level. This finding signals a need for the library media specialist to establish a role as a consultant to that decision-making process.

Research suggests that the degree to which principals share decision making with staff members develops over time as a result of specific factors. Yukl and Fu (1999) found that competence, job level, goal congruence, and time together with the principal were determinants in the level of management participation. The library media specialist who pays attention to these factors is then more likely to have influence on the principal's decision making. The influence-seeking library media specialist can make particular effort toward two of these: goal congruence and time together with the principal. Aligning the goals of the library media program with those of the principal is an obvious step toward greater influence. Equally important is communicating this alignment explicitly so that the principal recognizes and appreciates the sense of common purpose between the library media specialist and himself or herself. Similarly, these findings suggest that time spent with the principal can yield greater influence. This is not to say "hanging out" in the principal's office is a good idea, but it does suggest that frequent substantive communication with the principal beats "hiding out" in the library media center.

A participative decision-making culture demands special skills on the part of the principal. Team building, conflict identification and resolution, consensus building, communication, persuasion, and diplomacy are important skill areas for a principal in a participative management environment. Principals are still expected to have a vision for the school, but the implementation of that vision depends on the principal's ability to promote ownership of the vision among all the stakeholders of the school. Reconciling the principal's authority with staff participation poses a leadership challenge to principals (Broadwell 1996). The principal be-

ENHANCEMENT IN ACTION:
SHARED DECISION MAKING

Consider a setting in which a library media specialist perceives that students are not reading enough and that one possible solution is to establish a sustained silent reading time throughout the school. The library media specialist takes this idea to the decision-making team, which includes various teachers, other specialists, and the principal. One approach is for the principal to state the problem (too little reading among students) and then state the potential solution (give students reading time every day for the last 15 minutes of the school day). A second approach is to state the problem and offer alternative solutions such as, "We could agree to a silent reading time for the whole school or we could agree that students would all get 15 minutes of sustained silent reading during their language arts class each day." Another approach is to state the problem and ask for potential solutions, allowing the group to propose possible solutions. Which approach will engender the most ownership? Which approach will most likely result in implementation? Will the problem—too little independent reading—be solved?

comes a participant in decision making, functioning not as the decision maker but as facilitator, advisor, and executive officer (Heath and Vik 1996). The principal must work as a facilitator and a guide; actively listen to the ideas of others; incorporate those new ideas into the assumptions, principles, and values already ingrained; and keep "all eyes on the prize" (that is, to maintain the vision for the school).

Schoolwide participation in decision making increases the complexity for the library media specialist as well. Whereas in a hierarchical setting the library media specialist must work to align the library media program with the intentions of one person, the principal, in a participative management environment, that alignment must be evident to many more participants. Clear and concise communication, active listening, and big-picture thinking are important not only for the principal but also for the library media specialist. Taking into account the points of view of the various stakeholders is an important initial step in a participative management environment.

CONCLUSION

Some topics will be more difficult to address than others in a participative management environment, depending on the stakes. Budget allocations will require clear communication of the benefits to be accrued by all when dollars are allocated to any one program. Likewise, scheduling issues can carry high stakes, since these decisions affect the nature of the workday for teachers and have student-management implications as well. However, working in this kind of decision-making environment has many of the same requirements as alignment with the principal: consider the perspective of others and determine how the library media program can be aligned with the needs and wants of other programs within the school. The critical issue is to keep the mission and vision clearly in view—an important responsibility of both the principal and the library media specialist.

ACTION STRATEGIES

Information Access and Delivery

- Help the principal maintain current awareness of innovations, such as new technologies for instruction or management. E-mail can be useful, but beware of overload. Be selective and focus on that which is locally relevant.
- Arrange with the principal for opportunities to appear as a "regular" on staff meeting agendas and use the time well—share briefly information that relates directly to concerns of teachers.

Program Administration

- Educate the principal to the role of the library media specialist. Remember what the workday of the principal is—providing the principal with an unsolicited deluge of articles and books to read is not the best way. Instead, explain your work to the principal in terms of your profession. Use terms from the AASL/AECT guidelines, such as "instructional partner" and "teacher," to identify your roles. Make reference to collection maps as a professional tool for describing the state of the collection and show how your professional skills relate to those of the teacher and the principal.

- Consider the principal's style when deciding whether to encourage drop-in visits or make formal invitations.
- Make opportunities for meaningful communication with the principal. Given the nature of the principal's day, it makes sense to schedule a weekly or monthly 30-minute session with the principal to review issues related to the library media program. These must not be complaint sessions, but productive meetings of give and take, advice seeking, brainstorming, and activity reporting. Provide documentation that shows what is occurring in the library media center. Use e-mail for updates, but don't overload the principal's mailbox.
- Read the same journals your principal reads (for example, *Bulletin of the NASSP*, *Principal*, and *Educational Leadership*). This practice will increase your familiarity with "principal terminology."
- Be attuned to the vision the principal holds for the school and seek ways to communicate the relationship of the library media program to that vision.
- Help teachers understand how the library media program benefits them, so that they too can advocate for support from the principal.
- Help make the principal and the school "look good" by showcasing the library media program to constituents—parents, community members, school board members, and school district officials.

SCENARIO FOR DISCUSSION

The principal at Smith Memorial Middle School takes her role as instructional leader very seriously. She is determined to focus staff meetings on professional growth issues. At the end-of-the-year meeting, she announces her goal for the coming year: a series of staff development meetings focused on how to improve student performance on standardized tests. Mr. Brown, the library media specialist, is worried that this emphasis on tests means that the library media program will be completely "written out" of staff meetings for the coming year. He recalls that research studies indicate a positive correlation between library media programs and student achievement. He also has concerns about test items about information literacy. Should he approach the principal to ensure that the library media program is part of the year's staff development agenda? If so, how should he approach the topic with the principal?

REFERENCES

American Association of School Librarians and Association for Educational Communications and Technology.(1998). *Information Power: Building Partnerships for Learning*. Chicago: American Library Association.

Blase, J. and J. Blase (2002, December). "The Dark Side of Leadership: Teacher Perspectives of Principal Mistreatment." *Educational Administration Quarterly 38* (5) 671–728.

Broadwell, D. (1996, January/February). "Situational Leadership and the Educator of the '90s." *Emergency Librarian 23* (3): 21–27.

Bryant, M. (2002). "The Role of the Principal in the Evaluation of the School's Library Media Specialist," *School Libraries Worldwide 8* (1): 85–91.

Bryk, A. S., V. Lee, and J. Smith (1989, May). "High School Organization and Its Effects on Teachers and Students: An Interpretative Summary of the Research." Paper presented at "Choice and Control in American Education conference," University of Wisconsin-Madison.

Campbell, B. (1994). "High School Principal Roles and Implementation Themes for Mainstreaming Information Literacy Instruction." Ph.D. dissertation, University of Connecticut.

Council of Chief State School Officers (1996). *Interstate School Leaders Licensure Consortium Standards for School Leaders*. Retrieved March 15, 2004, from www.ccsso.org/.

Donham van Deusen, J. and J. Tallman (1994, Fall). "The Impact of Scheduling on Curriculum Consultation and Information Skills Instruction." *School Library Media Quarterly 23* (1): 17–25.

Hartzell, G. (2003, October). "The Power of Audience: Effective Communication with Your Principal." *Library Media Connection 22* (2): 20–22.

Heath, J. and P. Vik (1996, January). "School Site Councils: Building Communities of Leaders." *Principal 75* (3): 25, 28.

Kennedy, C. (2001, March). "Splitting the Principalship." *Principal 80* (4): 60–61.

Leithwood, K. (1994, November). "Leadership for School Restructuring." *Educational Administration Quarterly 30* (4): 498–518.

Manasse, A. L. (1985, January). "Improving Conditions for Principal -Effectiveness: Policy Implications of Research." *Elementary School Journal 85* (3): 439–463.

National Association of Elementary School Principals (2001). *Leading Learning Communities: Standards for What Principals Should Know and Be Able to Do*. Alexandria, VA: National Association of Elementary School Principals.

Pierce, M. (2000, September/October). "Portrait of the 'Super Principal.'" *Harvard Education Letter Research Center*. Retrieved September 28, 2004, from www.editor.org/post/issues/2000-50/principal.shtml.

Somech, A. (2002, August). "Explicating the Complexity of Participative Management: An Investigation of Multiple Dimensions." *Educational Administration Quarterly 38* (3): 341–371.

Vroom, V. H. and P. W. Yetton (1973). *Leadership and Decision Making*. Pittsburgh, PA: University of Pittsburgh Press.

Wilson, P. P. and A. J. MacNeil (1998, September 1). "In the Dark." *School Library Journal 44* (9): 114–116.

Wilson, P., M. Blake, and J. Lyders (1993, September/October). "A Study and a Plan for Partnership." *Emergency Librarian 12* (1): 19–24.

Yetter, C. (1994). "Resource-Based Learning in the Information Age School: The Intersection of Roles and Relationships of the School Library Media Specialist, Teachers, and Principals." Ed.D. dissertation. Seattle University.

Yukl, G. and P. P. Fu (1999). "Determinants of Delegation and Consultation by Managers." *Journal of Organizational Behavior 20* (2): 219–232.

Chapter 4

The School District

This chapter:

- describes the school district's influence on the school library media program
- considers site-based decision making and centralized decision making
- identifies specific contributions that a library media specialist can make to district planning and policy
- identifies action strategies for working within the school district context

School districts vary in size, number of schools, and number of students. Some districts cover expansive countywide areas, and others govern a single K–12 school. Some districts have an extensive hierarchy of central-office administrators, specialists, and support staff, while others have a single chief officer and a small support staff. Fewer and fewer districts have a district-level library media director. In 1987, the *School Library Journal* survey of school library media specialists reported that 40 percent of respondents had a central office position; by 2001, that number was down to 30 percent (Miller 2001). Many districts assign a central office administrator (such as a curriculum director or an assistant superintendent) oversight for the library media program, and many have no central office representative for the library media program at all. In each setting, the person who takes responsibility for relating the library media program to the district's direction and policy varies, and in many small districts, it is the building-level library media specialist. Whoever acts as liaison between the district's central decision-making authority and the school library media program must contend with four major organizational issues: funding, personnel, curriculum, and technology.

FUNDING

Funding is allocated in different ways in different school districts. More centralized districts allocate a per-pupil amount earmarked specifically for library media resources. Many library media specialists appreciate this automatic allocation to their program for its reliability and equity across the district. However, where site-based decision making has brought spending decisions to the building level, staff members and principals work together to make decisions about resource spending. Wohlstetter and Buffett (1992) studied five major decentralized districts. In those districts, allocation to the schools was based on enrollment. Each school had a total FTE (full-time equivalency) staffing allotment to be "spent," based on building-level decisions, and a total dollar amount for each of several budget categories to be spent, again based on building decisions. As site-based decision making has become more prevalent, this practice is closer to the norm than the centralized budget process. An exception may be those situations where a districtwide priority is set for improving school library media programs. The Houston Independent School District is a case in point (McCaffrey 2003). When such a district priority is set, it is often the result of an awakening to the fact that the school library media programs are in dire circumstances (as in Houston where the average book collection was 23 years old and where catalogs were not centrally automated across the district).

While site-based decision making has caused anxiety among many library media specialists, it may benefit the library media program to have funding decisions made "closer to home." In site-based management, some would say that what the principal considers important is often what happens (Beasley 1996). In surveying Indiana library media specialists, Callison (1994) found a strong relationship between how frequently the library media specialist and principal conversed about budget and the number of dollars per pupil invested in library media materials. The differences are summarized in Figure 4.1.

FIGURE 4.1

Per Pupil Allocations for Books Based on Frequency of Media Specialist and Principal Interaction (Callison 1994)

		Interaction with Principal			
	State Average	None	Annual	Monthly	Weekly
Elementary	$5.91	$5.53	$5.92	$6.79	$9.45
Junior High	$5.85	$5.60	$5.94	$6.21	$6.75
Senior High	$5.43	$4.65	$6.03	$6.57	$6.51

The more frequent the conversations, the higher the dollars. Thus, placing responsibility for allocations at the building level may be an opportunity to increase resources, if the library media specialist communicates with colleagues, including the principal. To learn how well the library media collection responds to teachers' needs, a simple chart can be given to each teacher listing the major units they teach for which the library media program should be a resource. Teachers can then complete the chart and return it to provide the library media specialist with indications of their perceived needs. This information starts the conversation with teachers about how the library media program can improve its support. Next, the library media specialist must take action based on the teachers' responses and communicate with each teacher about how his or her input is being used. An example of such a chart appears in Figure 4.2.

Site-based decision making calls for increased responsiveness and accountability to the library media program's clients. It calls for justifying the library media center's budget based on program outcomes. Such built-in accountability holds real promise for library media programs because many curriculum innovations depend on strong collections, and the people most aware of that dependence are classroom teachers who will be participants in budgeting decisions. In a school where resource-based teaching and learning are occurring, the library media specialist does well to provide justification for the program's budget proposal to the entire staff. Figure 4.3 shows an example of a proposal presented at

---

FIGURE 4.2
Teacher Input for Collection Development

To: Mr. Holmes
From: Your library media specialist

How well is our collection working for you? How can we improve?

Please fill in the chart below and return to me by March 1.

Unit	Rating (Excellent Good Fair Poor)	Suggestions for improvement in our library media center	Outside sources I use to supplement
The Short Story			
Romeo and Juliet			
To Kill a Mockingbird			
Expository Writing			
Quests			
Castles			

---

a staff meeting where the building's budget for the coming year is under discussion.

Providing direct information to teachers helps them make decisions based on information; when they can see how library media allocations have been spent, how they will be spent, and the benefit to them and their students, they are much more likely to be supportive. In an environment of shared decision making, providing data is crucial if decisions are to be rational.

Any teacher who has embraced resource-based teaching or who uses multiple resources to supplement a textbook can readily appreciate having locally available the resources he or she needs. Only when teachers feel disenfranchised or underserved by the library media program will they question supporting library media resources. Library media specialists must take the initiative to reach out to teachers, to increase their use of the library media center and its resources, and to make the resources as accessible as possible. Often teachers want to create their own classroom libraries because they consider the library media center too

FIGURE 4.3
Budget Proposal—
Elementary School Library Media Center

Expenditures This Year

Item	Comment	Spent
Books	Reading themes, grades 5–6	$1369
	Reading themes, grades 3–4	$1,211
	Children's Choice Award Books	$235
	Books to support author residency	$116
	Books to support social studies, 5–6	$118
	Books to support social studies, 3–4	$165
	Books to support social studies, 1–2	$50
	MC/NS collection building	$178
	Professional books	$55
	Reference books (almanac, author biography)	$125
	Award winners, student interest	$191
	Pattern books (kindergarten)	$425
Total Books		**$4,238**

Note that there was very little purchasing for books for student self-selection; most purchases were curriculum-related.

Item	Comment	Spent
Supplies	Laminating film, transparencies, transparency pens, printer cartridges, computer paper	$574
Subscriptions		$395
AV Software	Audio and DVD	$120
Computer Software	*Kidspiration*, Replacements	$375
Total		**$1,465**
Grand Total		**$5,702**

PROPOSAL FOR NEXT YEAR

Books	
Books for reading themes, Grades 3–6	$1,600
Books for reading themes, Grades K–2 (includes some science and social studies literature)	$2,000
Science trade books	$1,300
Social studies trade books	$600
Books for student self-selection	$500
Total Request for Books	**$6,000**
Computer networked resources	
Tumble Books subscription for read-alongs	$450
Virus protection	$500
Total Software Request	**$850**
Supplies	
Computer paper, printer cartridges, laminating film, DVD	$450
Subscriptions	$400
Total Supplies Request	$850
Grand Total Request	**$7,700**

remote or inaccessible. The benefits of centralizing resources need to be publicized:

- Circulation and inventory control systems already exist; it will not be necessary for teachers to create a record-keeping system.
- Cataloging reduces duplicate purchases so that more resources can be available.
- Pooling dollars for a central collection, rather than dividing them among classrooms, makes it possible to buy expensive items when the need arises.
- Access to all materials is improved for both teachers and students.

Budgets for capital investments are typically centralized. These are larger, long-term expenditures, and concern for equity among schools is perhaps one justification for retaining these decisions at the central office. These expenditures affect library media specialists because they typically include equipment (such as projectors, computers, furniture, and peripherals). Centralized decisions typically include which computer platform to use, how many computers should be purchased, what capacity is really needed at each level, what peripherals schools need, how frequently overhead projectors need to be replaced, and when it is time to move to the next video format. Yet they all have impact on the school library media program.

To influence capital expenditure, either the district library media coordinator or, if there is not one, a school library media specialist must develop and nurture a working relationship with the district's financial officer responsible for capital purchases. Finance officers want to spend money wisely, and so do library media specialists. With expertise on equipment specifications and reasonable replacement cycles, library media specialists can improve the value the district gets for its money. It is important to accept some assumptions in working with finance officers. Their charge is to conserve, to spread the funding over the many demands from groups throughout the district; unreasonable demands are detrimental. This situation calls for the library media specialist to accept the spending parameters, and then work within those parameters to acquire the best equipment possible. The advantage of quantity purchase is substantial, so working to amass orders is worthwhile. This one simple strategy will be appreciated by the finance officer, and the library media specialist can quickly be seen as a valuable colleague at the district level. Finance officers are also concerned about equity; be-

ENHANCEMENT IN ACTION:
LIBRARY MEDIA PROGRAMS AS A SUPERINTENDENT'S
PRIORITY

April 2003: Media centers nationwide are being hit with the worst budget crisis in recent history, but that hasn't stopped Bill Harner from updating his Greenville County (SC) school district's aging library collection or buying new Dell computers for 42 media centers. "While we are facing financial struggles, media centers will remain a priority. Media services are an integral part of the education plan," Harner says. "We strive to be the best." Indeed, Harner's accomplishments in his three short years as superintendent are impressive. He worked with the school board to pass a budget allocating $1.2 million annually over five years to build new library collections, and he secured more than $400,000 for 418 new computers. Harner, who heads 84 schools in South Carolina's largest school district, regularly visits library media centers and attends faculty meetings to explain the importance of weeding old collections (Whelan 2003).

cause they are accountable to a governing board, fairness across the district is important to them. By maintaining awareness of the biases at work at the district level, the library media specialist can increase library media program resources.

Even in tight financial times, it is important to maintain optimism and commitment to the belief that library media programs really make a difference in student learning. It is easy to become discouraged when one reads of districtwide and statewide cuts in library media funding. Yet, regardless of the situation, districts have money, and the question that remains is, "What are the best programs to invest in?" The library media program needs to be seen as such a program, and thi can happen only when library media specialists work closely with administrators at both the building and district levels. There are exemplary districts where superintendents and library media specialists are working together even in tight financial times. These examples need to be showcased where district-level support is needed. The American Association of School Librarians identifies these exemplary administrators with its School

Administrator of the Year Award. Library media specialists can share the stories of these individuals with their own districts to show what can be done. A recent example, which hails from Greenville, South Carolina, is highlighted in the shaded box.

PERSONNEL

Of the four major district-level functions, the library media specialist may have the least involvement in personnel matters. However, some aspects of district-level personnel practice affect the library media program. Two particularly significant ones are staffing allocations for library media professional and support staff and district policies on personnel evaluation. In highly centralized districts, staffing allocations for teachers are determined for each building at the district level. This practice, which seems to persist even as districts move to site-based management, is reasonable since staffing accounts for a large percentage of the district's budget—often approaching or exceeding 80 percent (Wohlstetter and Buffett 1992). Such a large investment demands close governance and accountability to the governing board. However, the building principal, who may or may not ask staff to participate, usually determines exactly how the allocation is spent (for example, how many teachers will be assigned to each grade level or how many paraprofessionals there will be and where those paraprofessionals will work).

Specialized staff positions, such as guidance counselors, principals, and library media specialists, often continue to be district-determined, even in districts with high commitment to site-based decision making. The district value for equity across schools accounts for this practice, at least in part. District-level policy thus directly affects the library media program in setting its staffing level. Often districts assign one certified library media specialist per school, regardless of size, or they determine staffing by ranges of student enrollment, so that, for example, schools with an enrollment of up to 700 have one library media specialist, schools from 700 to 1,200 have 1.5, schools over 1,200 have two, and so on. When staffing allocations depend on district policy, the library media program needs high visibility of its effect on teaching and learning so that district policy supports (or increases) those allocations. Without such visibility, the line item for library media personnel in the district budget can be vulnerable whenever administrators need to respond with dollars to a new demand.

Performance appraisal is a process typically managed at the district level and implemented at the building level. Many school districts fail to provide a specialized performance appraisal form or process for library media specialists and instead use a generic form designed for classroom teachers. Clearly, this practice creates significant problems in comprehensive performance assessment because there are many unique aspects in the library media position. Advocating for performance appraisal practices that address all dimensions of the library media professional's position is important. A tailored appraisal tool and process not only affords the opportunity for review of the complete school library media specialist position, it also provides a communication tool for helping school administrators understand the work of the school library media specialist.

Each district typically develops its own appraisal format. The tools used to evaluate the library media professional will need to be consistent with the district format. Some appraisal forms are somewhat open-ended, providing opportunities for the professional to set goals or targets and then submit documentation to describe how these goals have been met. Others are more prescriptive. In situations where a prescriptive model is in place, the library media specialist will want to ensure that all aspects of the position are represented in the criteria: management, teaching, curriculum involvement with teachers, collection development and maintenance, and technology leadership and support. The Missouri Department of Elementary and Secondary Education has developed a comprehensive example of performance appraisal for school library media specialists (Missouri State Department of Education 2002).

CURRICULUM

Consistency, stability, innovation, and equity are values that drive district-level curriculum decisions throughout the district, vertically and horizontally. Consistency calls for curriculum articulation, so that common beliefs about such topics as literacy or hands-on science or using calculators in mathematics guide all teachers' practice, and so that the sequence of learning experiences is appropriate. Likewise, stability is a value; while change is a common topic among schools, long-term and effective change in schools tends to be evolutionary. Innovations, while sometimes initiated by teachers or principals, tend to concern the district bureaucracy because they require coordination and resources for implementation. Equity is the fourth value that district-level curriculum specialists strive to maintain. It is important to recognize the difference between equal and equitable. Equal suggests that each entity has the same, whereas equity connotes fairness, taking all factors into account. Sometimes, schools in lower socioeconomic neighborhoods need more resources, or different kinds of support to balance disadvantages they might have. Often, district-level curriculum directors become the arbiters of fairness. School library media specialists often base decisions on the same considerations within the school context. Acknowledging the similarities between the perspective of the district-level curriculum specialist and the school library media specialist improves the likelihood that these two professionals can work together toward common ends.

Whatever happens with curriculum at the district level has important influence on the library media program. If new science units are being developed and promoted, new foreign languages are being taught, or new courses are being added to the social studies program, library media resources may need to change dramatically to support these new developments. Likewise, if new strategies are being considered (like using manipulative materials in mathematics, or replacing the formal research paper with an I-Search paper, or moving toward performance assessment requiring student production in various media), then library media programs need to change dramatically to provide appropriate materials and develop requisite skills.

While a traditional curriculum development model may be a top-down design, in fact, research suggests that truly effective school systems simultaneously provide opportunities for top-down and bottom-up influence (Cuban 1984). Still, in larger districts, leadership in curriculum often comes from district curriculum generalists and specialists. They maintain awareness of new trends and directions in their specialties, following the literature and attending conferences and workshops to keep up to date. Often these central-office specialists provide staff development to share new ideas with teachers.

The standards movement in curriculum has intensified the centralization of curriculum development. State and district testing programs call for a common curriculum across districts, and in some cases across states. This trend begs for proactive library media specialists who will advocate for curriculum design that incorporates learning to learn, learning to use technology effectively, critical thinking, and literature. Implementing district-level curriculum development and change typically begins through committees led by district-level curriculum specialists. Committees tend to be a primary vehicle for increasing the ownership of new ideas and for disseminating ideas throughout a district. District-level curriculum directors and specialists are initiators and facilitators, and committees are useful for both roles. Curriculum cycles tend to focus on a different content area each year; in districts with a more integrated curriculum, multiple areas, such as mathematics and science, or language arts and social studies, are reviewed simultaneously. Or, the focus may be cross-disciplinary and emphasize a strategy such as assessment or technology integration.

However it is organized, most districts have a schedule for curriculum review. Participation in such reviews is crucial for library media specialists. These committees offer opportunities to learn what and how teachers will be teaching. The library media specialist can be the information specialist for the committee (for example, searching professional literature about the topics under discussion, locating relevant teaching resource material, and searching for new trade books or electronic resources to support curriculum innovations). By actively participating when curriculum change is being planned, the library media specialist can help teachers anticipate topics or strategies for which there will be a wealth of materials or for which material will be scarce. This level of participation is clearly preferable to waiting until all curriculum decisions have been made and then responding by saying, "It will take three months to get what you need," or, "What you are asking for doesn't seem to exist!" Simply put, proactive is better than reactive, and participation from the beginning allows the library media specialist to be proactive. In some settings being appointed to such curriculum committees will require some initiative from the library media specialist. If central-office curriculum specialists are unfamiliar with curriculum-involved school library media programs, they may not even think of including a library media specialist on such a committee. So, initiating contact and articulating why library media specialists should participate in curriculum at the district level may be necessary.

Central-office instruction or curriculum supervisors perceive their positions as invisible (Pajak 1989). They see their role as working to make those in more visible positions—superintendent, principals, and teachers—look good. That invisibility may be something that library media specialists share with curriculum specialists. Both roles involve facilitating the work of others—working behind the scenes. Having this role characteristic in common can bring the library media specialist and curriculum specialist together, since both focus on supporting the work of the "front line." It can also generate competition as each seeks to be a helper. Making the distinction between the content specialist and the resource and instruction specialist is important to foster working relationships.

TECHNOLOGY

Technical support from the district level is an essential ingredient in school districts of all sizes. Networking increases the technical knowledge needed to maintain and upgrade equipment, telecommunication systems, and software. For student production in multimedia, technical knowledge is needed to help building-level library media specialists buy appropriate equipment and learn to use it effectively. Increasingly, districts are employing network specialists and technicians to assist in these specialized needs. Library media specialists can help these technical support people; often technicians are naive about teaching and learning, but highly skilled in the technology itself. Library media specialists can be important intermediaries to help technical support people understand how various technologies will be used so that they can select and deploy equipment in ways that will work most effectively for educational applications.

For district-level planning to be implemented, there must be effective links between the district and building. On many matters, the principal provides that link, particularly in areas of staffing, facilities, personnel management, grade reporting practices, and other managerial topics. The library media specialist can also serve as liaison between district and school by serving on district committees for policy, curriculum, or planning issues. One topic that particularly warrants involving the library media specialist as a liaison is technology.

The library media program should be a highly visible component of the school district's Web presence. Links to the library media center's Web page should be prominent from the school's home page. Ideally, the district's Web pages will include information about the library media program districtwide.

Building-level library media specialists need to design Web pages that serve all the district's clientele—students, teachers, parents, and citizens. Portals for each client group may be one possibility for design. The library media specialist needs to consider what information resources

ENHANCEMENT IN ACTION:
THE LIBRARY MEDIA SPECIALIST AND TECHNOLOGY PLANNING

Planning for instructional and information technologies is complex. District-level planning encourages equity among schools and consistency in vision, program, and platform. The district plan provides the parameters for technology uses. Components of the district plan usually include a mission statement for technology, recommended applications, software guidelines or criteria, hardware, and staff development plans (Langhorne, Gross, Rehmke, and Donham van Deusen, 1989). Then, each building develops its implementation plan, using the district technology plan as its framework. For example, it is likely that a district would determine technology-related competencies for students. At the building level a technology planning team must take those competencies and determine how, when, and by whom they will be taught. The library media specialist is a natural participant on the district's technology planning team. After all, this is the person who uses technology for information seeking; this person is accustomed to tracking reviews of new titles, previewing materials, and determining their fit in the school's program. This person has the bird's eye view of teaching and learning. The ideal is for the district technology planning committee to include people who work in school buildings and continually learn more by observing technology-related activities, by reading professional literature, and by attending technology-rich conferences and institutes. Such activities constitute a substantial part of the library media specialist's work.

At the building level, the library media specialist again is an ideal person to lead in translating the district technology plan into an action plan for the school. The building plan includes identifying specific applications and software and correlating with specific units or courses of study at the building level; deploying and scheduling hardware, whether in labs, minilabs, clusters, or individual classrooms; and providing staff development opportunities on the applications and software to be used in the school. The library media specialist has much to contribute to each of these issues, and can be particularly helpful if he or she has been a member of the district's planning committee, so that the building implementation accurately reflects the district committee's intentions. Besides planning, the library media specialist is responsible for acquiring and managing software and hardware, for providing building-level staff development, for seeking ways to integrate into technology instruction, and for advocating appropriate technology uses. By performing these roles at the building level, the library media specialist gains experiences and insights that result in increasing importance as a member of the ongoing district planning process. Active participation by the library media specialist at the district level brings important visibility to the library media program.

the library media center's Web site can provide. The following possibilities are worthy of consideration:

For students and teachers

- Links to the library media center's subscription databases
- Off-site access to databases, where licensing agreements allow and where password protection can be provided
- Aids for student researchers, such as citation style formats
- Reading suggestions with highlights of new books

For parents and community

- Guides and links to age-appropriate Internet sites
- Information about the library media center's programs
- Links to educational resources on the Web, such as museums
- Links to college planning information, especially for secondary schools
- Links to the local public library and other local agencies, such as museums and recreational/cultural centers

A WORD ABOUT SMALLER DISTRICTS

This chapter has focused on the impact of the district on the school library media program and the influence that the library media program can have at the district level. While there are many very small school districts with skeletal central offices, nevertheless, there is an organizational unit known as the school district. That entity, however small, has its own mission and goals, its own beliefs about teaching and learning, and its own relationship to its community. Where districts are very small, perhaps a regional agency provides leadership, particularly in areas such as curriculum or technical support or staff development. Regardless of district size, each library media specialist has an overarching organization where visibility and advocacy for the library media program constitute an important responsibility.

ADVOCACY

While it may seem intuitively obvious to those in the library media profession that library media specialists belong on district committees, can be key players in implementing district programs, and have contributions to make to district-level work in finance, curriculum, personnel, or technology, these roles are rarely obvious to key decision makers at the district level. Thus, the importance of taking initiative cannot be overemphasized. Library media specialists must make the case for what their specialization can offer, and then must act on their promises. When we say we can provide information, we must provide it in a timely fashion. When we say we can contribute to the conversation about curriculum articulation, we must produce. When we say we have ideas about using technology, we must articulate them. When we suggest that we can save the district money, we must come up with purchasing recommendations that accomplish that. The "say-do ratio" must be high.

WORKING WITHIN THE SYSTEM

More than 40 years ago, Robert Presthus (1962) published an interesting analysis of how people work within organizations. His theory is particularly relevant for the school library media specialist working within the school district context. The responses Presthus described are those of the upward mobile, the organizational indifferent, and the organizational ambivalent. An upward mobile person is optimistic about the organization and plays roles within the organization to advance. Such individuals identify closely with the organization—the success of the organization is their success. An upward mobile person is able to overlook inconsistencies in the system. Accepting the organization's goals commits the upward mobile to conform to whatever the powerful influences in the organization want. The organizational indifferent is a disenfranchised person who does not identify with the organization. An indifferent focuses on his or her own job and remains aloof from the larger system. The organizational ambivalent speculates what the organization ought to be rather than what it is. This type is ambivalent toward his or her status in the organization—in contrast to the upward mobile. The ambivalent wants success but does not want to pay the organizational price—this price is often compromise. Often the ambivalent is characterized as something of an outsider who may lack the political finesse needed to work within the system. Each of these is a pure type, but rarely do people fit into only one category. Indeed, the behavior is often situational. Deciding how to respond to organizational demands requires reflection about stakes and potential consequences.

As an example of a library media specialist playing a role in the larger system, assume that a districtwide decision has been made that no R-rated movies are to be shown in schools. This decision will eliminate showing several films that have been used in high school classes for several years, for example, *The Killing Fields* used in a social studies course on war. How the high school library media specialist accommodates this decision can be classified by Presthus's theory. The upward mobile will support the decision unquestioningly. Or, this type might diplomatically point out, via a carefully developed and annotated list, those videos for which exceptions might be made. The organizational indifferent will have no opinion. The organizational ambivalent may question the decision based on principles of intellectual freedom, feeling that a class of materials ought not to be censored and that such a ruling violates teachers' and students' rights. An organizational ambivalent would probably openly state his or her concerns about the ruling and would be likely to contact the American Library Association Intellectual Freedom Office for an opinion.

As another example, consider a district technology committee that is determining where to allocate computers and decides to place computers in kindergarten rooms for the first time. Parents of young children, early childhood teachers, and the school board have expressed their desire to increase the young children's access to technology. The library media specialist on the committee believes that it would be more developmentally appropriate for computer use and instruction to begin at third grade when children can begin to take advantage of the computer's capabilities for more sophisticated uses, seeing the computer as a tool rather than a reward. The upward mobile will recognize that the influential forces in the organization want young children to access computers and will accept this allocation, despite needs in upper grades. The organizational indifferent will have no opinion, and probably would not participate on the committee in the first place. The organizational ambivalent might oppose the idea and express concerns about developmental appropriateness or the needs at other grade levels and may appeal to literature from early childhood education to support his or her position.

Deciding how to respond to district-level issues challenges the library media specialist. Each response must be weighed in terms of what is at stake, what are the consequences of agreeing or not agreeing with the district, and what will benefit students and teachers most in the long run. There will be times when performing as the upward mobile may seem to be the long-run best choice, and there will be times when, - despite the consequences, the organizational ambivalent's posture is called for. Assessing the situation each time challenges the library media specialist to consider repeatedly his or her position within the district context.

The library media specialist contributes to the work at the district level and is affected by district-level policy and planning. As districts adopt more site-based decision making, the district's role shifts toward providing a vision and parameters within which building decisions are made. When decision making moves to the building level, the potential for the library media specialist to influence decisions may increase, if other participants in the process have benefited from the library media program and see its value in improving teaching and learning. Responsiveness to the local clientele increases in consequence as decision making gets closer to the action.

ACTION STRATEGIES

Program Administration

- Participate in district-level policy and planning when you have special expertise. Examples include:
  —materials selection policy
  —copyright policy
  —acceptable use policy
  —privacy issues
  —networking for access to information
- Develop a positive professional relationship with the district's chief financial officer. Demonstrate to him or her your insight into the budgeting process, the importance of differentiating between *needs* and *wants*, the necessity of compromise, and the importance of fiscal accountability.
- Work to ensure that administrators place you on district committees related to curriculum development and revision. Emphasize your knowledge of resources and technologies as a potential contribution to the process.
- Develop a network among educators across the district. Present yourself as a problem solver.
- Be a friend to the district's physical plant—it is easier to get electrical connections where they are needed, move furniture to accommodate new technologies, and make other physical plant improvements when workers know they are appreciated and respected.
- Develop and maintain a library media Web presence within the district's Web site. Consider all constituents in designing and organizing pages.
- Periodically provide the superintendent with "good news" to share with the board. Choose substantive items to share, but remember that such news as major increases in circulation, visiting authors, minigrants received by the library media center, or participation in library media events by local "celebrities" might also be good items because they show increased use, community involvement, and initiative.

SCENARIO FOR DISCUSSION

The district has embraced a whole-language approach to reading for at least ten years. During this time, all reading instruction in the classroom has been based on trade books rather than a reading textbook. As a result, the library media specialist has lobbied for funding to purchase multiple copies of titles used in classroom reading instruction. In addition, single titles have been purchased to support themes taught as part of the reading program. Now the district has adopted a new reading textbook series for all elementary schools. Materials for each grade level include anthologies and selected lists of books for extended reading.

The shelves in the library media centers hold many sets of books, and many individual titles that may no longer be used with the new program. With the added expense to the district for the reading series, it is likely that funding for library books will diminish. What should library media specialists be doing at the building and district levels to sustain their own collections and to support the new program?

REFERENCES

Beasley, A. (1996, November). "Becoming a Proactive Library Leader: Leadership 101." *School Library Media Activities Monthly 13* (3): 20–22+.

Callison, D. (1994). "The AIME Statewide Survey of School Library Media Centers: Relationships and Associations from the Data." *Indiana Media Journal 17* (1): 103–162.

Cuban, L. (1984). "Transforming the Frog into a Prince: Effective Schools Research, Policy and Practice at the District Level." *Harvard Educational Review 54* (2): 129–151.

Langhorne, M. J., J. Gross, D. Rehmke, and J. Donham van Deusen (1989). *Teaching with Computers: A New Menu for the '90s.* Phoenix: Oryx Press.

McCaffrey, M. (2003, February). "The Change Master." *School Library Journal 49* (2): 55–56. Retrieved May 4, 2003, from *Academic Search Elite.*

Miller, M. (2001, October). "New Money, Old Books." *School Library Journal 47* (10): 50–60.

Missouri State Department of Education (2002, July 29). *Guidelines for Performance-Based Library Media Specialist Evaluation.* Retrieved March 16, 2004, from www.dese.state.mo.us/divimprove/curriculum/library/.

Pajak, E. (1989). *The Central Office Supervisor of Curriculum and Instruction: Setting the Stage for Success.* Boston: Allyn and Bacon.

Presthus, R. (1962). *The Organizational Society: An Analysis and a Theory.* New York: Random House.

Whelan, D. L. (2003, April). "SC Librarians Laud Top Administrator." *School Library Journal* 49 (4): 19.

Wohlstetter, P. and T. Buffett (1992, March). "Decentralizing Dollars Under School-Based Management: Have Policies Changed?" *Educational Policy* 6 (1): 35–54.

Chapter 5

The Community

This chapter:

- describes the purposes of community involvement
- identifies ways for the library media program to communicate and cooperate with community entities
- identifies action strategies for cooperative community activities

While the school plays a central role in children's development, they benefit when there is interaction between the school and its community. Parent organizations, school boards and parent-teacher conferences represent typical school-to-home connections, but these relationships are limited primarily to parents of school-age children or to select community members. The greater community can also share in raising its youth. Businesses, social agencies, museums, and libraries have human, physical, and fiscal resources that can complement the school's resources.

PURPOSES OF INVOLVEMENT

Community involvement in the school library media program can serve several purposes (Gorton and Schneider, 1991). Through involvement, parents and other citizens become informed about how the library media program helps students. Understanding the program helps people support it verbally and fiscally. Most important, when parents are involved, they are able to help their children academically and socially.

Community participation also provides the school library media program with new ideas and expertise.

FAMILY INVOLVEMENT

The family is the core of the school's community. Teachers and the school principal communicate directly with families through parent-teacher conferences, parent organizations, and newsletters. The library media program lacks the direct visibility of the classroom or the football field. Making presentations to parent and community groups is one way to share information about the library media program and gain support from people who have influence on either the school or the district.

For example, a library media specialist can make presentations to parents about choosing materials for the library media center. Often, parents are rather naive about the materials selection process. That naiveté can lead to challenges or concerns about materials in the school library media program, particularly at the elementary school level. Worse can be a sentiment that the library shelves are full, so why keep spending money on more materials? Topics could be the selection policy, including criteria for selection; reviewing sources and selection tools; or procedures for parents, teachers, and students to suggest items for the collection. Naive parents may think that purchasing for a library is akin to a shopping spree, but a presentation like this can help them understand the complexity of collection building. Another area that may interest parents is Internet use. Since the mass media have raised public concern about inappropriate Internet activities, the library media specialist can alleviate this concern with a session in which parents access the Internet and experience appropriate use. Sessions that address child safety on the Web may be of particular interest. During such a session the library media specialist could explain local policies for responsible Internet use or demonstrate use of subscription databases and help parents see the value they offer in contrast to "free" information. To leave these topics unaddressed opens the door for criticism from parents who have too little information from less reliable sources than the library media specialist. Such informative meetings are likely to increase knowledge, confidence, and communication.

A library media specialist can also offer parents, particularly at the middle school level, programs about homework and study skills. Strategies for note taking, examples of ready-reference materials appropriate for the home, and school library media resources available to students to help students with their homework can all be topics for such a presentation.

Literacy programs are a natural family-school library media center connection. Such programs can target special populations. For example, if a school has English-as-a-second-language students, then a program might include sharing books that will help children build their English vocabulary, such as picture dictionaries and pattern picture books. It might include demonstrating audiobooks or e-books and encouraging parents to join their children during a set-aside after-school time to use these materials in the library media center. It might be a program offered cooperatively with the public library to raise awareness of materials and services available there.

Another target audience is families with preschoolers. A research study by Gregory and Morrison (1998) revealed some very specific outcomes from parents reading to preschool children. Among those outcomes were higher cognitive levels of the questions they asked their parents, improved structure of their oral language, and increased general knowledge that prepares them for school. A report by Morisset (1993) cites research findings that an effective way to promote language skills and develop strong social interactions among young children is through storybook sharing. She reports that the frequency of listening to stories in the home was found to be directly related to literacy and teacher ratings of students' oral language skills at ages five to seven. These studies underscore the value of reading in the home. The school library media specialist might share tips on reading aloud to young children or suggest books appropriate for the very young, e.g., books with repetition, pattern books, rhymes, and concept books, or share strategies for reading to and with children, e.g., paired reading where parent and child take turns reading or chanting refrains together. Programs like this are an investment in future students who will have benefited from listening to literature and will have gained language experience.

Presentations such as these can be a part of monthly parent meetings or school open houses. Or, these can be podcast via the school's Web site. Perhaps even more effective are meetings of local service groups. In these settings, the audience includes parents as well as other community members. Program chairs of Lions Clubs, Kiwanis, Rotary, League of Women Voters, and other service groups are frequently looking for ideas. A library media specialist may find an eager response to an offer for a presentation for such groups. It will be important to make the presentation entertaining, informative, and upbeat. This is no place for whining, but rather an opportunity to showcase the skills and knowledge of the library media specialist and the value to education afforded by the library media program. Reading from children's literature as part of the program or providing slides showing young people at work in the library media center are examples of ways to make the program engaging.

The need for communication between the school library media program and the family extends beyond special presentations. No school newsletter should go home without at least one meaningful item from the school library media program. Brief, readable articles can include suggesting good books to read as a family, describing student activities in the library media center, promoting events in the community, or advising about computers or software for the home. Library media program visibility is key, and the message must be that the library media program is fundamental to learning.

The school's Web site and e-newsletters provide important avenues for communication. The library should aim to be visible on school Web pages directed toward parents. Items to be included can include volunteer opportunities, a calendar of events, recommended Web sites, activities in the library media center, or book reviews. A blog can be a useful format for pushing news out to parents. Using an open source product like edublogs (www.edublogs.org), LifeType (www.lifetype.net) or b2evolution (www.b2evolution.net) as an authoring tool provides a readily accessible tool for frequent communication. The blog can appear on the school or library home page.

Another way to involve parents is through advisory committees; for example, if the school is developing its technology plan, the committee should include a parent. Periodically, the library media program needs to be evaluated. Districts often have a review cycle in which each program or curricular area has a major evaluative review every five or seven years. Usually, the review process begins with naming a committee or team. When such a team includes parents, they gain important insight into the program, and, as a result, they often become advocates. Moreover, they provide an important perspective on whether the program is really reaching students as intended.

A typical review process includes these steps:

- reviewing the current literature to determine "the state of the art";
- assessing the existing program to determine its status, often ac-

complished by means of surveys to several groups: students, teachers, administrators, and parents;
- comparing the results of the literature review and assessment; and
- developing a vision statement, goals, and an action plan.

Surveys should be tailored for each audience in order to get the
clearest responses from each. A sample parent survey for a library media program review appears in Figure 5.1. Parental involvement through
the survey and in the review process helps give parents information
about the program and a way to express their viewpoints on its effectiveness. Imagine that communicating with parents is communication
with the boss—the person paying the bills—because in some ways, it is!

BUSINESS INVOLVEMENT

Local businesses have a real interest in the quality of local education.
First, their future employees may come from the local schools. Besides,
good schools can be a "selling point" for chambers of commerce in at-
tracting new businesses into the community. Community pride helps
keep local business thriving; business benefits from a sense of confidence within a community. All these factors mean that business cares
about its schools. Every chamber of commerce has an education committee—an indicator of the importance business places on quality local
education. When real estate brokers market homes to families, one common question is whether the schools in the neighborhood are considered "good" schools. Bankers in the home mortgage market want to be
able to assure families that the investment in the community is a good
one for them and their children; "good" schools are central to that assurance. Business and education are likely partners.

Businesses enter into partnerships with schools for two reasons: (1)
to contribute to the public good and improve the quality of the school
and (2) to increase their own standing in the marketplace. Schools seek
business partnerships for two purposes: (1) to increase their resources
and (2) to improve the community understanding and respect for their
programs.

There are two important principles to guide school-business partnerships: maintaining a focus and maintaining the school's authority
over substance. Focus allows any given business to have a niche for its
marketplace advantage; for example, a business can become known as

FIGURE 5.1
Parent Survey—
School Library Media Program

Item	Strongly Agree	Agree	Disagree	Strongly Disagree	No Knowledge
Students are taught how to use information resources available in the school library media center.					
Students receive assistance in using the library media center.					
Our library media center has enough appropriate materials to meet students' needs.					
My son or daughter can use the library media center whenever he or she has a need.					
The library media center appears well organized.					
The library media center is inviting.					
I receive information about the activities in the library media center.					
I understand the role of the library media center in the school program.					
I would feel comfortable coming to the library media center.					
Additional comments or suggestions:					

the science partner or the fine arts partner or the reading partner, and this association gives them an identity in marketing. Focus allows the school to have special-interest staff members take on responsibilities for specific partnerships to nurture the relationships; for example, the library media specialist takes care of the reading partners or the networking partners and the art and music teachers take care of the fine arts partners. Perhaps even more important is controlling the substance of the project. One concern is whether the business brings its own special interests or biases to a project. It is the school that should decide the *what* of the partnership; the business's participation is in the *how*. Educators, after all, are responsible for what is taught in schools, and they should be protective of their right to determine content lest inappropriate bias influence instruction. Library media specialists must set standards for business participation in order to maintain the integrity of the school library media program (Tinnish 1996). In a case study of a Cincinnati school-business partnership, Abowitz (2000) emphasizes the importance of continuous monitoring to ensure that the power balance is governed so that the interests of business do not overtake the interests of educators.

Effective partnerships take time. A business partnership is a new relationship, and relationships can be demanding. School library media specialists considering such a partnership need to expect to give it time. Like any relationship, it will not survive without nurturing. That nurturing involves regular contact with a representative of the business; it requires reporting progress to the business, particularly impact on students; it requires public acknowledgment—the business marketplace purpose cannot be met if the public is unaware of the contribution.

COMMUNITY RESOURCES

In Sweden, a public institution known as a *kulturhus*, a house of culture, incorporates the public library, the local recreation center, and a fine arts center for courses in painting, sculpture, photography and other media. The *kulturhus* is used by the public and by neighboring schools as a resource for exploration. In the United States, we tend to isolate each of these activities in a separate entity; yet, cooperation among community resources makes sense. Each community has resources that can expand the vitality of the school library media program—and the school.

Miller and Shontz (2003) found that half of the school library media specialists they surveyed maintain ongoing communication by e-mail, telephone, or fax with their local public librarians. Furthermore, approximately 25 percent reported that they distribute and exchange newsletters with their public library counterparts, and 60 percent reported that they promote public library summer reading programs.

Supporting students' assignments and supporting literacy are two functions common to school and public libraries. For the most part, communication is key to these partnerships. One possibility here is a monthly telephone call or visit. The school library media specialist can report to the public librarian topics coming up in the curriculum. In a perfect world, this would be comprehensive, but the world is not perfect and this report will not be a complete summary of every assignment students will have. Still, a good faith effort is a start. Public libraries often host library card drives, especially in the fall when school is just underway. School library media specialists can help in promotion, perhaps hosting a representative from the public library who visits the school to encourage card sign-ups among students and teachers. The public librarian can report to the school library media specialist on programming planned for the coming month. The school can then relay this information to teachers and families. While a monthly set time may seem artificial, it is a way to open communication, and it may lead to additional contacts as the relationship develops. If students get better service and if families know more about programs to help children, then the efforts at cooperation have paid off.

On a larger scale, school and public libraries can both benefit from considering the subscription databases each makes available and looking for opportunities to mount the same resources in both environments; consistency will help students and teachers feel "at home" in each environment. Where the opportunity exists to consider matched catalog software the opportunities for cooperation are even greater. Librarians can team up to design instruction programs for both the public and school environments. The potential for a stronger position in price negotiation for purchase of common products should not be overlooked. And, looking for ways to negotiate licensing for complementary products—some in the public library, some in the school—is another possibility.

In small communities cooperation for library services has taken the form of shared use of facilities and resources. In rural areas, such a shared use of resources results in services that would not otherwise be available locally. While some would raise objections to shared resources because of their distinct missions and collection needs, a reality in rural

America is that very small communities may be unable to provide information resources and expertise to the community without creative solutions like school-community libraries. Governance, hours, and collection must be negotiated between the constituencies. However, the alternative of no local public library services where the small scale makes them fiscally impossible may encourage collaboration and compromise.

Cooperative activity with museums and other local groups is another means of community involvement. Art museums, science museums, natural history museums, and local historical societies have programs, exhibits, and outreach staff available to connect to the school. Library media specialists serve well as contact persons for these organizations because they know the whole curriculum. Besides organizations, every community has individuals with special knowledge, skills, or talents. One possible way to track community resources is to develop a "community talent bank." Such a resource directory could include these items for each entry:

**ENHANCEMENT IN ACTION:
SHARED FACILITY FOR HIGH SCHOOL AND PUBLIC
LIBRARY SERVICES**

In the city of Venus, Texas, population approximately 2,000, a partnership between the City of Venus and the school district provides for a school-community library. A director of libraries and three library aides staff the library. Opened in 1994, the Venus High School and Community Library is one of the few combination high school and community libraries in Texas. Because of shared resources the library's collection and services compares to that of libraries in cities much larger than Venus. This combination allows students the use of all resources of the high school library, plus the extra resources of a public library. The library has a completely automated circulation system, Internet access to the library catalog, TexShare databases, computer and copy services, popular periodicals, and more than 14,500 books and videos. The library is open to the public from 4:00 p.m. to 6:00 p.m. on Tuesday and Wednesday, from 8:00 a.m. to 6:00 p.m. Thursday and Friday, and from 9:00 a.m. to 1:00 p.m. on Saturday. The library Web site is www.venusisd.net/

- Contact person
- Address
- Telephone
- E-mail address
- URL
- Topics
- Curriculum area(s) (e.g., science, art)
- Description (e.g., a speaker, an exhibit, a demonstration)
- Limitations (e.g., age groups or group size limitations)

Developing such a directory can begin with the chamber of commerce education committee or with parent organizations. A simple form can facilitate collecting information. Then, the library media specialist can assemble it into a database and make it available to teachers. Of critical importance is that teachers must use the resources, once collected; some marketing may be required until the database becomes a standard resource. Such community involvement generates support and understanding of the school's program. In many communities the majority of voters are not parents; only about 25 percent of the adults in the United States currently have children enrolled in public schools. The majorities in most communities are young people without children or older citizens whose children are grown. Yet, schools depend on the support of these people for taxes and bond referenda. They need to feel some ownership of the schools. Library media specialists can put their program into the spotlight by taking a central role in the management and organization of a community resource directory. This is one way for the public to see the library media program's central role—something not intuitively obvious to those who remember their school library as a closet-sized room with a few books.

Some communities have community improvement foundations. These foundations can serve as a starting point for tapping into local resources. The Council on Foundations offers at its Web site (www.cof.org) a locator for finding local and area foundations. This database is searchable by state. When seeking support from organizations, it is essential to educate oneself about the foundation's giving programs. Each typically has priorities, and education is very often among them. Make a personal contact with the organization or write a letter of appeal. It is important to approach the foundation with a proposal tailored to its goals. To approach a local foundation for assistance, Hughes-Hassell and Wheelock (2001) offer a suggested outline that includes seven components:

- A request: What is needed and how will it be used?
- The need: What local area need will be met?
- The fit of the proposal with the foundation's initiatives: How will the library media program with these added resources help the foundation progress toward its goals?
- Comparative data: How does the status of the local library media center compare with other situations in the state or nation?
- A human face: Provide an anecdote that gives the proposal a human face.
- Proposal details: Provide a timeline and description of how improvements will be carried out if the request is granted.
- Conclusion: Invite further conversation. (p. 122)

Another important community resource is the local press. In small communities, contact local news media whenever events are occurring in the school library media center. In larger communities, send press releases to local media. By making these releases professional, the likelihood of their getting attention is enhanced. Often, larger newspapers and area television media have invitations on their Web sites for story leads. Bookmark the Web sites of local media to help remind you to contact them. In small to medium-sized districts, the local newspaper provides an excellent opportunity for a weekly or monthly newspaper column. Such columns can include recommended good reading for students of varying ages, information about research on the importance of good school library media programs for student achievement, information about using the Web for school work, and advice about study skills. The target audience here is parents, but the entire community will see what is going on in the school library media program.

ACTION STRATEGIES

Information Access

- Provide access to school library media center resources for parents, e.g., the collection and the technology.

- Initiate communication with the local public library to develop such collaborative programs as an after-school homework center, intergenerational reading, or Saturday dramatics.
- Explore opportunities for consortial database purchasing with public libraries.

Program Management

- Plan and present parent meetings: topics can include book talks on books for a specific age or topic, a film festival of videos about parenting borrowed from a local public library or other social agency, a "how to help your child study better" session, an introduction to computer software used at the school, a computer literacy session for parents who have never used a computer, or an introduction to the World Wide Web with emphasis on sites that have information pertinent to topics students are studying in school.
- Include something in each newsletter that goes home, e.g., book suggestions, Web addresses of interest to students, or brief descriptions of activities in the library media center.
- Use the school's Web site to communicate with the public about the library media program.
- Encourage parent or community-member volunteers, give options for weekly or monthly tasks as well as one-time projects, and seek volunteers from senior citizen ranks and business employees who are not parents, but who have talents or time to offer. Remember to acknowledge parent help in newsletters. Treat volunteers to special events periodically to convey appreciation.
- Make personal contacts with local businesses and identify ways they can be supportive; focus the request to any single business so that each has its own niche, if possible.
- Look for community foundations that can offer fiscal support to the library media program.
- Seek connections with local media to provide news about the library media program.

SCENARIO FOR DISCUSSION

A middle school serves a neighborhood with a large proportion of children whose parents speak Spanish and do not understand English. Also, some Spanish-speaking parents are not literate in Spanish. How does the library media specialist communicate with parents regarding the library media program, their child's performance with respect to library instruction, and ways to provide literacy development at home? How does the library media program support English language learners (ELL) families of global backgrounds? What is the relationship between the ELL program and the library media program? How is that relationship fostered?

REFERENCES

Abowitz, K. K. (2000). "Democratic Communities and Business Education 'Partnerships' in Secondary Education." *The Urban Review 32* (4): 313–341.

Gorton R. A. and G. T. Schneider (1991). *School-Based Leadership: Challenges and Opportunities.* Dubuque, IA: Wm. C. Brown.

Gregory, L. P. and T. G. Morrison (1998). "Lap Reading for Young At-Risk Children: Introducing Families to Books." *Early Childhood Education Journal 26* (2): 67–77.

Hughes-Hassell, S. and A. Wheelock, A. (2001). *The Information-Powered School.* Chicago: American Library Association.

Miller, M. and M. Shontz (2003). "The SLJ Spending Survey." *School Library Journal 49* (10): 52–59.

Morisset, C. E. (1993). *Language and Emotional Milestones on the Road to Readiness.* Baltimore, MD: Center on Families, Communities, Schools and Children's Learning, Johns Hopkins University.

Tinnish, D. (1996). "Big Business in the School Library." *Emergency Librarian 23* (5): 8–11.

PART II:

The Library Media Program

Chapter 6

Collaborative Planning

This chapter:

- describes the process of collaborative planning
- examines the role of the library media specialist as a member of the instructional team
- discusses how collaboration benefits students, teachers, and library media specialists
- identifies action strategies for collaboration

The increased complexity of today's world calls for teamwork. Robert Reich (1987) observes in *Tales of a New America:*

> Rarely do Big Ideas emerge any longer from the solitary labor of genius. Modern science and technology is too complicated for one brain. It requires groups of astronomers, physicists, and computer programmers to discover new dimensions of the universe . . . . With ever more frequency Nobel prizes are awarded to collections of people. (p. 126)

Increased complexity characterizes the teaching profession as well. Less dependence on basal textbooks, increased concern for students' learning styles, the explosion of information, advances in instructional and information technologies, advocacy for cooperative learning, and collaborative teaching are factors that increase the complexity in instructional planning. Teams of teachers are more likely to address productively the complex task of planning than individuals working alone.

Not all schools have evolved to team-based work. In many settings, long-standing tradition in schools has kept teachers isolated in their self-contained classrooms. Many teachers entered the profession expecting to work alone with their students, having autonomy over their own classroom and students. Yet, that image is out of step today with a society that recognizes that teamwork can increase effectiveness and productivity and can improve the work environment. Experiments like the General Motors Saturn Plant have received considerable attention as teamwork models to improve the product and the process of manufacturing. Underlying much of the discussion about collaboration is the work of Edward Deming, whose name is regularly associated with the "quality" movement.

In a *School Library Journal* survey, library media specialists rated the importance of what they do. They listed providing teachers and students with resource material as their top priority, followed by collection development, then recommending materials, and finally "information literacy planning and instruction" (Whelan 2003). The effectiveness of all of these tasks depends on working with other school professionals. Without collaboration, there is little purpose for the collection, the curriculum, or the staff of the library media program. So, library media specialists must seek to work collaboratively with classroom teachers in order to improve students' learning experiences.

THE COLLABORATIVE PLANNING PROCESS

Collaboration depends on effective communication and supportive relationships. Raspa and Ward (2000) describe collaboration as:

> the bond of belonging. . . . In collaboration, we are bonded to each other in acts of listening that endow enterprises with life and meaning. It requires hearing the other completely, waiting before speaking, re-creating in one's mind what was just said, and making sure it was understood. This way of listening holds judgment in suspension. Questioning about being right or wrong yields to questions about ways of thinking and acting on behalf of the enterprise. (pp. 1–2)

The "enterprise" is effective teaching and engaged learning.

Beyond communication and respect is the need for time. Since working together takes more time than working alone, there must be motivation to collaborate. Sometimes that motivation is intrinsic—people trust that the result of collaboration will be better teaching and learning, and it is worth their time. Sometimes, the motivation must be external because people lack confidence that collaboration will be beneficial. In these cases, administrators sometimes impose expectations for collaboration, setting team or department meeting times and attending those meetings whenever possible. Sometimes, principals build the expectation for collaboration into the personnel evaluation system. In cases where collaboration is an expectation held by the principal, it is particularly important that the benefits be quickly evident to participants.

In many schools, teachers have formed planning teams, based on grade level or academic discipline. Depending on the school culture, these teams may meet weekly, monthly, annually, or as needed. These teams plan "big-picture" curriculum, instructional units, individual lessons, and/or special activities together. Whatever the meeting pattern and agenda, library media specialists need to participate in order to be true collaborators with classroom teachers. As members of the planning team, media specialists need to help teachers understand what they can offer to the planning process. Often, teachers perceive the library media specialist as the person to approach *after* they finish their planning. It is important for the principal to support the library media specialist in the role of an instructional partner who should be part of curriculum planning from the beginning so that library media specialists and teachers are perceived as equal partners in instruction. When such understanding is lacking, the library media specialist may start a conversation like this:

> I can alert you to resources both here at school and elsewhere if I know what you are teaching and expecting your students to do. My goal is to help save you time, to help you locate the best resources for your instructional needs, and to help your planning be as effective as it can be. I also want to teach your students the skills necessary to locate and use information; if I am here at your planning meetings, then together we can decide on how best to give them the opportunity to develop these information skills.

Teamwork requires mutual trust in one another's contributions to the team's work, a no-risk environment for openly sharing ideas, and a shared commitment to the group's decisions. Establishing ground rules from the beginning that recognize these requirements will improve the potential for collaboration. Specific and explicit strategies are useful for helping teamwork proceed:

- *Pose questions using nonthreatening language.* To protect the no-risk atmosphere, phrasing questions so that they do not put others on the defensive is important. No one wants to speak in a group where ideas are at risk of being criticized or attacked; yet, open discussion demands that disagreement be voiced. Tact and sensitivity are important. Ask, "Might Steinbeck be too difficult for some kids to read?" rather than state, "Steinbeck is too difficult."
- *Ensure that all team members are heard.* Some people tend to be cautious about speaking up even in small groups. Someone must take responsibility for seeing that all voices are heard. A simple query like, "Mark, we haven't heard from you; what do you think of this idea?" is sometimes all that is needed. A round-robin approach, asking each person for comments, also works well.
- *Clarify terms.* Careful communication is important for teamwork, so think about assumptions and see that they are explicit. For example, a clarification like, "When we say consensus, do we mean agreement by the majority, or do we mean unanimous agreement?" may prevent a serious misunderstanding later on.
- *Keep the discussion focused.* "We began with talking about how we would assess students' learning at the end of the Civil War unit, and now we are talking about camcorders. We seem to have gotten off the track."
- *Engage in active listening.* Elements of active listening are the following: paraphrase what others say, ask probing questions, jot down important points, withhold advice until all information is shared, and listen to advice in full before reacting. (Holcomb 1996)

A team meeting must be organized in order to be more than a chat session. The group needs a facilitator. Meetings should begin with a stated purpose or an agenda, with opportunities for additions from participants. Likewise, meetings should have some kind of outcome—written and distributed minutes, or an oral summary of what was accomplished. These features help all participants know that the time was well spent.

THE INSTRUCTIONAL PLANNING TEAM

A team is a small number of people with *complementary skills* committed to a *common purpose, performance goals*, and an approach for which they hold themselves mutually *accountable* (Katzenbach and Smith 1993). This definition has several key concepts, each of which deserves exploration.

Common Purpose

For instructional planning teams, the common purpose is to provide effective educational experiences for students. Members of a team collaborate around a common purpose. An important aspect of teamwork is to "keep the eye on the prize." Sometimes, team members can become enthusiastic about the activities and events to be planned and lose sight of the purpose. To keep the purpose in focus, team members must ask "What do we want students to gain from these experiences? What do they need to know or be able to do?"

Performance Goals

Performance goals refer to what each member of the team will do—each teacher, the principal, and the library media specialist. For example, a kindergarten team was observed planning an upcoming unit that would involve several activities, including a field trip. As they talked, each member seemed to have established himself or herself as a specialist:

> The *artist* responds to "Will you draw us a pattern?"
> The *shopper* responds to "Will you call and bargain for a good deal on the fee for the field trip?"
> The *facilitator* asks, "Has everyone had a chance to share their ideas now?"
> The *challenger* asks, "Is that too difficult for our kids?"
> The *resourcer* responds to "Have we got any easy books about the presidents?"

In a follow-up conversation with the observer, the teachers acknowledged that these were typical roles for each of them to play as they planned units. Performance responsibilities will vary with the needs of the group, but clearly each member of the team has performance expectations. Just as members of an athletic team have primary assignments to call the plays or to cover second base or to kick the field goal, so in this situation each team member will have unique performance expectations.

Besides substantive responsibilities that help accomplish the work of preparing for instruction, there are affective responsibilities to the team as well. In *Team Players and Teamwork*, Parker (1990) provides a checklist of behaviors for collaboration:

- Help the team establish long-term goals and clarify its current objective or task.
- Help the team see how its work fits into the total organization.
- Regularly remind the team of the need to revisit goals and action plans.
- Encourage the team to establish plans with milestones and appropriate task assignments.
- Pitch in to help other team members who need assistance.
- Work hard to achieve team goals and complete tasks even when you do not agree with them.
- Do not gossip about other team members or share negative comments about the team process with nonmembers.
- Remain flexible and open to new ideas or data that may alter team goals. (pp. 74–75)

These behaviors are appropriate to consider in developing ground rules for formal planning teams. It is unreasonable to expect that people who have been accustomed to working in isolation will automatically know how to perform in a team situation. Explicit discussion of team behavior and team organization provides the groundwork often needed in making the transition to a collaborative planning process.

Accountability

Team members are accountable to one another for meeting their responsibilities. To ensure accountability, some kind of end-of-meeting summary of "who will do what" is necessary. Successful teams set high expectations for team members. Creating a culture of accountability to the team occurs when everyone takes team responsibility seriously.

Complementary Skills

The concept of complementary skills indicates that different team members are good at different aspects of the team's work. In an instructional team, sometimes those complementary skills relate to curriculum knowledge or teaching skills and strategies; sometimes they relate to group task rolls, like the *clarifier*, or the *tester*, or the *harmonizer*.

THE LIBRARY MEDIA SPECIALIST AS COLLABORATOR

Loertscher's (1988) taxonomy of involvement in curriculum provides a useful structure for envisioning the roles the library media specialist can play in collaboration with teachers. This taxonomy classifies involvement from minimal participation to central role. Loertscher contends that one's placement along the taxonomy is situational and that each level is appropriate at some time or other.

Level 1. No interaction. Some situations require no involvement from the library media specialist.

Level 2. Self-help warehouse. The "warehouse" represents the library media center's resources. Collection development is a collaborative process. Teachers give the library media specialist suggestions of topics, themes, or titles. The library media specialist negotiates with teachers to prioritize needs and determine what will be purchased. This collaborative process is an ongoing one in which information is continually being shared in both directions. Teachers are making requests, library media specialists are alerting teachers to resources that may be of interest, teachers and library media specialists are working together on setting priorities, and library media specialists are reporting to teachers what is being purchased or what has been received. Library media specialists are reviewing the existing collection and making decisions for weeding; these decisions too are shared with teachers to reduce the chances of withdrawing materials that have value. The "warehouse" extends beyond the physical collection to include resources available online and from other collections. And the organization and access systems of the "warehouse" are communicated clearly to teachers so that they can use it independently.

Level 3. Individual reference assistance. In the context of collaboration, the library media specialist works with the teacher to find an answer to a specific question. Reference work is a collaboration between the information seeker and the library media specialist. Active listening and probing questions are key to effective individual reference. It requires careful communication to determine a precise need.

The Reference and User Services Association (1996) of the American Library Association adopted a set of guidelines for successful reference transactions. Five qualitative measures are included in the guidelines: approachability, interest, listening/inquiring, searching, and follow-up. According to the approachability guideline, "the initial verbal and nonverbal responses of the librarian will influence the depth and level of the interaction between the librarian and the patron. The librarian's role in the communications process is to make the patron feel comfortable in a situation that may be perceived as intimidating, risky, confusing, and overwhelming." These guidelines are highly relevant to individualized reference assistance as a collaboration between library media specialist and teacher. Examples of *approachability* behaviors are smiling, establishing eye contact, and extending a greeting. Under the guideline for *interest*, behaviors include using both verbal and nonverbal cues to signal that the library media specialist is listening and understanding the query. For *listening/inquiring*, the library media specialist allows the teacher to fully state his or her information need before hurrying off to respond, rephrases the question or request, and seeks assurance that the request is fully understood. In addition, the library media specialist uses open-ended questioning to gain additional information. For example, the library media specialist might simply ask, "Can you tell me a little more about . . . ?" As a follow-up, clarifying questions help determine how extensive the information search should be or whether specific formats will be more useful. Under the guideline for *searching*, the library media specialist not only engages in the search for information, but also informs the teacher of the search process and explains how to use sources if the teacher shows interest. At this stage, the library media specialist works with the teacher to broaden or narrow the search if too little or too much information is identified. Finally under the guideline for *follow up*, the library media specialist asks the teacher if the question has been fully resolved and makes referrals to other sources if it has not. Careful, friendly, and thorough individual reference assistance may serve as a starting point for collaboration at higher levels of the taxonomy.

Level 4. Spontaneous interaction and gathering. At this level, teacher and library media specialist engage in minimal collaboration. The teacher suddenly discovers a need for something and sends a request, often by way of a student or e-mail, to the library media specialist: "I need a picture that shows the difference between a moth and a butterfly," "I need that videotape about how to deal with strangers because of an incident reported this morning." As collaboration increases, however, teachers grow more confident that the library media specialist will be able to respond to such requests.

Level 5. Cursory planning. Here, collaboration in the true sense of planning with teachers begins—but informally. Brief informal conversations occur in which teachers talk about what they are planning to teach, and the library media specialist may interject ideas or resources. Often, such conversations are essentially brainstorming; generally, they are brief and unstructured. Yet there is communication between the library media specialist and teacher and often some activity occurs as a result—the library media specialist locates some resource, a lesson is taught in the library media center, a time is set for more in-depth conversation, or an activity is designed.

Level 6. Planned gathering. As a result of communication between teachers and the library media specialist about upcoming instruction, the library media specialist gathers resources. Clear communication between teacher and library media specialist is vital. This interaction cannot be simply a teacher stating a topic and a library media specialist gathering everything available about that topic. That is not collaboration. Collaboration means that the teacher helps the library media specialist know what kinds of resources will be really useful. Several questions need to be answered:

> *How long will you be working on this unit?* The answer to this question will guide the library media specialist regarding how much to - collect.
> *How will you use the materials?* If the response is that the teacher will be using them as resources for himself or herself, then concern for reading level is not as crucial.
> *Is there a particular focus to the unit?* The response will help the library media specialist know, for example, whether to collect materials

related to causes of the Civil War or merely to collect information about the battles in the war itself, or both.

What kinds of activities do you anticipate? If the response is reading and writing, the kinds of resources considered will be different from those collected if the response is hands-on activities and field trips.

Gathering materials becomes collaborative only when these kinds of questions are pursued. If the library media specialist simply pulls all the books about classical mythology or World War II off the shelves, the process is not collaborative. More importantly it may not be particularly helpful, since providing teachers with more materials or the wrong materials may actually create unnecessary work for both teacher and library media specialist and ultimately be counterproductive to the most common purpose of collaboration—improving teaching and learning.

Level 7. Evangelistic outreach. Marketing might be another appropriate image for this level of involvement. Marketing requires clear understanding of the customers' needs and desires. By working closely with teachers, the library media specialist learns what will "sell" in terms of resources and services. In the school setting, one of the most effective approaches is providing in-service teacher training. For in-service training to be successful, teachers must have information about how and why such a program will be useful to them. Collaboratively planned in-service training—when the library media specialist and teachers discuss what is possible and what is appropriate for them and their school—may indeed be the most successful. The library media specialist can suggest menus of possible in-service programs and together the group can discuss the local value of each suggestion. Such discussions allow the library media specialist to introduce resources to teachers in the context of their own needs assessment. Marketing activities can also include book talks for teachers, focused on upcoming themes or topics. Again, the topic of the in-service training results from collaboration so that all teachers who participate have a sense of purpose about it.

Level 8. Scheduled planning in the support role. Formal collaborative planning occurs when the library media specialist participates in planning sessions with teachers and provides assistance in identifying resources or designing activities. In schools where collaboration is a part of the local school culture, formal team, department, or grade-level meetings occur routinely. Acting in the support role, the library media specialist responds to teacher initiatives, taking away from such sessions a "to-do" list that usually involves fetching resources or designing activities based on the directions of the teachers.

Levels 9 and 10. Instructional design. Here, formal collaboration with the library media specialist moves beyond the support role so that the library media specialist also takes part in designing the unit. This team relationship engages teachers and the library media specialist equally in collaborative planning, including determining the goals for the unit, perhaps some team-teaching, selecting resources, designing student assessment, and evaluating the unit at its conclusion.

Level 11. Curriculum development. Library media specialists have a legitimate place on curriculum development committees at the school and district levels. Their special expertise makes them important contributors to "big-picture" curriculum planning. Library media specialists are, after all, teachers with the same educational qualifications as other teachers. Beyond that, their special expertise about resources, technologies, teaching, and learning strategies makes them valuable participants.

SUBJECT SPECIALIZATION

What is the library media specialist's subject specialization? One specialty is information processing, from articulating the information need through communicating information or applying information to solve a problem. Another is resources; the library media specialist must be able to locate resources of high quality to meet the needs of teachers. Knowing the literature for children and young adults is a particular strength of the library media specialist. Finally, technology, both instructional and informational, can be perceived as the library media specialist's specialization. Library media specialists thus must approach teamwork with the confidence that they have something special to contribute. Next, they must make substantive contributions to the work.

GROUP TASK ROLES

The library media specialist has a unique position on a team as both an insider and an outsider (Donham van Deusen 1996). The library media specialist is a regular member of the team, and a member of the school staff, and as such is an insider. However, as a library media specialist rather than a classroom teacher, he or she is an outsider who brings a different perspective to the planning table—a perspective that incorporates what is being taught throughout the school in different grades or in different departments, a perspective influenced by technology and by a broad variety of resources. This unique insider-outsider view of the planning process creates an opportunity for raising questions that can be at once naive and challenging—questions like, "How does this new fifth-grade unit relate to the existing sixth-grade unit on space exploration?" or "What do you really want to accomplish in this unit?" This outsider can pose such questions as naive queries that cause the teachers to reflect on their planning, to refocus, or to alter their direction.

Variations on the lists of group task roles exist. Drawn from the classic work of Benne and Sheats (1948), these roles can be summarized as follows:

The *clarifier* gives relevant examples, offers rationales, restates problems.

The *initiator* suggests new or different ideas.

The *opinion giver* states pertinent beliefs about discussion and others' suggestions.

The *summarizer* reviews discussion, pulls it together.

The *tester* raises questions to test whether the group is ready for a decision.

The *compromiser* yields when necessary for progress.

The *elaborator* builds on the suggestions of others.

The *encourager* praises and supports others.

The *gatekeeper* keeps communication open, encourages participation.

The *harmonizer* mediates differences, reconciles points of view.

The *tension reliever* uses humor or calls for breaks at appropriate times to draw off negative feelings.

Because of the library media specialist's unique insider-outsider status, five of these roles are particularly suited to the library media specialist as a member of the planning team: clarifier, initiator, opinion giver, summarizer, and tester. As *clarifier*, library media specialists can pose questions to teachers, "What do you want children to learn?" or "*Friendship* is a very broad topic; what might be the focus of this unit on friendship?" Such questions encourage teachers to reassess their planning and

---

ENHANCEMENT IN ACTION:
TEAM TEACHING

A team of fifth- and sixth-grade teachers is meeting to plan a new unit on oceanography. They are brainstorming subtopics to be covered—ocean animals, sea plants, waves and tides, folk tales and sea chants, and navigation and map reading. The library media specialist, as something of an outsider, asks, "What do you want students to learn in this unit?"

With that one question, the library media specialist begins to bring focus to the unit. Later in the discussion, a teacher suggests that the unit should have a research component, and wonders whether the library media specialist could teach students to look up current literature about environmental concerns for ocean species. The library media specialist responds that the collection does not include enough current periodicals or appropriate indexes for students to look up articles; however, he can provide students with preselected articles from which they could extract information.

The library media specialist has changed the focus of instruction from using indexes to locate information to developing skill in extracting information from resources and using note-taking strategies. Later in the discussion, teachers wonder what they will use to assess learning. After hearing ideas like developing a unit test or requiring an essay, the library media specialist suggests that the class develop a multimedia production about the ocean, with groups responsible for different aspects of the topic. Finally, the group assigns tasks—what will each teacher do and what will the library media specialist do?

---

to focus on their goals. As *initiator*, the library media specialist can offer suggestions and alternatives to teachers. Benne and Sheats (1948) state that the initiator may suggest a new organizational structure to address a difficult issue. Perhaps a library media specialist might suggest, and subsequently facilitate, a faculty technology study group to examine educational technology issues and to determine in what direction the school should proceed. Or a suggestion for a short course for students on "netiquette" might be in order. These are behaviors of an initiator. As *opinion giver,* the library media specialist might bring in a different view-point or perspective based on the resources or on the professional litera-ture. For example, the library media specialist might suggest that stu-dents should be using a word processor to do their initial drafts, not just their final drafts, when teachers see the computer as a publication tool rather than as a writing tool. The library media specialist might also suggest that dependence on e-mail for communication among teachers may not be appropriate until everyone has in-room access to the net-work, or he or she might remind teachers to be aware that English-as-a-second-language students cannot depend on text-only resources for in-formation. As *summarizer,* the library media specialist can share the re-sults of listening to teachers, often teachers from various teams. As *tester,* he or she can measure what teachers say or do against the mission and philosophy of the school. All of these team task roles involve the library media specialist's ability to step away from the group and become an "outsider" to offer a perspective that could help direct, redirect, or focus the team's efforts. Such a perspective is uniquely valuable to the poten-tial for the team to adhere to its mission and to maintain awareness of its larger context.

The other group task roles may be played by some library media specialists, but their appropriateness is related largely to personal char-acteristics; some people are natural tension relievers or clowns; others are not. The gatekeeper role may be a role sometimes taken on by li-brary media specialists depending on the issue at hand. Generally, these roles are less "mission-critical" for performing the work of the library media specialist on the team, when compared to the first five roles.

Figure 6.1 displays the task assignments adopted by the group de-scribed in the Enhancement in Action shaded box. This list is an ex-ample of the outcome of a planning meeting—a testament to the pro-ductive use of time.

FORMAL AND INFORMAL COLLABORATION

Collaboration has been described primarily in terms of formal meetings as teams. Less formal, less involved activity might be considered coop-eration. A teacher stops into a library media center and shares an idea about an upcoming unit, and the library media specialist responds with a suggestion, question, or idea. Collaboration has begun. Where this in-formal interaction leads depends largely on the kind of response the

FIGURE 6.1 Sample Team Member Assignments	
Teacher	Tasks
Library Media Specialist	• locate articles on ocean ecology and environmental issues for exploration • teach lesson on note taking, providing students with two alternative formats • create a template for the class multimedia project • teach students how to use HyperStudio • locate video on whales, including whale songs
Ms. A, Teacher	• design lessons on waves and tides • gather supplies for hands-on waves activities
Mr. B, Teacher	• design lessons on sea mammals • arrange for speaker from local aquarium to discuss dolphins and their communication systems
Ms. C, Teacher	• design lessons on saltwater plant life • set up plant experiments with seaweed
Mr. D, Teacher	• work with library media specialist to design assessment rubric for final project

library media specialist makes. In this situation, the image of Loertscher's taxonomy should appear in the mind's eye of the library media specialist, who then says to himself or herself, "How much involvement does this teacher want from me? How much involvement is appropriate for this instance? Do I offer a few books to help the teacher out? Do I suggest that I search for a variety of materials to support this unit? Do I suggest that we sit down and do a little brainstorming about possible activities to engage kids for this unit?" These informal opportunities for collaboration can have the same impact as more formal group meetings; indeed, in many schools where collaborative planning is not a part of the local school culture, this is the only kind of collaborative opportunity.

BENEFITS OF COLLABORATION

Collaboration requires time and energy and it is more complicated than working alone. The benefits of collaboration make it worth the effort in planning for instruction. In particular, three outcomes are likely benefits of collaboration that includes the library media specialist: reflective thought, schoolwide coordination, and improved teaching and learning.

Reflective Thought

A number of scholars and educators—for example, Feiman (1979), Tom (1985), and Zeichner and Liston (1987)—have written about reflection, based in large part on Dewey's (1910) concept of reflective thinking. Schön's (1983) work brought reflective thinking to the forefront. Reflective teachers consistently assess the origins, purposes, and consequences of their work (Nolan and Huber 1989). Pugach and Johnson (1990) describe reflection as an art of mediated thinking. They propose that reflection among teachers can be mediated and enhanced by collegial dialogue. They suggest that to facilitate reflective thinking, one practices restraint and allows teachers to think aloud. Their proposal that a facilitator can promote reflective thinking is relevant to the role that a library media specialist plays in helping teachers plan. The library media specialist can raise questions to generate reflective thought among teachers, whether it is a question of how they would define their thematic unit on friendship, why and when their students should learn keyboarding, or what they want their students to learn about war.

Kottkamp (1990) distinguished between prescriptive and descriptive communication in his discussion of how to facilitate reflection. He emphasized the importance of avoiding prescriptive communication as a facilitator (that is, messages in the form of "you should . . .") and instead using descriptive language that avoids judgment. The intent of the library media specialist is not to tell teachers what to do, but rather to encourage them to verbalize, to think aloud. Such thinking aloud can lead them to insights of their own and help them communicate with one another. Because of the "outsider" status, the library media specialist can pose naive questions that encourage deliberation among teachers, thus functioning as a catalyst for reflective thought. Holt (1993) encourages a deliberate climate in schools where teachers consider and determine both what and how to teach. The collegial relationship he describes reflects the exchange of ideas generated in planning sessions; the library media specialist can facilitate that exchange by being an "insider" (a member of the staff), yet a somewhat naive participant as an "outsider."

Costa and Garmston (1995) state that cognitive coaching provides a safe format for professional dialogue and develops the skills for reflection on practice, both of which are necessary for productive collaboration. The library media specialist acts as a clarifier. By probing for his or her own clarification, the library media specialist encourages the teachers to clarify their thinking and planning for themselves. Poole (1994) describes this phenomenon when she characterizes one teacher as learning not from suggestions of a coach but from the process of reflection that was necessary to articulate her ideas to the colleague. Because the library media specialist is an "outsider," teachers need to articulate quite clearly what they are thinking. As in Poole's case, this process forces clarifying their thinking as well.

Schoolwide Coordination

The library media specialist has the advantage of serving the entire school community—all grades, all subjects. By working in collaboration with teachers throughout the school, he or she can share knowledge of the total system with others and help teachers broaden their view of their students' total school experience. The model of self-contained isolated teaching was based on the assumption that a textbook series would provide the articulation students needed from year to year within a discipline as well as consistency across grade levels. As schools move away from textbook-based learning, the need for coordination is greater. Teachers are designing instruction based on curriculum goals, but the potential is great for gaps and redundancy. Collaboration helps counteract both of those concerns. In his description of the basic school, Boyer (1995) asserts that teachers are leaders who work together. He advocates perceiving the school as a community of learners. The concept of community carries with it the connotation that people are working together in the learning process. Library media specialists can be important community members.

Improved Teaching and Learning

It seems intuitive that when more than one mind is put to a task, better ideas, better planning, and ultimately better teaching and learning will occur. Each member of a team brings special kinds of talents, knowledge, experience, and intelligence to the table. It seems difficult to believe that any one of those people can produce better planning than the group working together. In a case study of collaboration in high schools in California, teachers maintained reflective logs during research units. They affirmed the value of collaboration with librarians, noting the benefit of two teachers available to work with individual students and the more systematic approach to research taken by students with guidance from the library media specialist (Lange, Montgomery, and Magee 2003). Of key importance is the ability of a team's members to behave in ways that take advantage of the synergistic potential of teamwork.

ACTION STRATEGIES

Learning and Teaching

- As a collaborative partner, whether working with an individual teacher or a whole team or department, leave each interaction with a to-do list and complete the tasks promptly so that teachers gain confidence in collaboration.
- Avoid being merely a "go-fer" for a team; library media specialists have more than "things" to deliver. Ideas for teaching and learning strategies, offers to teach or team-teach, particularly when information processes are a part of the learning, are ways to contribute substantively to the quality of learning.
- Be sensitive to the requests of teachers. When a teacher asks a question, it may not be the *real* question, and an opportunity for collaboration may be presenting itself to one who is poised to notice it. For example:
  — When a teacher says, "Do we have a copy of *Little House in the Big Woods?*" might he really be asking, "Can you suggest a good read-aloud for my class?"

— When a teacher asks, "May I bring my class to the library media center on Friday?" she might really be saying, "We are going to do some 'research' and I don't think my students know where to begin to find the information they will need."

— When a teacher asks, "Do we have any books on Canada?" the real message is, "I am about to begin a unit on Canada, and I have no materials."

— Of course, sometimes the simple question is merely seeking the simple direct answer; effectively tuning in and knowing which kind of response is needed is an important first step toward becoming a partner.

Information Access and Delivery

- Share resources about teamwork. For example:
  Patrick Lencioni. *The Five Dysfunctions of a Team.* San Francisco: Jossey-Bass, 2002.
  Harvey Robbins and Michael Finley. *The New Why Teams Don't Work: What Goes Wrong and How to Make It Right.* San Francisco: Berrett-Koehler, 2000.
  Carl Larson and Frank LaFasto. *When Teams Work Best: 6,000 Team Members and Leaders Tell What It Takes to Succeed.* Vienna, VA: Sage Communications, 2001.

Program Administration

- If collaboration is not already a characteristic of the school culture, initiate conversations with individual teachers and include offers to brainstorm ideas or to search for materials. Deliver high-quality information or resources promptly so that the teacher can see the benefit of working together.
- Share with the principal intentions to collaborate with others in the school and seek help for ways to become more involved in planning with teachers.

SCENARIO FOR DISCUSSION

At Washington Elementary School, the new school library media specialist is new, and in her first school media position. The school faculty consists of many seasoned teachers and a principal waiting to retire within the next three years. The previous librarian retired after more than 20 years at this school. The collection is top-notch, and the facility is modern and conducive to learning and teaching. The computer lab has recently been updated. Students come from homes that value education and support the school. It is November and the teachers are still mourning the loss of their previous librarian. They are reluctant to accept a new person in the role, and the principal is not about to make waves with the staff. What steps should the new library media specialist take to create a climate that's conducive for collaboration in this school?

REFERENCES

Benne, K. D. and P. Sheats (1948, Spring). "Functional Roles of Group Members." *Journal of Social Issues 4:* 42–47.

Boyer, E. (1995). *The Basic School: A Community for Learning.* Princeton, NJ: Carnegie Foundation for the Advancement of Teaching.

Costa, A. and R. Garmston (1995). *Cognitive Coaching.* Norwood, MA: Christopher-Gordon.

Dewey, J. (1910). *How We Think.* Boston: Heath.

Donham van Deusen, J. (1996, Spring). "The School Library Media Specialist as a Member of the Teaching Team—An 'Insider' and an 'Outsider.'" *Journal of Curriculum and Supervision 11* (3): 229–248.

Feiman, S. (1979, Spring). "Technique and Inquiry in Teacher Education: A Curricular Case Study." *Curriculum Inquiry 9* (1): 63–79.

Holcomb, E. (1996). *Asking the Right Question: Tools and Techniques for Teamwork.* Thousand Oaks, CA: Corwin Press.

Holt, M. (1993, Winter). "The High School Curriculum in the United States and the United Kingdom." *Journal of Curriculum and Supervision 8* (2): 157–173.

Katzenbach, J. R. and D. K. Smith (1993). *The Wisdom of Teams.* Boston: Harvard Business School Press.

Kottkamp, R. B. (1990, February). "Means for Facilitating Reflection." *Education and Urban Society 22* (2): 182–203.

Lange, B., S. Montgomery, and N. Magee (2003, June). "Does Collaboration Boost Student Learning?" *School Library Journal 49* (6): 4–5.

Loertscher, D. V. (1988). *Taxonomies of the School Library Media Program.* Littleton, CO: Libraries Unlimited.

Nolan, J. F. and T. Huber (1989, Winter). "Nurturing the Reflective Practitioner Through Institutional Supervision: A Review of the Literature." *Journal of Curriculum and Supervision 4* (2): 126–145.

Parker, G. (1990). *Team Players and Teamwork.* San Francisco: Jossey-Bass.

Poole, W. (1994, Spring). "Removing the 'Super' from Supervision." *Journal of Curriculum and Supervision 9* (3): 284–309.

Pugach, M. and L. J. Johnson (1990). "Developing Reflective Practice through Structured Dialogue." In R. Clift et al., ed. (2004), *Encouraging Reflective Practice in Education: An Analysis of Issues and Programs.* New York: Teachers College Press (pp. 187–204).

Raspa, D. and D. Ward (2000). *The Collaborative Imperative: Librarians and Faculty Working Together in the Information Universe.* Chicago: Association of College and Research Libraries.

Reference and User Services Association. (1996). *Guidelines for Behavioral Performance of Reference and Information Services Professionals.* Chicago: American Library Association. Retrieved September 25, 2003, from www.ala.org/RUSAMAINTemplate.cfm?Section=RUSA.

Reich, R. (1987). *Tales of a New America.* New York: Time Books.

Schön, D. (1983). *The Reflective Practitioner.* New York: Basic Books.

Tom, A. R. (1985, September/October). "Inquiring into Inquiry-Oriented Teacher Education." *Journal of Teacher Education 36* (5): 35–44.

Whelan, D. L. (2003, September). "Why Isn't Information Literacy Catching On?" *School Library Journal 49* (9): 50–53.

Zeichner, K. and D. Liston (1987). "Theory and Practice in the Evolution of an Inquiry-Oriented Student Teaching Program." *Harvard Educational Review 57:* 34–48.

Chapter 7

Scheduling Library Media Activities

This chapter:

- describes alternatives for scheduling instruction and information work in the library media center
- reviews the benefits and liabilities of flexible scheduling
- examines the prerequisites for flexible scheduling
- highlights the potential that block scheduling offers in secondary schools
- identifies action strategies for scheduling

Scheduling students for instruction or activities in the library media center can be a challenge for the school library media specialist. In many schools, going to the library media center is no different from going to the art room or the music room. While it is good to consider the library media center a classroom because teaching and learning occur there, it is important to recall that the library media center is *more* than a classroom. While the library media program has a curricular agenda of its own for information literacy, it is best when integrated into the rest of the school curriculum. And, of course, the resources of the library media center support instruction throughout the curriculum.

Scheduling for students to use the library media center differs between elementary and secondary schools. Elementary school library media centers have a long-standing tradition of functioning as a "special classroom" analogous to other special subjects like music or physical education. One might speculate that this association arose because "special" teachers for art, music, or physical education gained popularity in elementary schools at a time when schools were also beginning to hire more elementary school librarians. Secondary schools, on the other hand, seem to have followed a more traditional library model, where students visit when they have a need. Unlike the elementary level, secondary school library media centers have had to assert themselves as a teaching space.

In elementary schools, the weekly visit to the library media center is very common. Sending students to the library media center each week for a 30-minute class on "information skills" or literature meets several other needs: it meets the teachers' need to have added planning time, the need for all students to have access to the library media center frequently, the need for library media specialists to know the students in the school, and the need to "cover" the information skills curriculum. However, there are inherent problems in counting on a weekly class schedule to achieve what should be a library media program's goal—making students independently effective information consumers. The work students do in the library media center and the lessons they learn ought to have application to real information problems. Information-processing skills are not analogous to music or art curricula where there is disciplinary content. In the library media center, students learn about the intellectual tools needed to accomplish work within content areas. Designing schedules so that library media instruction occurs within the context of content area instruction makes the teaching and learning meaningful.

Regardless of the school level, learning theory supports flexibly scheduling library media instruction at the point of need for the student. Learning skills to access, evaluate, and use information requires the opportunity to apply the learning to a problem or need. Such a context allows students to reflect on the specific skill and take action to use it, in keeping with constructivist theory of learning (Donham, Bishop, Kuhlthau, and Oberg 2001). Students need to participate in information literacy instruction in the context of information problem solving. Most frequently, such a context is created by assignments from the classroom. As students engage in these assignments, they have a need for information literacy skills and knowledge and will be motivated to gain those skills because the learning will be relevant to their need. Further, they will learn these skills because they will construct their own understanding as they integrate them into their own active processes.

ELEMENTARY SCHOOL SCHEDULING ALTERNATIVES

Most commonly, the literature describes *flexible scheduling* and *fixed scheduling* as the two classic alternatives; in addition, there are variations. *Fixed scheduling* is arranging classes to meet in the library media center on a regular basis, usually once a week or once a scheduling cycle. Classes meet for perhaps 30 minutes, and activities might include direct teaching by the library media specialist, story times, book talks, book selection and checkout, or work on information-based projects. With fixed scheduling, library media specialists can print up their year's schedule, showing when each class will come to the library media center. Space left in the schedule becomes time for specific library media tasks (such as cataloging and processing, preparation, meeting with teachers, and reference work), or it can be offered to teachers for scheduling other library media center activities.

On the other hand, *flexible scheduling* is a plan by which the library media specialist teaches classes when students have a specific activity driven by a need in their classroom; these classes do not have library media instructional time unless they have a need. For example, a class might come to the library media center every day for five days, or for two weeks in a row, for instruction or work on an assignment or project, and then they may not have any instruction in the library media center for three weeks until a class activity requires it again.

Concern about retention of learning from one session to the next is one good reason to support flexible scheduling. When a library media specialist sets out to teach a complex process, it may take more than one class period to develop the skill. In weekly scheduled classes, seven days intervene between the first and second lessons. How likely is it that students will retain learning from the first week in order to build on it the second week? Another factor is transfer of learning. Application to real needs is less likely in weekly scheduled classes where the activities are unrelated to classroom work. What is the likelihood that students will automatically transfer what they learn about indexes to using the index in their American history textbook, unless there is teaching for transfer and the teaching in the library media center is integrated?

Weekly classes can prolong activities over several weeks; such scheduling can decrease students' enthusiasm. If a library media specialist is teaching about keyword searching or the Dewey Decimal System, for example, it may take a month of weekly lessons or more to complete the instruction. By the third or fourth installment, students' interest can easily decline. Although they have only spent 50 or 75 minutes on the topic, the spread over several weeks makes it feel much longer.

One critical attribute of flexible scheduling is that some classes come to the library media center several days in a row in order to accomplish a task, whereas in other weeks these classes might not come to the library media center as a class at all. Also, the work that students do during the flexibly scheduled class time grows out of assignments from their classroom teacher so that library media center activity is timely—students have genuine concern about what they will learn because it has immediate relevance. In a flexibly scheduled library media program, no two weeks are alike.

Some people describe what they are doing as flexible scheduling, when in fact their schedule variations lack some of flexible scheduling's critical attributes. For example, half a class might come to the library media center once each week to work with the library media specialist on classroom-generated topics. While this approach departs from the fixed schedule plan because it does not involve the whole class coming for instruction all at once and it does not provide the teacher with release time, it is still a once-a-week time slot filled by a scheduled commitment and that slot is not available for a point-of-need request. This schedule limits the students' instruction in the library media center to once a week even when more complex tasks would benefit from multiple sessions scheduled closer together.

Another variation reserves each class a time slot at the beginning of the year and assures teachers that whenever they want to schedule their class into the library media center, that time slot is theirs. While this practice fits the flexible scheduling model in that classes do not come to the library media center every week, it does not provide teachers the same degree of flexibility. For example, when science class is doing information work, they can come to the library media center only during science class, and for social studies they can come only during social studies class, for however many days are needed. In other words, the point of need is not really considered. While these alternatives to flexible scheduling have advantages, they should not be confused with true flexible scheduling, where "flexible" is a literal term and where the teacher can schedule the class into the library media center for instruction or for guided and independent work at the point of need and until the need is met.

BENEFITS OF FLEXIBLE SCHEDULING

Flexible scheduling is supposed to improve both student and library media specialist performance because it supports students' learning and practicing information processing skills *in context* while it supports flexibility in library media specialists' schedules to work collaboratively with teachers. For students, then, the flexible schedule allows them to work and learn information skills just in time (that is, when they need to apply them to class work they are doing), rather than just in case they might need them some day. For library media specialists who have a fixed schedule, the time when they meet with students is typically the time when teachers are free to plan. They are therefore unable to participate, even briefly, with teachers during planning. Flexible scheduling should allow them to book themselves with teachers for collaborative planning. Flexible scheduling allows library media specialists to teach complex skills by having classes meet daily when needed in order to build understanding from one day to the next, rather than from one week to the next. Flexible scheduling is not intended to reduce the library media specialists' teaching, nor is it intended to reduce contact with students. In fact, a study of time use among elementary school library media specialists found no significant difference in how much time was spent teaching between those with fixed schedules and those with flexible schedules (Donham van Deusen 1996). So, flexible scheduling is not a strategy to reduce teaching. If it does reduce teaching, then its implementation should be examined to determine if some prerequisite factors have not been met.

PREREQUISITES FOR FLEXIBLE SCHEDULING

While there may be no one right formula, some conditions may make flexible scheduling more likely to succeed. Six key elements are the following:

- Information skills curriculum matched with content area curriculum

- Flexible access to the library media center
- Team planning, including the library media specialist
- Principal expectations for collaboration between teachers and the library media specialist
- Commitment to resource-based learning
- Support staff in the library media center (Donham van Deusen 1995)

If these elements are lacking, it may be premature to advocate for flexible scheduling. Without the appropriate conditions, a move away from fixed scheduling can become a move toward no scheduling (that is, children having little or no access to the library media center and little or no library media instruction).

Information Literacy Curriculum

The library media specialist must have a clear plan for what he or she intends to teach. Several models for information process curricula exist; widely known models include those by Eisenberg (Eisenberg and Berkowitz 1990), Kuhlthau (1994), Stripling (1988), and Pappas (1995). These models underpin information literacy curriculum design. Classroom teachers must also have a clear curriculum plan for their own teaching. Through collaboration and negotiation, classroom teachers and library media specialists match the information skills agenda to the content area goals so that information skills are learned within the context of the content area curriculum. This planning involves designing appropriate instructional activities to support integration and laying out the timeline for the school year. Such planning can occur between individual teachers and the library media specialist, or between teams (grade-level or discipline-based). The crucial fact is that such collaboration must occur to map the integration. If this process is not comprehensive—every teacher, every grade or team—the information process curriculum is hit or miss. We would probably not allow math to be hit or miss, so how can we in good conscience settle for an information curriculum that is hit or miss?

This preliminary planning and mapping requires sustained sessions. One possibility is to set aside workshop time before school. Another possibility is to hire substitute teachers for a few days during the school year so that teachers and the library media specialist can collaboratively map the integration. The principal's support for a truly integrated information skills curriculum is important in facilitating the planning phase.

Flexible Access

Implementation of flexible scheduling raises concern about opportunities for book checkout and reading guidance. While we see an increasing emphasis on information processing and information technology, the elementary library media program aims to encourage children to become readers, to guide them in selecting appropriate reading materials and provide access to those materials. When the weekly class period is eliminated, it must be replaced with some way to meet these reading goals. The library media center offers opportunities for children to use a variety of information technologies for browsing or searching. Flexible access is perhaps the best solution. Flexible access is complex; its implementation must be systemic. It is not enough to simply say to everyone, "The library media center is open all day. Children may come whenever they wish." Classroom teachers must enable access *from* the classroom and *into* the library media center. Some teachers establish systems for allowing free-flow between the classroom and the library media center. For others, concern about student accountability demands more formalized systems. Systems as simple as creating laminated passes for use in each classroom can govern over how many students arrive at the center at once and how many leave a given classroom at one time. Two to four passes per classroom, depending on school and center size, may meet the needs. One would hope that whenever a student has an information need, there is a way to seek the solution in a timely fashion.

Regularly scheduled book checkout/browsing time is another way to provide access. For example, each classroom might have a designated 15-minute period per week to come to the center with the teacher so that each child can explore and check out materials. This arrangement differs from weekly scheduled classes in two important ways: the purpose is not direct instruction, and the teacher accompanies the class to assist. Daily checkout times for primary grade classes may be appropriate in many settings. This allows children to develop a sense of responsibility in a consistent pattern of borrowing and returning (Fox 2001).

If possible, the library media specialist may want to try to schedule these browse-and-checkout times during periods when it is unlikely that other teachers would be requesting flexibly scheduled instruction (for example, when classes are having mathematics, physical education, or other activities less dependent on library media center use). Whatever the system, access for all must be addressed.

Team Planning

Research suggests that in schools where teachers plan as teams (by grade level or content area), flexible scheduling particularly enhances the consultation role (Donham van Deusen and Tallman 1994). The relationship was not determined to be causal, but is clearly correlative. This finding suggests that the library media specialist ought to provide some leadership toward teachers working together as teams if this structure is not already in place.

Principal's Expectations

Research has found that where some form of flexible scheduling was in place and principals had expectations for the library media specialist to participate in instructional planning with teachers, more such participation occurred (Donham van Deusen 1993). The importance of the principal perceiving that the library media program is a collaborative partner in classroom instruction cannot be overlooked. The library media specialist must help the principal see the relationship between the library media program and the classroom and demonstrate that relationship in practice.

Commitment to Resource-Based Learning

Flexible scheduling can facilitate the library media specialist's ability to work as an instructional consultant with teachers. In that role, library media specialists identify appropriate electronic and print resources and recommend ways those resources can be used in teaching. Resource-based learning fits a constructivist approach to learning; it facilitates student engagement and active learning. If there is no commitment to resource-based learning, it is difficult to envision flexible scheduling serving much of a purpose; the library media specialist may have less to offer as a consultant in a textbook-bound approach to teaching.

Support Staff

Support staff will almost inevitably enhance a program with flexible scheduling. Research suggests that when library media specialists have support staff, they do significantly more consulting (Donham van Deusen 1995). In that report the operational definition of the consulting role included five tasks: gathering materials for teachers, helping teachers identify instructional objectives, helping teachers plan learning activities, team teaching, and evaluating the instruction. Three groups were analyzed: those with no paid support staff, those with up to 20 hours per week, and those with 20 hours or more per week. Those library media specialists who had more than 20 hours of paid support staff in their library media centers reported over 150 percent as many instances of four of the five consulting tasks (all except gathering materials) than those who had no support staff. With support staff available in the library media center, the library media specialist can meet with a teacher or a team, and students can still access the center and locate and use resources there. While flexible scheduling can occur without support staff, there may be no one available to help students when the library media specialist is working with classes or teachers. In a 1993 flexible scheduling study, library media specialists reported that they often gathered materials upon request of teachers; this study included no measure of support staff availability (Donham van Deusen 1993). Gathering material may only require a note or e-mail message, or brief conversation between library media specialist and teachers. However, more extensive collaboration must occur for media specialists to join in designing instructional objectives or activities, whereas gathering materials can occur based on a note or an e-mail message. Of course, building size must be considered in determining an appropriate number of support staff. No significant differences were found between those with no support staff and those with fewer than 20 hours of assistance. These findings suggest that, at a minimum, it may take 20 hours per week of support staff to begin to make a difference in consulting.

MIXED SCHEDULING

A compromise between fixed and flexible scheduling bears examination. It incorporates both kinds of scheduling. With totally flexible scheduling, there is the concern that many students will never come to the library media center. Perhaps their teacher is reluctant to schedule the class into the library media center periodically, perhaps the student's class schedule limits the opportunities to visit the library media center, or perhaps the student has no motivation to go to the library media center. These students, then, are missing out on opportunities to learn information access and use skills. They are also missing out on browsing—a particularly important activity for younger children who are less independent library media center users. Another concern is teacher's release time. In many schools, teachers have grown dependent on the release time provided while the library media specialist takes their classes, and teachers are understandably reluctant to give up that time.

In response to these concerns for students and teachers, the library media center can schedule weekly or regular visits to the library media center for classes, and in addition offer flexible scheduling. In creating a mixed schedule, setting the times for the regularly scheduled classes is affected by several factors. Ideally, they should be scheduled during times when other classes are having "specials" (such as art, music, physical education, or foreign language) or mathematics when it might be less likely that those classes would need flexibly scheduled class time. Also, these classes can be short, say 15 minutes in length, because their purpose is scheduled access, not teaching. It is likely that during this time the library media specialist will do no formal instruction beyond a few brief booktalks or a brief introduction to some new resource in the center. These visits are single-purpose: to ensure that all students have regular and frequent access to the library media center. The majority of the library media schedule remains flexible so that when a class needs sustained instruction or guided information work, that need can be met. The flexibly scheduled time remains a high priority for the library media specialist and for the center. If space allows, flexibly scheduled classes can be double-booked during weekly checkout visits once regular visitors establish an appropriate level of independence, or if support staff can monitor these visitors so that the library media specialist can work with classes who need "the expert" for instruction or assistance. Supervision of regularly scheduled checkout groups can even be a volunteer activity; the times are predictable and the skills needed can be taught to volunteers.

Although many library media specialists feel that it is a stop-gap measure, research suggests that the mixed schedule option is indeed worthy of consideration. In their national study of scheduling, Donham van Deusen and Tallman (1994) found that compared to library media specialists with fixed scheduling, those with mixed schedules participated in significantly more consultation with teachers. Furthermore, in the same study those library media specialists with mixed schedules significantly outperformed those with both fixed and flexible scheduling in how frequently they incorporated information skills instruction with classroom curriculum activities. These research results highlight the potential for combining fixed schedule classes, perhaps at certain grade levels, and flexibly scheduled classes.

An example of a mixed schedule appears in Figure 7.1, which requires some explanation. This is a schedule for a three-section K–5 school. Each class has a weekly scheduled checkout time to ensure that all students have regular access to the library media center. These 15-minute periods are shown on the schedule in italics. The teacher may or may not accompany the group, depending on local priorities for teacher release time. Generally, these regular sessions are scheduled at times unlikely to be sought for flexible scheduling, because they come at the beginning or end of the day, around the lunch hour, or during times when special area or mathematics classes meet.

The example shows that the two succeeding weeks are not alike, except for the weekly circulation times. It is of particular importance that some classes come to the library media center daily for extended work on a project. Some classes come to the center for a single class meeting. Some classes are scheduled for two 30-minute modules; others are scheduled for only one. Many activities involve the whole class, but some involve small groups. Teachers do not have designated time slots for their flexibly scheduled classes. Instead, they schedule classes to fit their teaching needs; for activities in reading, a given class may come to the media center in the morning, but when that class has a project requiring media center resources in science they may schedule to come in the afternoon. The classroom schedule drives the library media center schedule. All these variations are driven by the students' immediate needs—not by a set schedule.

BLOCK SCHEDULING

Secondary schools are rethinking the daily schedule for classes, to seek a system that will provide opportunities for greater depth in instruction. Block scheduling is one structure that may provide a solution. In a review of secondary school reforms in *School Library Media Researcher Online*, Gary Hartzell (2001) describes some of the advantages of block scheduling:

> For students, fewer classes at any given time enable them to concentrate their efforts and to prepare more thoroughly for each class than they could if they were taking seven or eight. Over the run of

FIGURE 7.1
Sample Mixed Schedule

Week 1

	Monday	Tuesday	Wednesday	Thursday	Friday
8:00-8:30	Meet with Kdg leam			Meet with Grade 1 leam	
8.30-8:45	Grade 3 Circ Berger		Grade 3 Circ Barr	Grade 3 Circ Denison	
8:45-9:00	Grade 2 Circ Berger		Grade 2 Circ Barr	Grade 2 Circ Venison	
9:00-9:30	Kdg. Story/Circ Smith	Kdg. Story/Circ Jones	Grade 3 Denison Index Lesson Animals Unit		Kdg.Story/Circ Johnson
9:30-10:00			Grade 3 Denison Index Lesson Animals Unit		Grade 5 Roy 6 students to work on magazines
10:00-10:30					Grade 5 Roy 6 students to work on magazines
10:30-11:00	Grade 5 Bell Social Studies Culture Proj.	Grade 5 Bell Social Studies Culture Proj.	Grade 5 Bell Social Studies Culture Proj.	Grade 5 Bell Social Studies Culture Proj.	
11:00-11:30	Grade 5 Bell Social Studies Culture Proj.	Grade 5 Bell Social Studies Culture Proj.	Grade 5 Bell Social Studies Culture Proj.	Grade S Bell Social Studies Culture Proj.	
11:30-11:45	Grade 4 Circ Gorman	Grade 4 Circ Flynn			Grade 4 Circ Hedge
11:45-12:00				Lunch	Lunch
12:00-12:15	Lunch	Lunch	Lunch	Lunch	Lunch
12:15-12:30	Lunch	Lunch	Lunch Golf	Grade 5 Circ Hart	Grade 5 Circ Roy
12:30-1:00			Green ESL Project	Green ESL Project	
1:00-1:30	Grade 4 Flynn Science HyperStudio Groups	Grade 4 Flynn Science HyperStudio Groups	Grade 4 Flynn Science HyperStudio Groups	Grade 4 Flynn Science HyperStudio Groups	Grade 4 Flynn Science HyperStudlo Groups
1:30-2:00	Grade 4 Flynn Science HyperStudio	Grade 4 Flynn Science HyperSlndio	Grade 4 Flynn Science HyperStudio	Grade 4 Flynn Science HyperStudio	Grade 4 Flynn Science HyperStudl

FIGURE 7.1 (Cont.)				
	Monday	Tuesday	Wednesday	Thursday	Friday
2:00-2:30	Grade 3 Berger Native Am.	Grade 3 Berger Native Are.		Meet with Grade 2 Team	Meet with Grade 3 Team
2:30-2:45	Grade 1 Circ Burke	Grade 1 Circ Burke			Grade 1 Circ Burke
2:45-3:15			Grade 5 Circ Bell	Grade 5 Circ Roy	Grade 5 Circ Travis

Week 2

	Monday	Tuesday	Wednesday	Thursday	Friday
8:00 -8:30	Meet with Grade 5 Team				
8:30-8:45	Grade 3 Circ Berger		Grade 3 Circ Barr	Grade 3 Circ Denison	
8:45-9:00	Grade 2 Circ Berger		Grade 2 Circ Barr	Grade2 Circ Denison	
9:00-9:30	Kdg. Story/Circ Smith	Kdg. Story/Circ Jones			Kdg Story/Circ Johnson
9:30-10:00	Grade S Roy 6 students to work on magazines		Grade 4 Gornian State History Research	Grade 4 German State History Research	Grade 4 Gorman State History Research
10:00-10:30	Grade 5 Roy 6 students to work on magazines		Grade 4 German State History Research	Grade 4 German State History Research	Grade 4 German State History Research
10:30-11:00	Grade 3 Barr Poetry Search	Grade 3 Barr Poetry Search	Grade 3 Barr Poetry Search	Grade 3 Deniss Poetry Search	Grade 3 Daubs Poetry Search
11:00-11 :30	Grade 3 Berger Poetry Search	Grade 3 Berger Poetry Search	Grade 3 Berger Poetry Search		
11:30-11 :45	Grade 4 Circ Gorman	Grade 4 Circ Flynn			Grade 4 Circ Hedge
11:45-12:00			Grade 5 Circ Adams	Lunch	Lunch
12:00-12:15	Lunch	Lauch	Lunch	Lunch	Lunch
12:15-12:30	Lunch	Lunch	Lunch	Grade 5 Circ Golf	Grade 5 Circ Hart
12:30-1:00	Grade 1 Burke Farm Animals	Grade 1 Burke Farm Animals	Grade 5 Roy Booktalks: Biography		Grade 5 Bell Booktalks: Biography

FIGURE 7.1 (Cont.)				
	Monday	Tuesday	Wednesday	Thursday	Friday
1:00-1:30	Grade 4 Hedge Science HyperStudio	Grade 4 Hedge Science HyperStudio	Grade 4 Hedge Science HyperStudio	Grade 4 Hedge Science HyperStudio	Grade 4 Hedge Science HyperStudio
1:30-2:00	Grade 4 Hedge Science HyperStudio	Grade 4 Hedge Science HyperStudio	Grade 4 Hedge Science HyperStudio	Grade 4 Hedge Science HyperStudio	Grade 4 Hndge Science HyperStudio
2:00-2:30		Grade 4 Flynn Booktalks: Survival Stories			Grade 4 German Booktalks: Family Fiction
2:30-2:45	Grade 1 Burke Circ	Grade 1 Barnes Circ	G/T Inventions Research	G/T Inventions Research	G/T Inventions Research Grade 1 Holland Circ
2:45-3:15			Grade 5 Circ Bell G/T Inventions Research	Grade 5 Circ Roy G/T Inventions Research	Grade 5 Circ Travis G/T Inventions Research

their high school careers, students usually can take more classes than they could in the traditional pattern. Students are able to receive greater individual attention because teachers are dealing with fewer students each day and they have a longer period of time with each student each day. Teachers in block scheduling typically teach in three of the four blocks and use the fourth for planning or conferences. Because up to one-quarter of the staff is not committed to class at any given time, there is increased opportunity for teacher collaboration. (n.p.)

Some schools have created variations on the block schedule concept, but one common arrangement is to offer a six-period day over two days, with Day A (when three classes will meet) and Day B (when three different classes will meet). Other options exist, but the commonality among them all is fewer but longer class periods, and elimination of study halls. Extended class periods allow for more varied teaching/learning strategies to be employed beyond lecture, a method that has been pervasive in situations where there was not enough class time for cooperative learning, hands-on learning, or project work.

Block scheduling offers secondary school library media specialists the opportunity to teach information literacy skills and strategies in greater depth. More research occurs at this level, and class periods are long enough to accommodate direct instruction and hands-on engagement in the context of a real need (Richmond 1999). An informal survey of library media specialists who have block scheduling indicated from 30 to 100 percent increases in class use of the library media center. They cite a change in teaching methods, including more student research activities (Gierke 1999). Many will, in fact, be searching for ways to change their teaching behaviors, and the time is ideal for library media specialists to team up and initiate projects and activities for classes in the library media center.

With conventional scheduling, by the time a class arrives in the center and receives brief instructions about a task, there will often be only a few minutes left to carry out work. Or, students will just begin to use the information they have located and it is time to pack up and move on. Block scheduling can alleviate these frustrations. In a 90-minute class period, the teacher can explain the assignment, the library media specialist can teach relevant skills and strategies, and students can work while both teacher and library media specialist make themselves available for one-on-one consultation. The time advantage of 90 minutes instead of 45 or 50 is significant. Because there is enough time to make significant progress and do meaningful work, students are more likely to engage than in settings where the assignment and instruction segments might leave 10 minutes or less for student work—clearly not enough time to do work substantial in either quality or quantity.

The concern elementary library media specialists have for supporting free voluntary reading within flexible scheduling is shared in settings with block scheduling at the secondary level. High school librarians reported that fiction circulation declined, speculating that immersion in subject matter decreased free reading time (Gierke 1999). This "red flag" calls the library media specialist into action to devise ways to market free-reading books to students and to collaborate with teachers to facilitate students continuing to be readers.

ACTION STRATEGIES

Perhaps the greatest challenge in a fixed schedule is making the transition toward a more flexible schedule. Since every school is different, there is no formula for making that happen, but there are some strategies to consider in light of the local situation.

Learning and Teaching

- Provide in-service teacher training about the information skills curriculum, including information access, use, and production. Demonstrate with local examples how these skills can be incorporated into what teachers are teaching. Show an example of a class that could come to the library media center every day for, say, five days in a row to complete a project (compared to dragging a project out over weeks because it is done one period per week).
- Take a proactive stance to work closely with teachers who are changing to block scheduling. Design lessons that incorporate use of the library media center and help students develop increasingly sophisticated information skills.
- Engage teachers in discussion of free voluntary reading and identify ways to help keep students reading (such as by infusing trade books into curriculum and assignment expectations, finding times for book talks and other "marketing" techniques, and identifying browsing times for students).
- Serve on study committees in schools that are considering a transition to block scheduling, and thus initiate thinking about how to use the library media program better within instructional programs.

Information Access and Delivery

- Consider mixed scheduling in elementary schools as an appropriate way to accommodate as many needs as possible.
- In schools with block scheduling, offer book talks during classes to encourage students to use the library media center for reading. These sessions can be 15-minute segments of the longer class periods. In some classes book talks might be thematic to fit classroom units; in other cases, book talks may be aimed at recreational reading interests.

Program Administration

- Meet with the principal to discuss the concerns about weekly classes. Point out the advantages and disadvantages of fixed scheduling, as outlined in Figure 7.2.
- Discuss teacher release time, especially if it is a contractual matter, and look for alternative ways to provide the time without fully

booking the library media specialist (for example, enlist a teacher associate or volunteer to supervise weekly visits for browsing, develop a long-range schedule showing that teachers actually will have as much (or more) release time *on average* if classes come to the library media center on a flexible schedule).

- When teacher release time is a barrier to flexible scheduling, explore the idea of having other specialists provide some teacher release time. Group guidance classes are one example.
- Given the opportunity for some flexible scheduling, make a monthly report to the principal, documenting the activity in the library media center. The report should indicate:
  —classes regularly scheduled and their activities
  —classes flexibly scheduled and their activities
  —evidence of student access to the library media center
  —services provided to teachers
- Review the list of prerequisites for flexible scheduling with the principal:
  —information skills curriculum matched with content area curriculum
  —flexible access
  —team planning
  —principal's expectations
  —commitment to resource-based learning
  —support staff

Work with the principal to develop an action plan to address each of these requirements.

- Accept some compromises at the beginning. For example, while the ideal is that teachers would accompany their classes to the library media center for instruction, it is likely that some teachers will believe that they are free to leave if the library media specialist is teaching the students. Indeed, it would be helpful for the teacher to know what students have learned. On the other hand, is the teacher's presence worth losing a scheduling scheme that will make library media instruction meaningful for students? Probably not. The optimist will say that over time, teachers may begin to believe it is worthwhile to attend when the library media specialist is teaching, as they see what their students learn. Meanwhile, the library media specialist does well to keep the teacher informed about the lesson content, and encourage teacher attendance. Certainly, many teachers will want to be present, and will enjoy the opportunity to

FIGURE 7.2	
Advantages and Disadvantages of Fixed Scheduling	
Advantages	**Disadvantages**
Teachers have release time.	Library media specialist is "tied up" when teachers have planning time and is often unavailable to collaborate with teachers.
All students get to the library media center every week.	Students cannot retain what they learned a week ago; the library media specialist cannot build on that knowledge for complex processes.
All students get exposure to information skills.	Skills taught in isolation are usually not mastered because students see no relevance.
The library media specialist's work day is filled with easily documented activity.	The library media specialist may not be available when teachers need help or when students need instruction.
Weekly classes are predictable.	Once-a-week sessions limit the complexity of activities. For example, producing television commercials as a part of a unit on advertising or creating a historical newspaper based on information collected from various sources requires considerable time; such a project accomplished in weekly 25-minute segments drags on and students lose their enthusiasm.

collaborate. Still, it may be necessary to accept the decision of those who do not. In some grades, teachers may see little use for flexible scheduling; often kindergarten teachers focus on building habits in their children and the once-a-week class meets their needs. They may feel that there is little need for flexibly scheduled classes because their children have not attained the literacy skills needed for some information work. In response, the library media specialist can accept their position, and yet share with them the possibilities for production activities that may be highly appropriate for kindergarten children (such as creating an electronic alphabet picture "book," or creating finger puppets and performing puppet plays in the library media center). These are activities not easily accomplished in weekly classes, but with flexible scheduling they occur in a timely fashion that maintains children's enthusiasm.

SCENARIO FOR DISCUSSION

The Hughes High School has transitioned to block scheduling, which is now in its second year. The library media specialist keeps a calendar on the circulation desk where teachers can reserve space in the library for classes. The calendar asks them to key in whether they want space (S), instruction (I), or guidance (G) while they are there. Now that classes are longer, two social studies teachers have begun to schedule their classes into the library media center routinely for "research time." Their typical practice is to meet with their class in the classroom for 20 minutes and then parade them to the library media center to "do research." They mark S on the library media calendar, indicating that they just want to use the space. Each class has arrived in the library at least twice a week for the past month. The library media specialist has asked the teachers whether she can provide specific guidance or instruction for the projects students are doing. Both teachers have said, however, that their seniors probably don't need any help—they just need to be in the library where they can get at resources they need. Meanwhile, the students from these classes are at workstations around the library surfing the Web. What next?

REFERENCES

Donham, J., K. Bishop, C. C. Kuhlthau, and D. Oberg (2001). *Inquiry Based Teaching: Lessons from Library Power*. Worthington, OH: Linworth Publishing.

Donham van Deusen, J. (1993, Spring). "Effects of Fixed Versus Flexible Scheduling on Curriculum Involvement and Skills Integration in Elementary School Library Media Programs." *School Library Media Quarterly 21* (3): 173–182.

Donham van Deusen, J. (1995, September/October). "Prerequisites for Flexible Scheduling." *Emergency Librarian 23* (1): 16–18.

Donham van Deusen, J. (1996, Winter). "An Analysis of the Time-Use of Elementary School Library Media Specialists and Factors that Influence It." *School Library Media Quarterly 24* (2): 85–92.

Donham van Deusen, J. and J. I. Tallman (1994, Fall). "The Impact of Scheduling on Curriculum Consultation and Information Skills Instruction." *School Library Media Quarterly 23* (1): 17–25.

Eisenberg, M. B. and R.E. Berkowitz (1990). *Information Problem-Solving: The Big Six Skills Approach to Library and Information Skills Instruction.* Norwood, NJ: Ablex.

Fox, C. J. (2001, January/February). "Designing a Flexible Schedule for an Elementary School Library Media Center." *Library Talk 14* (1): 10–13.

Gierke, C. (1999, September/October). "What's Behind Block Scheduling?" *Book Report 18* (2): 8–10.

Hartzell, G. (2001). "The Implications of Selected School Reform Approaches for School Library Media Services." *School Library Media Researcher Online 4.* Retrieved July 27, 2004, from www.ala.org/aasl/SLMR.

Kuhlthau, C. C. (1994). *Teaching the Library Research Process.* Metuchen, NJ: Scarecrow Press.

Pappas, M. (1995). *Teaching Electronic Information Skills Series.* McHenry, IL: Follett Software.

Richmond, G. (1999, September/October). "Block Scheduling: From Principles to Practice." *Book Report 18* (2): 12–14.

Stripling, B. K. (1988). *Brainstorms and Blueprints: Teaching Library Research as a Thinking Process.* Englewood, CO: Libraries Unlimited.

Chapter 8

Collection

This chapter:

- discusses selection criteria and policies
- describes trends in collection development that reflect more interaction with the context of the library media program
- considers the demands of special populations for accessible resources
- discusses the demands on collection planning associated with electronic resources
- discusses collection maintenance and evaluation
- describes the process for reconsideration of challenged materials
- identifies action strategies related to collection

Although the library media program is far more than a warehouse of materials, still the collection is important. In a time when the mass media predict the demise of print, when people speak of virtual libraries replacing print collections, when funding for resources is challenged by those who suggest that there is no need for a collection because all the information is "out there" on the World Wide Web, it may be more important than ever to discuss and justify the library media collection. Electronic access will certainly continue to change the nature and emphasis in collections. Nevertheless, collecting resources to be locally available continues to be important. Naively, administrators sometimes assume that electronic access to information will justify reducing the budget for materials. For several reasons, this is simply not true. For example, the elementary school's reading program demands print resources for children, and the mathematics program demands manipulative materials (such as items to count and sort or items with which to measure). Students in science classes will continue to use models to understand scientific principles. Students seeking a quick answer to a fact question will often find it most efficient to look in an almanac or another fact book. Furthermore, not all information is readily accessible online. In many schools, the amount of online access is limited to one or a few workstations. Voluntary reading will most likely continue to occur between covers rather than on screen. Some nonfiction will continue to be better explored in print rather than electronic resources. A collection that includes both electronic and print resources is likely to continue to characterize school library media centers, despite the growth of online access.

If the library media program is characterized by close collaboration with teachers, involvement with students and their diverse needs, and communication with principals, parents, and the community, then collection use warrants continued fiscal support. High-use patterns should be documented to show that teaching and learning are dependent on the center's physical collection as well as its access to online information. Each year *School Library Journal* publishes the average book price for that year. For 2002, the average book price was listed there as $18.78 (St. Lifer 2002). This compares to a 2005 average price of $20.52 (St. Lifer 2005)—a 9.3 percent increase in three years. The constant rate of book publishing for children and youth promises no imminent demise in print materials, and the infusion of books into content-area learning signals a continued demand; budgets will need to keep pace with the market prices. Budgets for local collections continue to be needed for books, DVDs, and other formats in addition to online access.

SELECTION CRITERIA AND POLICIES

Each school district should have a formal, board-approved policy governing materials selection and reconsideration. In research on reconsideration of materials, Hopkins (1991) found that in those schools where a formal policy exists, library media specialists felt less pressure to be cautious in their selection practices. The selection policy should include the following features:

1. Statement of responsibility for selection. This statement is often a delegation of authority to a particular staff member. Bartlett (1980) offers this model statement of responsibility:

 > The responsibility for the selection of library information and materials is delegated to the library media specialist(s) employed by the District. Responsibility for selection of text materials is delegated to ad hoc and standing text selection committees proposed by the administration and approved by the Board. While the responsibility for final selection and recommendation for purchase rests with the licensed school media personnel for library materials and with designated committees with text materials, suggestions will be welcomed from principals, teachers, students, supervisors, and community members.

2. Criteria for selection. General criteria might include the following qualities:
   - Consistent with the general educational goals of the district and the objectives of specific courses
   - High in quality of factual content and presentation
   - Appropriate for the subject area and for the age, emotional level, ability level, and the social development of the students for whom the materials are selected
   - Of aesthetic, literary, or social value
   - Authored by competent and qualified authors and producers
   - Fosters respect for women and minority and ethnic groups
   - Selected for strengths rather than rejected for weaknesses
   - Suitable in physical format and appearance for intended use
   - Provides ideological balance on controversial issues

3. Selection procedures. Procedures for selection should accomplish the following:
   - Ensure quality by advocating use of reviewing media and professional selection tools
   - Provide for gathering input from the library media program's constituencies
   - Establish gift criteria consistent with those applied to new purchases
   - Guide weeding and periodic replacement of both materials and hardware

4. Reconsideration process. It is essential to have a written procedure for any community member to request formally that an item be

reconsidered for inclusion in the collection. This process should include the following elements:

- The composition and operation of the reconsideration committee
- A description of the review process
- A statement of the next course of action in the event of a failure to resolve the concern

The research of Diane Hopkins (1993) indicates that "support for retention of challenged materials from persons/organizations within or outside the district was greater for written challenges" and that written rather than oral challenges predominate when there is a selection policy in place (p. 29). One can expect the due process afforded by a written selection policy is more likely to result in retaining challenged materials. These findings underscore the importance of insisting on a written, board-approved policy in order to protect intellectual freedom.

TRENDS

Collection development in school library media centers is affected by collaboration with faculty, resource-based learning, tightening budgets, increasing prices for books, demand for materials accessible for all students, and demand for electronic formats.

Focus

Librarians have traditionally developed collections, in part, with a "just-in-case" mind-set; that is, they have tried to maintain a balanced collection that covers the breadth of potential information needs. A trend toward more focus and away from balance relates to three simultaneous events. First, online access is providing the balance in the collection in place of locally available physical resources. As online access becomes more widespread and more efficient with faster connectivity and better search engines, more reference questions are being answered online. Second, school library media budgets are not growing in step with the increasing costs of materials. Reduced buying power means that library media specialists must prioritize; they cannot maintain broad-based collections and support curricular topics in depth. Third, school library media collections are becoming more curriculum-driven as programs grow more integrated with the school curriculum and as teachers depend more on trade resources.

Curriculum-driven collections tend to have depth in those topics that the curriculum emphasizes. For example, middle schools where American history is taught are likely to have library media collections with substantial depth in that topic, while those same collections may have very little, if any, specialized resources on Asian history if it is not represented in the curriculum.

Curriculum mapping and collection mapping are two strategies useful for measuring how well the collection fits the curriculum. Curriculum mapping is a strategy for identifying the instructional content for each grade level or course and summarizing it on a chart to show the spectrum (Jacobs 2000). Charting the curriculum shows the articulation from grade to grade and course to course. If there are gaps, they become more obvious, and if there are inappropriate repetitions, they too are evident. In addition, curriculum maps can identify potential areas for integration. For example, when *My Brother Sam Is Dead* is being taught in a middle school language arts program, the curriculum map for the social studies program may reveal study of the American Revolution in the history curriculum, suggesting possibilities for curriculum integration. A curriculum map can help align curriculum with district or state standards. A curriculum map is a valuable tool for the library media specialist—it facilitates anticipating topics so that appropriate materials can be selected to support instruction. While there are commercial products for curriculum mapping (such as *TechPaths: A Curriculum Mapping System* accessible at www.perfpathways.com), the process is essentially one of creating a school-wide chart of the curriculum. The map should include three types of data: content (key concepts/essential questions), specific skills, and assessments. These data are charted according to grade level, teacher, discipline, or other data elements useful for articulation within a school or a school district.

Collection mapping is a technique for identifying topics and determining the depth of holdings on those topics. Karen Lowe (2001) recommends that library media specialists print out their shelf list from the library automation system. Essential fields to include are the call number, the title, and the copyright date. The data in this report can be compared to the curriculum to determine where resources align with curriculum needs and where they do not. By examining the Dewey range relevant for a particular curricular area, the library media specialist can

FIGURE 8.1 Collection Map: Dewey Range 570 to 585		
Call number	Title	Copyright
574.5	Hidden Life of the Forest	1988
574.5	Conserving Rain Forests	1990
574.526	At Home in the Rain Forest	1991
574.526	Garden	2007
574.526	Grassland	1996
574.526	The Coniferous Forest	1997
574.909	Forest Life	2006
575.6	Flowers, Fruits and Seeds	1999
575.7	Flowers for You	1993
577.3	A Forest's Life	1997
581	Incredible Plants	1997
581	Eyewitness Visual Dictionary of Plants	1992
581	Green Plants	1993
581	How Seeds Travel	1982
582	Flowers	2003
582.016	From Flower to Fruit	1986
582.016	How a Seed Grows	2007
582.13	Freaky Flowers	2002
582.13	A Child's Book of Wildflowers	1992
582.16	Are Trees Alive?	2002
582.16	How Trees Help Me	1992
582.16	Crinkleroot's Guide to Knowing the Trees	1991
582.16	The Big Tree	1991
582.5	Douglas Fir	2005
583.2	Insect-Eating Plants	1995
583.322	Bean and Plant	1986
583.55	Dandelion	1987

FIGURE 8.2
Collection Data for Curricular Emphases

Category	Average Copyright Date	Number of Volumes
Science 590s (Animals)	1970	160
Science 520s (Space Science)	1995	65
Science 550s (Earth science)	1988	55
Science 580s (Plants)	1993	27
Science 590s (Animals)	1989	110
Technology 600s	1991	190
Social Studies 910s (Geography)	1990	130
Social Studies 970s (American History)	1987	310

determine both how extensive and how current the collection is to meet the demands of the curriculum. Most library automation systems provide a report option that includes call number, copyright, and title. Figure 8.1 shows an example of a report that maps a small section of a collection. The report can be sorted by call number to match the collection with the curriculum, or by copyright to examine the need for updating within the selected call number range. For a more comprehensive collection map, reports for various call number ranges can be summarized, as shown in Figure 8.2, a summary collection map for an elementary school.

Identified gaps become targets of a purchase plan. Library selection tools (such as *Senior High Core Collection*, Neal-Schuman's *Guide to Recommended Children's Books and Media for Use with Every Elementary Subject*, or *Children's Catalog*) or specialized books (like *A to Zoo: Subject Access to Children's Picture Books* or *Best Books for Young Teen Readers*) can then be used to identify quality resources to fill these gaps.

Focusing collection development on curriculum can pose some challenges. A focused collection will have gaps. When the collection does not respond to a query, the library media specialist must use outside sources to provide assistance. Seeking information on the Web is one avenue. Interlibrary loan with neighboring schools or public libraries is also a possible solution. Curriculum changes from time to time, and when it does, the changes will affect the collection. For example, when teachers who have taught a thematic literature unit on the Middle Ages for several years abandon it in favor of a thematic unit on heroes and heroines, few of the resources that have been collected for the former theme will apply to the new one, and many items about the Middle Ages will go largely unused, except for the rare independent request. Such a curriculum change calls for a supplement to the library media budget to accommodate the new in-depth demands on the collection.

Collaboration

Library media specialists usually have the primary responsibility for selecting resources, yet the importance of teachers and library media specialists collaborating on collection decisions cannot be overlooked. In the past, library media specialists read reviews and based their selections largely on what the reviewers said, with an eye to what they thought their clients wanted. In integrated library media programs, collection decisions shift toward what the clients are asking for, and secondarily toward what the reviewers say. When library media specialists are working with teachers as they plan, they are in very close communication with what is being taught. That information helps them to prioritize according to curricular demands. As units are discussed they learn what units were frustrating for teachers and students because of resource deficiencies, and they learn where the collection has worked well. Direct involvement with teachers in planning and evaluating instruction is key to ensuring that the library media specialist is making good collection development decisions.

Collection development can be collaborative in another way also. In districts with multiple schools, some collaborative collection development can occur among schools. By comparing collections and demands and identifying common needs, it is quite possible to share resources. This strategy is particularly useful for curriculum-based purchases used only once a year. For example, thematic literature units often call for purchase of multiple copies of some titles for common readings. If more than one school within a district will teach a unit on conflict and will use some of the same titles for common reading, is it necessary for every school to purchase the multiple copies? Could the units be coordinated so that they are not taught at the same time and materials could be shared? The cost of materials and the increasing expenditures for online subscriptions, coupled with minimal increases in budget—in part because of the increasing demands for hardware and technology infrastructure—makes cooperative purchases particularly attractive where possible.

Quality

Collaborating with teachers and encouraging their involvement in collection decisions does not mean that the library media specialist abdicates the overall responsibility for the collection. While teachers may indicate areas they perceive to be deficient or strong in the collection, the library media specialist has data to confirm what the collection includes. Also, the library media specialist can identify external sources to supplement the local collection, particularly for infrequent requests. Maintaining a high standard of quality is of particular importance for the library media specialist. When teachers suggest specific items, library media specialists need to apply the criteria listed in the selection policy. Reviewing media and selection tools continue to be essential resources for final selection decisions. If a teacher requests an item that lacks quality or has been reviewed unfavorably, the library media specialist has a responsibility to communicate that to the teacher and, if possible, identify a substitute of higher quality. It is essential that teachers receive feedback about the recommendations they make—both affirmative and negative.

Student Needs and Interests

Results from the National Assessment of Educational Progress show that significant gaps in reading performance continue to exist between racial/ethnic subgroups and between male and female students (National Center for Educational Statistics 2002). These data signal the need for providing collections of reading materials that are accessible for students reading below level. Besides accessibility, the library media center must include in its collection materials that appeal to students for whom reading is difficult. Graphic novels represent one format that appeals to challenged readers. This book format gives the reader more visual than textual information. While they are more accessible for students who find reading difficult and more appealing to less-motivated readers, they are socially acceptable among young people (Kan 2003). YALSA (Young Adult Library Services Association) launched its first "best" list of graphic novels in 2007. The YALSA Web site is an excellent resource for recommendations for this genre and others. (www.ala.org/yalsa). Because the audience for this genre spans a wide age range, school library media specialists should seek reviews and information to ensure the age appropriateness of specific titles.

Nonnative speakers present another challenge for the library collection. One of the most salient features of this population is their diversity; they vary in native language, world experience, cultural values and norms, and socioeconomic status. Peregoy and Boyle (2000) describe this population and its challenges in the context of reading:

> What differ between native and non-native English readers are the cognitive-linguistic and experiential resources they bring to the reading task, especially in terms of those variables that relate directly to reading comprehension in English, i.e., (a) English language proficiency, (b) background knowledge related to the text, and (c) literacy abilities and experiences, if any, in the first language. (p. 238)

One striking example is the challenge for the native speaker of Chinese who must adjust from symbols representing whole words or concepts to phonemes. Similarly, Arabic-language speakers must overcome a very different set of conventions as they approach a new alphabet. For the school library to provide resources that are age-appropriate and yet also developmentally appropriate for this group of students requires a conscious effort at seeking advice from teachers who specialize in teaching English-as-a-second-language students.

Electronic Resources

In a national survey, Shontz and Farmer (2007) found that online products represented an average expenditure of $2.16 per student, while only 90 cents was being spent per student on CD-ROMs and software combined. This trend suggests a transition away from a local physical collection to a subscription-based online collection. Changing from ownership of information sources to accessing them online represents a significant change in the meaning of collection. This trend has implications for budget. Online subscriptions are analogous to rent; the library media program pays for access to these resources for the year, but at the end of the year owns nothing. Hence, if the budget for these resources declines and forces discontinuation of some subscriptions, the void left in available information is even greater than in the days of owned physical resources.

ENHANCEMENT IN ACTION:
AUDIOBOOKS IN THE SCHOOL LIBRARY
MEDIA COLLECTION

In her middle school, Beers (1998) provides audiobooks to accompany trade books for students to read along and follow the
text as they listen. Read-alongs have long been common in
elementary schools, but the increased popularity of the
audiobook as an adult format has reduced the stigma that might
have once been associated with this practice for middle
schoolers. In Berkeley, California, 13 percent of Berkeley High's
student body comes from homes where English is not the primary language. These students participate in a group called
"Earphone English" in which they listen to books on tape in
English and then engage in discussion about them (Goldsmith
2002). Audiobooks provide a way for these students to develop
"listening English." While some students follow a text as they
listen, many do not, choosing to read the book later if at all.
Audiobooks may constitute an expanding portion of the collection, especially in secondary schools, as part of the solution for
meeting the needs of readers challenged by native language,
learning disabilities, or cultural situations.

Funding is finite, so it is unreasonable to expect that substantially
more dollars will come to the library media budget. Instead, a change in
attitude about collection is in order. The top priority for the collection is
curriculum support. Access to information via the World Wide Web needs
to be considered in collection decisions. What is available online to meet
the need? How readily accessible is it? Topics not frequently studied
may be voids in the local collection to be filled by online information.

While the general criteria listed in the selection policy apply to electronic resources as well as to print, there is still a call for specialized
criteria for electronic resources. Informational electronic products can
provide students the opportunity to learn by exploration and to have
considerable choice in what they investigate. Their organizational structure usually places a great deal of control in the hands of the user. Software evaluation needs to take into account beliefs about learning, design of the product, and technical quality. Figure 8.3 provides an ex-

---

FIGURE 8.3
Electronic Resource Evaluation Form

Program: _____

Hardware requirements: _____

Intended audience: _____

Producer: _____

Learning Features

Criteria	Comments
Is active learning emphasized?	
Are the concepts age appropriate?	
Is the child "in control" of the software?	
Are concepts represented concretely?	
Is there room for creative or divergent thinking?	
Is the learning intrinsically (rather than extrinsically) motivated?	
Do the content and design represent a "low entry" and "high ceiling? Is there expanding complexity?	
Is the software open-ended?	
Does this medium suit the content better than any other medium?	
Is there a focus on process?	
Are "powerful" ideas addressed rather than low-level skills?	
Is there a fit with the library's or school's program needs?	

---

ample of criteria to be considered for evaluating these products. Criteria related to learning are consistent with those recommended by the National Association of Young Children (Shade 1996).

Electronic resources involve licensing issues: Is off-site access permitted? Are there limits on the number of concurrent users? What are the costs of updates? Does the product reside on a local server or does

FIGURE 8.3 (Cont.)	
Design/Performance Features	
Criteria	Comments
Is the reading requirement appropriate to the age?	
Do music, motion, and sound add to the substance, or are they gratuitous?	
If speech is used, is it authentic and interesting, or mechanized and monotonous?	
Does it operate without error?	
Is installation straightforward and simple?	
Is navigation intuitive?	
Does the navigation allow choices for the user, e.g., ability to go back, ability to move from topic to topic?	
Does the documentation provide additional information that enhances the use of the software?	
Is the wait time for loading graphics or accessing data acceptable?	
Is telephone support available?	
Is there online help?	
Are there printing capabilities when desired?	

the vendor host it? Visual media call for specific criteria for selection. Suggested criteria to consider are shown in Figure 8.4.

It is important that library media specialists help administrators understand that providing online resources is a subscription transaction—not a purchase transaction. The implications in terms of budgeting are significant. When library media specialists build physical collections owned by the school, a budget shortfall for a year is problematic, but the library still has the accumulated collection of previous years to provide information. As the collection is built on a subscription basis, there is no development of equity in resources; the dollars must be available every year, or all of the information goes away. The advantages of online resources are significant, including simultaneous use by many students, the possibility of access from classrooms and homes, and availability of

FIGURE 8.4
DVD Evaluation

Title: _____

Producer/Distributor _____

Intended audience: _____

Content

Criteria	Comments
Is information accurate and up-to-date?	
Is there evidence of bias?	
Will the content maintain the viewer's interest?	
Are performance rights available if needed?	
Does the content fit the programming needs of the school or library?	
Does documentation indicate sources of information?	
Is the production of significant educational, social or artistic value?	
Are the language and visual elements appropriate to the intended age group?	

Design

Criteria	Comments
Is this the most appropriate medium for the content?	
Is pacing appropriate to the content and the audience	
Are visuals well produced and effectively used?	
If there is text, is it readable? Does it stay on the screen long enough to be read?	
Is the sound acceptable, e.g., good fidelity, realistic sound effects, synchronized to the visual?	
Is information accessible in useful ways?	
Are voices easy to listen to and to understand?	
Are accompanying guides useful?	

authoritative and very current information. Librarians will need to pay attention to usage reports provided through these subscriptions in order to gauge use and make annual decisions regarding this online "collection."

Besides subscription resources, the World Wide Web offers access to a vast array of free information resources, but they vary widely in quality, reliability, and stability. A good strategy for assuring access to quality information is for the library media specialist to use Web-authoring software to create pages for specific courses or assignments. This strategy is particularly useful when a class is researching a topic that is stable in the curriculum and when many students will be seeking information on the topic. Web pages take time to create, but they can help to organize an otherwise inefficient, maybe chaotic, search for information.

Questions to consider in reviewing sites to be bookmarked or linked to a course home page are listed in Figure 8.5. While it is important for library media professionals to apply specific criteria to Web sites, it is also important to share those criteria with teachers and students (Symons 1997).

COLLECTION MAINTENANCE

Maintaining a collection is as important as developing it. Collection maintenance involves two major processes: inventory and weeding. Inventory ensures that the materials included in the catalog are indeed in the collection. Automation systems provide for efficient inventory with a bar-code scanner. High-use collections may deserve annual inventory. At a minimum, sections of the collection should be inventoried each year so that over a three-year period the entire collection is checked. During inventory, besides ensuring that materials are physically present, the library media specialist can check for condition and appearance to see whether items should be withdrawn or replaced.

A few years ago, a library media specialist boxed up her entire collection over the summer so that her center could be repainted and carpeted. After the shelves were back in place, she began to unbox the collection. After two years in the school, she knew that the collection needed serious weeding, and she now felt that she knew the curriculum and clientele well enough to proceed with that task. With *Children's Catalog* and *Elementary School Library Collection* at hand to ensure that she did not remove a classic or a title that authorities suggest is the best avail-

FIGURE 8.5
Web Site Evaluation

URL: _____

Couroc/Aooignmont: _____

Teacher: _____

Content	
Criteria	**Comments**
Who is the audience?	
What is the purpose of the page—to inform, persuade, educate, explain?	
Is the scope clear?	
How complete and accurate is the information?	
How does the page compare to other sources of information on this topic?	
How comprehensive is the site?	
Are the links relevant and appropriate for the site?	
Is the site truly informative?	
Is the information current?	
Authority	
Criteria	**Comments**
Who is the author?	
What is the authority or expertise of the person(s) responsible for the site?	
What corporate entity (organization, government agency, university) supports the information?	
Is there evidence of bias?	
Are there reference citations to support the information?	
When was the site last revised?	
Is the site commercial? Is this a problem?	

FIGURE 8.5 (Cont.)	
Structure	
Criteria	**Comments**
Does the site employ good graphic design principles?	
Are the graphics functional, or are they decorative?	
Is the site well organized?	
Is the site searchable?	
Are there links back to the homepage from lower level pages?	
Does the homepage have a directory?	
Performance	
Criteria	**Comments**
How reliable are the links?	
Are there links that do not work?	
Has the URL changed? How frequently?	
How readable is the text?	
Are font choices good?	
How efficient is the loading of graphics?	
Does it do more than print could do?	
Do the pages fit your screen or do they require scrolling?	
Are icons consistent and intuitive?	

able for its purpose, she began unboxing and considering each title. By the time she had finished, she had reduced the collection by more than one-third, ridding it of a 20-year accumulation of books now dusty, dirty, tattered, and dingy. At the opening of the school year, students arrived in the library media center and remarked that they knew they would see new carpet and paint, but they didn't know they were getting so many new books too. In fact, the new books had not yet arrived; it was only that the existing collection looked so much better now that the newer books were visible and the worn-out ones were gone.

This example highlights some of the reasons why collection maintenance is important. First, a collection needs to contain accurate and current information; it is better to have no answer than to have an inaccurate or incorrect answer to a question. Second, weeding is important in making the collection attract users and in communicating that it is a recent and useful collection. Third, a collection needs to be attractive to its potential clientele, and eye appeal is particularly important to the young. A collection that goes unweeded, simply grows, uses more space, and fails to serve the clientele.

Access to the World Wide Web changes the weeding process. In the past, library media specialists were inclined to keep an out-of-date item just to have "something" on a topic—the information available on the Web makes this practice far less justifiable (Graf 1996). Offering no information is probably better than offering inaccurate information. A schedule for weeding can coincide with the inventory schedule so that the collection is reviewed periodically for content as well.

Figure 8.6 provides a general guide to using circulation data and age in the weeding process. The age column suggests an age to consider in the pre-weeding process; those materials older than the age posted here can be pulled from the shelf and reviewed using other considerations such as circulation data, physical condition, quality of the illustrative matter, etc. In some topic areas, age may not be relevant at all, e.g., anatomy or general art books. Weeding can be approached in a relatively objective way:

- Establish a cutoff date for circulation (for example, five years), and identify all titles that have not circulated within that period. If an automated circulation system has been in place for that long, this task should simply be a matter of generating a report from the system.
- Pull from the shelves materials not circulated since the cutoff date.
- Ask teachers to examine materials in their areas and flag those items to be retained.
- Evaluate the remaining items by checking to see whether the titles appear in selection tools, as appropriate for the grade levels served, as well as other bibliographic tools. See *The Collection Program in Schools: Concepts, Practices and Information Sources* (Van Orden and Bishop 2001) for additional suggestions of tools for collection evaluation. If a title appears in one of these resources, it is likely to be the best currently available title on the topic and probably should not be weeded. Review it for accuracy and currency.

- Evaluate for physical condition.
- Withdraw the bibliographic records for those items to be weeded.
- Discard materials according to institutional policy. Generally, items weeded from the library media collection ought not to be distributed to teachers for their classroom. If they are not suitable for the library media collection, they are most likely not suitable for classroom use either. In some districts, weeded titles are sent to a central facility for recycling or disposal. Cooperate with the custodial staff and principal to develop a method for disposal of weeded items.

RECONSIDERATION OF CHALLENGED MATERIALS

Earlier in this chapter, the components of a materials selection policy were outlined. One important component of that policy is a set of procedures for reconsideration of challenged materials. Responses to materials challenges must strike a balance between the individual's right to protest the inclusion of a particular item in the collection, the library media specialist's responsibility to select materials based on objective criteria rather than on personal beliefs or biases, and the institution's right to remove material deemed inappropriate after reasonable due process. Due process is a critical factor in reconsideration cases, and lack of due process has been the turning point for cases taken to the judicial system. The intent of due process is to avoid arbitrary decisions based on an individual's viewpoint or bias. Challenges represent freedom of expression and should not be labeled as inherently harmful. By providing a procedure for reconsideration of challenged materials, the institution is in effect stating that it will indeed reconsider a decision and give that reconsideration due attention and due process. This is a circumstance that brings the library media program and its various constituencies together, and mutual respect is the intended result. The intent of the principle of intellectual freedom is to ensure the right of any person to hold any belief and to express such beliefs or ideas. Censorship, on the other hand, is a denial of the right of freedom of expression; it is a negative act and a way of imposing one's beliefs on everyone. Library media specialists strive to provide to their users a full range of information and ideas and to protect their free access to information and various perspectives.

In schools, the issue of challenged materials is complicated by the

FIGURE 8.6 Weeding Timetable				
Class	Subject/Format	Age	Last Circ.	Comments
000	General	5	NA	
	Computers	2–5	2	
020	Library Science	10	3–5	
030	Encyclopedia	5–10	NA	Retain not longer than 10 years.
100	Philos/Psych	10	3–5	
200	Religion	5–10	3–5	Retain basics; weed or do not accept propaganda.
290	Mythology	10–15	5	Be cautious of classics.
300	Social Science	10–15	5	Retain balance on controversial topics.
310	Almanacs	2–5	NA	Have the latest; may store back issues for class use.
320	Poli. Sci	5–10	3–5	
340	Law	10		
350	Government	5–10	3–5	
360	Welfare	10	5	
370	Education	5	3	
380	Commerce	10	5	
390	Etiquette	5	3	
	Customs/Folklore	10–15	5	Retain basics; classics.
400	Language	10	3–5	Discard texts; retain basics.
500	General	5	3	Retain classics.
510	Math	10	3–5	
570	Biology/Nat.History	10	3–5	
580	Botany	10	3–5	
600	General	5	3	

Class	Subject/Format	Age	Last Circ.	Comments
	FIGURE 8.6 (Cont.)			
610	Anatomy/Physiology		5	
	Other 610	5–10	3–5	
620	Applied Science	5–10	3–5	
630	Agriculture	5–10	3–5	
640	Homemaking	5–10	3	Retain cookbooks.
650	Business	10	5	
660	Chemistry/food	5–10	3–5	
690	Manufacturing	10	3–5	Retain material of historical interest.
700	General			Keep basics, especially art history.
745	Crafts		5	Keep well illustrated.
770	Photography	5	3	Avoid dated techniques or equipment.
800	Literature			Keep basics, check indexes before discarding.
900	General	15	5	Demand accuracy, fairness.
910	Travel/Geog.	5–10	3–5	Retain expensive, well illustrated.
920	Biography	3–5		
F/E	Fiction/Everybody		2–5	Keep high demand; literary merit; well-written; well illustrated. Check indexes.

Source: Adapted from *Weeding the Library Media Center Collections* by Betty Jo Buckingham, Iowa Department of Education, 1984.

definition of a public forum. A classroom is not a public forum; students are required to attend school and the curriculum is under the purview of the school board. In *Minarcini v. Strongsville City School District* (1976) maintenance of a book on a library shelf and maintenance of material required for a course were considered two distinct issues. This case involved a class-action suit brought against a school board by five high school students when the board refused to adopt certain titles recommended by an English teacher for a course. The board also ordered removal of the books from the school library. At the appellate level, the two issues of library access and classroom requirement were separated. The court found that the board had oversight responsibility for selecting materials to be required of students, but that the library would continue to provide access to the books. This is an important distinction when addressing reconsideration requests.

Often in schools, issues of age appropriateness are central to reconsideration discussions. Parents, in sincere efforts to protect their children, may raise concerns about materials that are available in school library media collections. Often such concerns can be alleviated by conversations with parents to indicate that what one parent finds too mature for a child another parent finds ideal. The library media collection must be responsive to a larger public; if a parent has concerns about his or her child's selections, that is an issue to be addressed within the family. One effective, proactive approach to concerns about materials is for the library media specialist to offer a parent organization program about the process of materials selection. Parents can learn the criteria identified in the selection policy, the reviewing media the library media specialist relies on, and other sources of information and factors considered in purchasing decisions. Knowing the complexity of selection and the care taken in these decisions may be enough to alleviate many parents' anxiety.

Still, complaints will come. The library media specialist has six steps to take when a user raises a complaint about an item in the collection:

- Listen sincerely to the position of the complainant.
- Stress the need to respect diversity of the many people who use this collection.
- Inform complainant of how the material is used and how it was selected.
- Explain the procedure for formal reconsideration.
- Provide the appropriate form for a formal request for reconsideration.
- Inform the principal, because no principal wants to be blindsided by a potential controversy.

Remember two important factors about challenged materials: First, the citizen has the right to complain. Second, if a committee elects to remove an item, removal does not represent a failure on the part of the library media specialist, nor does it represent censorship when there is appropriate due process.

EQUIPMENT

Equipment is an important part of the library media collection. The International Society for Technology in Education (ISTE) is an excellent resource for the management of equipment. ISTE provides at its Web site (http://tsi.iste.org) an excellent *Technology Support Index* developed by Dr. Chip Kimball (International Society for Technology in Education 2001). This index offers a four-domain assessment tool for schools and districts to profile a technology support program. The first domain offers a rubric for equipment standards, including replacement cycle, brand and model selection, platform and operating system, application software, management of equipment and peripherals, surplus equipment, and security; thus it offers a framework for decision making. Four levels of equipment standards are described. The highest level includes the following criteria:

- Replacement cycle: Three years.
- Brand selection: The district purchases one brand of equipment.
- Model selection: Model selection is limited, with few exceptions.
- Platform: A common platform is used throughout the district, with few exceptions.
- Operating system: A consistent version of the OS is used across the district.
- Application software: Acceptable software is listed.
- Donated equipment: Equipment must meet district standards and be less than two years old.
- Granted equipment: Equipment purchased through grants must meet district standards.
- Peripherals: Brands and models are limited.
- Surplus equipment: Equipment is taken out of service when it reaches replacement age.
- Warranties: Equipment is warranted to cover its life expectancy.
- Security: Guidelines and a firewall are in place.

While these guidelines may seem restrictive, it is clear that the aim is consistency across a school district to facilitate support of both hardware and software.

The second ISTE domain covers staffing and processes. It offers such valuable benchmarks as a formula-driven technology staffing rubric. The third domain addresses professional development, and the fourth domain covers intelligent systems. This index provides an excellent and comprehensive approach to assessing the status of technology in a school district, and it offers specific guidance to equipment management.

Selecting equipment requires attention to details. Comparison among brands and models is important because equipment is expensive, it will be expected to last a long time, and it will get hard use in schools. When one purchases a new stove or iron for home use, usually one or two people at most will be using it. The fact that school equipment will have many users makes the decision particularly weighty. Ease of use, reliability, durability, safety, and performance are all important factors. By creating a checklist for these five criteria and examining various makes and models side by side, one can make sound decisions. A final factor to consider carefully in equipment purchase is the reputation of the vendor. When negotiating for volume discounts, when equipment problems arise, when warranty work must be done, when it would be helpful to have a demonstration of a new piece of equipment, the vendor is the first contact. In most districts, cost is the primary consideration, and bids often go to the lowest bidder, but vendor service must still be considered somehow. It is possible to request that specific desired services be included in vendor bids. For volume purchases, it may be appropriate to include in the proposal a price and turnaround time for repair or parts. Demonstrations or in-service training sessions could also be written into the proposal. The inclusion of some of these services may eliminate a few low-cost bidders, but the result may lead to better service in the long run.

Leasing is an alternative method of providing up-to-date technology in schools. Lease agreements can provide for more frequent refreshing of the equipment in a school. An important consideration here is that hardware expenses must be budgeted annually. When a district purchases equipment, there is the option to postpone purchase. Leases will require routine renewal or renegotiation, forcing districts to budget regularly for equipment acquisition (Kinnaman 1998). Donated equipment can often be more of a liability than a real benefit. The selection policy should include a disclaimer, granting the school the right to use it or dispose of donated equipment, and stating the maximum acceptable age for donated equipment. In considering whether to accept donated equipment, consider these factors:

- Opportunity costs: Will accepting the donations preclude the purchase of more current technologies?
- Software licensing: Does licensing require that any accompanying software be transferred to the school?
- Hardware: Does it work? What maintenance challenges does it present (e.g., cost, availability of parts)?
- Training: Do staff members know how to use this equipment?
- Networking: Is the hardware compatible with your network?
- Location: Where in your school will this equipment meet a need? (Reilly 2003)

Equipment maintenance and repair are essential to good service. Districts can either contract with an outside agency or employ an in-district repair technician. Periodic maintenance primarily involves cleaning equipment. Lenses need to be cleaned, fans need to have dust removed, overhead projectors need to be opened up and blown out to remove dust, heads on video equipment need to be cleaned. In most cases, equipment manuals explain how to clean and maintain the equipment. Clean equipment lasts longer and performs better.

An equipment inventory is necessary for insurance coverage. Some library media centers create catalog records for their equipment and even bar code the equipment for circulation. Another approach is to set up an equipment database. For each item, the minimum fields of information are item name, make, model, date of purchase, repair history, bulb/battery type, and cost. Generating reports from the inventory will provide information for making solid proposals for replacement funds and sound decisions regarding equipment replacement.

Replacement

A plan for equipment replacement helps to maintain a functioning equipment collection (Donham van Deusen 1995). A replacement cycle is simply a schedule identifying which machines to consider for replacement each year. A five-year cycle is often workable, so all types of equipment are distributed across the five years. The replacement cycle cannot be perceived as taking the place of decision making. However, by having a cycle, the library media specialist can assure that the status of each type of equipment is reviewed on a routine basis. This arrangement precludes, for example, overlooking the LCD projectors for years and then realizing that all of them are eight years old and unreliable. Another advantage of a replacement cycle is that purchasing equipment can be batched for more competitive prices. Furthermore, machines of like type will also be alike in make and model. This is an advantage in learning to use equipment; in maintenance, troubleshooting, and repair; and in parts inventory, especially bulbs and batteries. Each year, the library media specialist looks at what items are due in the replacement cycle and reviews the performance and condition of machines scheduled for that year. Staff input may indicate how much these machines are used, how well they meet the demands, and what features staff members would like replacements to have. Competitive bids can then be prepared for purchase.

Any replacement plan must have some flexibility so that funds are not spent on equipment simply because it is the year to buy it. Less use and good care can extend life expectancy. Criteria for replacement will be:

- machines scheduled to be reviewed in that year;
- machines at or beyond their life expectancy according to standard expectations; or
- machines that users report as unreliable.

Once machines are identified, professional judgment guides the process. Evaluating equipment being considered for replacement is relatively intuitive. The condition and durability of the equipment will vary with frequency of use and with frequent movement of equipment. These factors all help determine which machines will be replaced each year.

Computers and related devices create a special set of problems for replacement; they are likely to need upgrading after three years. This assumes that the equipment was purchased with some "growth room" at the beginning. After three years, typically, upgraded software requires more RAM, or the software offers capabilities (such as speech or video) that require added equipment features, or the speed of the processor is no longer acceptable. The three-year point calls for a decision: should we upgrade the equipment, or should we downgrade its use? In other words, should we invest money in improving this machine, or should we reallocate it to a less-demanding activity and replace it for the function under question with a more powerful machine? What factors enter into this decision? First, what kind of upgrading is needed? If the machine simply needs more RAM, that tends to be an inexpensive upgrade. By increasing RAM, one might expect to get one or two more years out of the machine at that task—if RAM is the only needed upgrade. If disk space is called for, it is likely that an external storage device could be added for perhaps three more years of service. If increased processor speed or other features are needed, it may be time to reassign the machine. Consultation with those who use the machine most will indicate how well the machine functions for its intended purpose.

Approximately 10 percent of a machine's cost can be estimated for RAM upgrades, and 25 percent of the machine's cost can be estimated for disk space or processor upgrades. Assuming that all machines will be upgraded after their third year of service, the upgrade budget could be estimated at 15 percent of the initial purchase cost. For planning purposes, a computer's initial cost should be added to the replacement budget for six years post-purchase. In this way, a budget can be built for computer replacement.

Another replacement strategy is "tiering," or identifying the installations that require high-end computers and placing new machines there perhaps every two years and then passing those machines down to installations where power and speed can be lower yet still serviceable. While there is often a complaint of receiving hand-me-down equipment, this practice does maximize the use of available equipment.

Computer peripherals (such as printers, modems, scanners) generally have a functional longevity of approximately five years. That is not to say that new and desirable models don't become available more frequently, but the functions for which the devices were purchased can typically be met for about five years. A replacement budget for peripheral equipment can be estimated by adding the purchase price to the replacement budget for five years hence.

Remember, the replacement cycle is a guide, not a rule. The library media specialist must make decisions about whether equipment really needs to be upgraded or replaced; the cycle serves only to encourage equipment review in a proactive manner.

ACTION STRATEGIES

Information Access

- Route publications with materials reviews to teachers and encourage them to initial those items that they would like to see in the collection. This allows them to consider quality from the beginning; for many teachers, catalogs have been their primary source of information about new materials.
- At the end of units, particularly those demanding student research or resources for the teacher, ask teachers how well the collection met their needs.
- Reserve a special amount from the budget for student-initiated purchases. One library media specialist brought together a committee of students to review the sports section of the collection one year and to help her spend funds on titles of interest to students. She met with the committee, gave them reviews to read as well as some books to preview, and worked with them to arrive at a list of titles for purchase.
- Involve staff members in decisions about replacement of equipment (for example, gather feedback on how the equipment is used and what features it should have).
- For both purchasing and weeding decisions, take into account information accessible via the World Wide Web. Consider whether a specific materials request can be adequately served online or whether it demands local materials.
- Offer parent information programs on the materials selection process to help parents understand the complexities of this process and to help them respect the need for diversity in point of view and level of difficulty within a collection.

Program Management

- Identify times for cleaning equipment—at least annually.
- Provide information (such as collection mapping data) about the condition of the collection to teachers and the principal so that they can make informed decisions about allocating the school's resources.
- Use the *Technology Support Index* (http://tsi.iste.org/techsupport/) to assess the status of equipment acquisition and management in

the school and/or district (International Society for Technology in Education 2001).

SCENARIO FOR DISCUSSION

A sixth-grade student in a middle school that serves grades six, seven, and eight was very ill as a toddler and may have had long-term memory loss. She has a significant learning disability, and reads comfortably at a primer or preprimer level. Her favorite book is *Green Eggs and Ham* because she can read it, and she was very excited because she could also read *Biscuit* books. It is common for her to check out four or five hard books at a time, including *Harry Potter*—most likely because of her peer and self-esteem issues. She returns them the next day. How can the library media specialist help her?

REFERENCES

Bartlett, L. D. et al. (1980). *Selection of Instructional Materials. A Model Policy and Rules*. ERIC Document Reproduction Service. ED192769.

Beers, K. (1998). "Listen While You Read." *School Library Journal 44* (4): 30-35.

Donham van Deusen, J. (1995). "Managing Equipment: A Proposed Model for Replacement." *Bottom Line 8:* 10–14.

Goldsmith, F. (2002). "Earphone English." *School Library Journal 48* (5): 50-54.

Graf, N. (1996). "Collection Development in the Information Age." *Technology Connection 3* (7): 8–10.

Hopkins, D. M. (1991). "Challenges to Materials in Secondary School Library Media Centers: Results of a National Study." *Journal of Youth Services in Libraries 4* (2): 131–140.

Hopkins, D. M. (1993). "Put It in Writing: What You Should Know About Challenges to School Library Materials." *School Library Journal 39* (1): 26–30.

International Society for Technology in Education (2001). *Technology Support Index*. Retrieved March 28, 2008, from http://tsi.iste.org/techsupport/.

Jacobs, H. H. (2000). "Upgrading the K-12 Journey Through Curriculum Mapping: A Technology Tool for Classroom Teachers, Media Specialists, and Administrators." *Knowledge Quest 29* (2): 25–29.

Kan, K. (2003). "Getting Graphic at the School Library." *Library Media Connection 21* (7): 14–19.

Kinnaman, D. (1998). "Leasing Has Never Looked Better." *Curriculum Administrator 33* (5): 64.

Lowe, K. (2001). "Resource Alignment: Providing Curriculum Support in the School Library Media Center." *Knowledge Quest 30* (2): 27–32.

Minarcini v. Strongsville City School District, 541 F2d 577 (6th Cir. 1976).

National Center for Educational Statistics (2002). *Digest of Educational Statistics, 2002*. Retrieved October 12, 2003, from http://nces.ed.gov/pubs2003/digest02.

Peregoy, S. F. and O. F. Boyle (2000). "English Learners Reading English: What We Know, What We Need to Know." *Theory into Practice 39* (4): 237–247.

Reilly, R. (2003). "Electronic Junk Dealer or Technology Wizard: Managing Donations." *MultiMedia Schools 10* (6): 61–62.

Shade, D. (1996). "Software Evaluation." *Young Children 51* (6): 17–21.

Shontz, M. and L. Farmer (2007). "The SLJ Spending Survey." *School Library Journal* Retrieved March 28, 2008, from www.schoollibraryjournal.com/article/CA6403260.html.

St. Lifer, E. (2002). "Enhancing Your Buying Power." *School Library Journal 48* (4): 11–14.

St. Lifer, E. (2005). "The 2005 Book Prices." *School Library Journal 51* (3): 11.

Symons, A. (1997). "Sizing Up Sites: How to Judge What You Find on the Web." *School Library Journal 43* (4): 22–25.

Van Orden, P. J. and K. Bishop (2001). *The Collection Program in Schools: Concepts, Practices, and Information Sources*. Westport, CT: Libraries Unlimited.

Chapter 9

Literacy

This chapter:

- explores three purposes of reading
- discusses the role of the library media program in a whole-language approach to reading and language arts
- reviews research that relates to nurturing readers
- discusses reading incentive programs and their impact on aliteracy
- identifies action strategies for encouraging and supporting reading

Literacy is the ability to gain information or vicarious experience from reading. When a student cannot only decode the words in a body of text but can also exhibit understanding by restating, summarizing, or questioning, then that student can begin to be considered literate. If we think of developing literacy as a continuum, then illiteracy represents a point on that continuum where the reader is not yet making meaning out of what is read. Where one sets the point on this continuum that divides the illiterate from the literate is debatable, but at some point the capability to make meaning from text becomes viable. Although the primary responsibility for addressing illiteracy lies with the classroom teacher, the library media specialist can play an important role in supporting literacy development.

Another dimension of the literacy issue is aliteracy—when one can read, but chooses not to. The mass media raise concerns regularly that

Americans are reading less. However, there are data to suggest that reading books is an increasingly common practice for the U.S. public. The Association of American Publishers (2003) reported that U.S. book sales totaled $25.4 billion in 2002, up 5.5 percent over the previous year. Furthermore, National Center for Educational Statistics (1997) data show that 53 percent of households with children reported going to the public library in the most recent month to borrow or return books.

These facts suggest that, at least for many, reading is alive and well. This is clearly good news, but it does not mean that all Americans are readers; moreover, it does not mean that all children and youth are readers, and it does not mean that schools have no need to nurture readers. In fact, a large-scale national study of more than 18,000 U.S. elementary school children found that both recreational and academic reading attitudes on average gradually but steadily declined throughout the elementary school years, beginning at a relatively positive point and ending in relative indifference (McKenna, Kear, and Ellsworth 1995).

Developing, extending, and sustaining enthusiasm for reading among children and youth presents a challenge. Both illiteracy and aliteracy are legitimate concerns for the library media program.

THE PURPOSES OF READING

Often the word "reading" brings to mind reading stories or fiction. However, reading serves three major purposes, and all three demand consideration in school library media programs—reading for literary experience, reading for information, and reading to perform a task.

Reading for literary experience occurs in free voluntary reading and the reading that students do in reading and literature classes—reading novels, short stories, poems, plays, and essays. The reader explores the human condition and the interaction among events, characters' emotions, and possibilities. Students gain insight into how a given author creates character and uses language. They experience vicariously.

Reading for information includes reading articles in magazines or newspapers, textbooks, entries in encyclopedias and other sources (both print and electronic), and nonfiction books. It requires that the reader be aware of the features found in informative texts, such as charts, footnotes, diagrams, and tables. Students usually acquire information to meet a specific information need and use such reading strategies as scanning and skimming, note taking, and paraphrasing to extract the needed information.

Reading to perform a task involves reading practical documents, such as schedules, directions, forms, recipes, warranties, and memos. Students must recognize the purpose and structure of practical documents to gain necessary information from them. The pragmatic approach of looking for information to accomplish a task differs substantively from savoring the style or intent of a text or literary work. The reader intends to apply the information to a task at hand.

Rosenblatt's (1978) work provides insight into how one engages in reading, depending on purpose. She describes a continuum of purposes one establishes as a reader. The continuum spans from *efferent* to *aesthetic.* The efferent reader approaches the text to take away information; the purpose is pragmatic, and the artistry of the writing is secondary to its content. From the efferent stance, the focus is on what will remain as residue after the reading experience. In contrast, the aesthetic reader attends to the reading experience itself. The text stimulates sensing, feeling, imagining, and thinking, and these behaviors make the aesthetic experience. Rosenblatt further emphasizes reader control—stance relies on what the reader does, not on what the text is. Many texts can be experienced from different points on the continuum. Historical fiction becomes an interesting case in point. It is common for teachers in social studies to ask children to read historical fiction as they study a historical period. For children reading historical fiction, it is important that the teacher know where along the efferent/aesthetic continuum their reading falls. In reading *Number the Stars,* to what extent is the purpose to learn information about the Danish resistance and to what extent is it to feel the experience of a young Jewish girl living through the horrors of those times? In reading *A Family Apart,* to what extent is the purpose to learn about the Children's Aid Society of the late 19th century and the movement of children to the West, and to what extent is it to feel the experience of siblings being separated from one another and from their birth families? An awareness of the reading purpose from the beginning can influence the reading experience. As trade books find their way into the curriculum, how teachers ask students to respond to their reading will influence the reading purpose, experience, and impact. Awareness of the reading stance continuum can increase the sensitivity in designing reading response activities. As students read fiction, they gain confidence in their knowledge because the narrative form complements students' understanding of the time and people portrayed in a historical novel. Asking students to glean information from historical fiction may not be an appropriate activity when the power of the novel is to generate a "feel" for the time—a substantively different experience from reading a textbook. The question to consider, then, is where along that continuum should the reader be to accomplish the current purpose?

Reading's power lies in its potential to develop in the reader new perspectives on times, people, and places, and to engender empathy for others' experiences and feelings. As students read fiction, they gain confidence in their knowledge because the narrative form complements and humanizes the factual.

THE LIBRARY MEDIA PROGRAM AND READING INSTRUCTION

Many schools use a basal reading series as the foundation for the reading instruction program. As statewide high-stakes testing has increased in response to national mandates under the No Child Left Behind legislation, basal reading series have experienced an increase in popularity. Still, many school districts use trade books as the foundation of their reading curriculum. Whether trade books comprise the core of the reading program or supplement the basal, they are important components of a reading program.

Reading instruction philosophy ranges from a phonemic approach (centered on teaching students an analytical method of reading grounded in phonics) to a more holistic approach to reading. Most schools engage in a moderate approach that encompasses both phonemic knowledge as well as emphasizing the meaning-making characteristic of "whole-language" approaches. Whole-language instruction is a philosophy more than it is a methodology. Its underlying construct is that learners construct meaning by interacting with text (Pearson, Roehler, Dole, and Duffy 1992) and relating the text to prior knowledge. Clarke (1987) describes the key to a successful whole-language program as the relationships one finds "between children and their reading/writing (one of enjoyment and ownership), between adults and the children (the former are "encouragers" as well as teachers, the latter "initiators") and among children (cooperative rather than competitive)" (p. 386). A goal of the whole-language philosophy is to develop an engaged reader who uses prior knowledge as a foundation for gaining information from new material, uses a variety of skills in a strategic way to gain information, is internally motivated to read for information and for pleasure, and interacts socially to make strides in literacy development.

While many schools describe themselves as whole-language schools, not all literature-based reading programs are alike. In her Arbuthnot Lecture in 1992 Charlotte Huck characterized three types of literature-based reading programs:

- *Literary reader programs*: The text contains selections from authentic literature. Huck responds to these, "I don't believe children become lifetime readers by reading selections of stories. Who ever developed a real love of reading by reading *The Reader's Digest*?" (p. 376). She further complains that these programs come with teacher's guides and workbooks filled with fragmented exercises, or as she describes it, "mindless busywork."
- *Trade books as basal reader program*: The teacher provides copies of a single title to all students and uses commercial or homemade guides to accompany the reading, providing black-line masters in place of workbooks to provide "activities" to accompany the reading. Huck comments, "these are used by teachers who do not trust the story to make a reader of the child" (p. 377).
- *Comprehensive literature program*: The teacher uses real books but gives children a choice of what to read. In these programs, as Huck describes them, children hear stories and books read aloud to them; they also read books in depth and discuss them, considering both the artistry and the meaning of the text.

The library media program plays a significant role in the teaching of reading, regardless of the approach taken in the classroom. All children must read in order to become better, more fluent readers. An important contribution for the library media program is providing access to a wide variety of excellent literature. Both quality and quantity are critical factors—and so is access. The books must be available to students at the point of need. Such access occurs when children can move in and out of the library media center as they need to; it also occurs when teachers can take armloads of books from the library media center to their classrooms for in-room collections and can return to exchange those for fresh titles periodically. Library media specialists have the reference tools, skills, background knowledge, and experience to identify quality in children's materials. Selecting materials that have substance, style, and rich language is crucial. Not just any old books will do to meet the goals of a reading program.

A caution may be in order here. With renewed commitment to standardized testing has come an interest in assessing the reading levels of library books and limiting students to reading "at level." Betty Carter (2000) urges caution in basing children's reading selection on readability formulas. She suggests that the Lexile score is not always an accurate indicator of readability; illustrative material may allow less facile readers to understand a text, and, conversely, unconventional text structures may make reading more difficult than the score indicates. Similarly, while students may have one reading ability score, the differences between reading fiction and reading nonfiction may not have been considered. She also expresses her worry that students will not automatically progress to increasingly difficult texts if they are classified at a specific Lexile level.

Beyond providing access to rich resources, the library media specialist offers consultation in developing thematic units. As a literature expert, the library media specialist can help teachers attain appropriate levels of sophistication in the development of their thematic units. For example, when the theme is families, the library media specialist can suggest some appropriate ways to focus such a topic into a true thematic unit: "Families is a rather broad topic, so how about focusing on sibling relationships, to create a thematic statement like 'Siblings can provide important support for one another in times of stress.'" From that point, the library media specialist can generate lists of possible titles to portray that thematic statement in both humorous and serious tones, and can generate possible open-ended questions to stimulate conversation about the treatment of the theme—questions beginning with "Why do you suppose . . . ?" "What if . . . ?" "What would you have done when . . . ?"

In the development of such thematic approaches, the library media specialist and teacher might consider several aspects of literary response. Miall and Kuiken (1995) identify six dimensions of reader response that might help to frame questions for student response to literature. They are summarized briefly as follows:

- *Insight*: relating the experiences and feelings portrayed in the text to one's own world experiences
- *Empathy*: developing sensitivity to the reasons for the behavior or beliefs of others

- *Imagery vividness*: sensing the places, people, and emotions portrayed in the text
- *Escape*: using literature to distract from the real world
- *Concern with the author*: relating the literature to the life and times of the author
- *Story-driven reading*: engaging in the story primarily to see what happens next.

Different readers approach text with different expectations. By keeping in mind these aspects of response, teachers and library media specialists can encourage each reader to respond to literature from a personally meaningful perspective.

Choosing books to read for oneself is a hallmark of comprehensive reading programs. Presenting a booktalk when students are selecting what they will read can generate enthusiasm among students about their reading. Besides formal booktalks, individual reading guidance can keep readers reading. Ideally, students read independently throughout the year. Teachers encourage children to vary the degree of difficulty of what they are reading. The level depends on the teacher's intent—to increase reading fluency or to increase reading capacity. Individual schools develop their own categories for levels of difficulty. Often, students learn to identify books at three levels of difficulty. An example of one local set of labels for difficulty levels is the following:

- *Vacation books*: easy books in which the reader knows all the words and easily understands the meaning; books read for fun and to develop reading fluency
- *Just-right books*: books in which the reader knows enough words to be able to figure out meanings; books read to practice reading strategies
- *Dream books*: interesting but challenging books that are difficult enough to affect comprehension; books best read with the assistance of another person or a tape recording; books browsed for captions and illustrations

Library media specialists can use such labels as they advise children in reading selection. Consistency between the classroom and the library media center will help children assess their reading choices.

Library media specialists need to provide professional resources to assist teachers, whether those resources are bibliographic tools, poetry anthologies, collections of stories and songs, or professional books to guide teachers in designing reading instruction. Effective reading programs thrive when the library media program supports them with resources and professional collaboration.

READING NONFICTION

Fiction often dominates the reading classroom landscape. There may be several reasons for this bias in favor of the narrative (for example, teacher preference, the preponderance of fiction in preservice courses in literature for youth, or the prevalence of narrative in the book-reviewing media). This bias in favor of fiction is also common in school library media collections and in the booktalks and promotions that occur there. However, the literacy demands of adults are primarily aimed at obtaining information from nonfiction texts (Venezky 2000).

Moss and Hendershot (2002) conducted a two-year ethnographic study observing sixth-graders' motivation for selecting nonfiction books. They found that students chose their nonfiction based on "the need to know"—that is, they read to satisfy a personal curiosity about a topic. This internal motivation to get information provides the backdrop for developing critical reading skills in students—skills that will serve them well as lifelong learners. If reading is indeed a meaning-making process, then nonfiction provides an excellent opportunity to employ critical thinking and constructivism by engaging students in such thoughtful tasks as the following:

- Judging the accuracy of the content of books (ask students to verify factual information by searching for another authoritative source to confirm or refute)
- Investigating the author's credentials (have students examine publishers' Web pages for leads toward such information)
- Using concept mapping (work with students to construct graphic organizers of the information they discover in a text to see the relationships among ideas)

These critical reading skills are the foundation for developing the information literacy competencies necessary in a world that often offers too much information or unjuried information. While fiction reading offers excellent opportunities for developing such skills as drawing inferences, analyzing motivation, and predicting outcome, reading non-fiction can develop complementary skills of questioning the accuracy or authority of the source, assessing the importance of currency of information, comparing and reconciling differences among sources of information, and observing potential bias. Together, fiction and nonfiction offer reading experiences that will make literacy instruction comprehensive. The library media specialist can play an important role in selecting quality nonfiction, marketing nonfiction to students, discussing nonfiction with students, engaging them in critical assessment of what they read, and advocating for nonfiction in the reading curriculum.

NURTURING READERS

Children arrive at school eager to join the community of readers. The anticipation of learning to read is part of the joy children feel about going to school. How can we sustain that desire to be a reader? There are a number of ways in which enthusiasm for reading can be nurtured and a number of ways that it can be squelched. Berglund (Berglund et al. 1991) surveyed college students to determine what teacher behaviors had supported their interest for reading and what behaviors had detracted from interest in reading. The list of detractors is particularly worthy of note:

- "Round robin" reading
- Lack of choice
- Irrelevant reading assignments
- Failure to accommodate for diverse reading abilities
- Book reports

Nurturing readers is a responsibility shared by teachers, parents, children and youth, the greater community, and library media specialists. Often, though, the library media specialist or the public librarian must initiate and guide the collaborative effort. Motivation to read is multidimensional. Wigfield and Guthrie (1997) propose a framework for reading motivation with three categories of motivational dimensions:

- *Competence*: Do I believe I can be a reader? Am I willing to take on a challenge?
- *Purposes and goals of reading*: Do I read for curiosity or recognition or enjoyment?

ENHANCEMENT IN ACTION:
CREATING A COMMUNITY OF READERS

The idea of a community of readers is characterized in the Community Reading Project, a winner of the John Cotton Dana Award for Public Relations in 1995. This project, supported largely by a local bank in Iowa City, Iowa, has for many years worked to turn an entire small city into a "community of readers" to help young people see that being a member of the community requires being a reader (Donham van Deusen and Langhorne 1997). There are no prizes and no incentives beyond the opportunity to explore and enjoy reading. The development of that community spirit occurs in part because the event has wide sponsorship; participants, besides the bank, include the area public libraries, local bookstores, other local businesses, the senior center, the university, and the community schools. Activities scheduled during a month in the fall include:

- *Booktalk lunches*: Each week during the month, the public library hosts a booktalk luncheon for a special target audience (such as parents of young children, parents of adolescents, adults, business people). Local librarians and booksellers as well as general community members are among those presenting the book talks.
- *Visiting author*: The bank supports a children's book author in residence for one week each year. In anticipation of the visit, teachers and library media specialists develop a guide to the author's work and use the guide to prepare children for the visit by having the children read works of the author, or by reading works of the author to them. Guest authors have included Jerry Spinelli, Chris Crutcher, Ashley Bryan, Pat Cummings, Brian Jacques, Phyllis Reynolds Naylor, and Penny Colman.
- *Read-In Day*: One day is identified each year as Read-In Day, when schools devote a 15-minute period to reading. Organizations such as the local senior center host activities for Read-In Day. Various businesses have identified people to be readers in their lobbies or other areas for the event. Restaurants and delis encourage customers to

read as they dine. Families choose an hour or so in the evening on a given date to turn off the TV and read together.

- *Newspaper insert*: Another way to extend the invitation to join the local community of readers is a special insert in the newspaper. The Iowa City *Press Citizen* prepares a special newspaper insert for Community Reading Month. The insert includes information on the visiting authors, articles about reading to children, book lists, and other materials to promote reading. The insert is paid for by ads sold to businesses in the community. The ads often feature a child or someone associated with the business describing a favorite book or reading experience.

Events are advertised widely in newspapers, through service clubs and the chamber of commerce, on radio stations, and in displays in businesses. Each year has its own special events as well, but the intent is to arrive at a number of activities that focus attention on reading, to reach that threshold where a majority of the community feels a part of the reading event, so that it is indeed a community of readers and belonging is its own reward.

- *Social aspects*: Do I want to share my reading experiences with others?

The experiences that develop reading motivation, then, influence all three of these categories. Development of confidence as a reader, helping create intrinsic purpose for reading, and providing the opportunities for social engagement about reading need to be among the conscious efforts of both school and home.

A simple fact is that enthusiasm is contagious. The adults with whom young people interact most at school are their teachers. Enthusiasm for reading among teachers provides an important model for students. Teachers can exhibit that enthusiasm by reading aloud to students, by offering booktalks—both formally and informally—or by making frequent references to books. Library media specialists, in turn, can engender enthusiasm among teachers in both formal and informal ways. A few good book talks at the beginning of faculty, departmental, or team meetings can be a step toward creating a community of readers among teachers. Sharing reviews or recently acquired books with specific teachers, based on their personal or professional interests, often generates interest in reading among faculty members, and offering to do booktalks in classes is a way to reach out to teachers as well as students. In the end, creating among the teaching staff a community of readers can be a major contributor to creating a community of readers among students.

Too often, young people perceive reading as a solitary rather than a social activity. Creating the spirit of a reading community transforms the perception of reading from a solitary activity in which only the loner retreats into a social activity that engages participants in conversation. The Iowa City project has been ongoing for more than 15 years. It has gained momentum and become a "rite of autumn" for the community. Students anticipate the author's residency; early in the fall, community members begin asking at the bank for information about the booktalks. Attendance at the booktalks increases each year. Library circulation and bookstore sales of books featured in booktalks and author visits persist beyond the duration of the project.

Book Discussion

Several studies—for example, Johnson and Gaskins (1992) and Manning and Manning (1984)—cite meaningful book discussion as an important contributor to positive attitudes toward reading. Student discussion is important to learning. Research shows that students' verbal exchanges about content improve their learning and increase their level of thinking (Marzano 1991). Peer interaction is particularly powerful; small-group and paired discussion about books that readers have chosen offer opportunities for meaningful interaction.

Encouraging students' personal response to literature improves their ability to construct meaning. With experience in reader response, over time, students develop increasingly complex responses to literature that help them become better at constructing meaning (Eeds and Wells 1989). When children's responses to literature are valued, they develop a sense of ownership, pride, and respect for learning. Out of this shared value of learning comes a sense of community. Reader-response strategies call for a much more open-ended approach to discussion of what has been read than the approach often found in novel unit guides or reading basal texts. The reader-response approach intends for readers' experience with text to be at the center of the discussion.

Langer (1994) laments that "literature is usually taught and tested in a non-literary manner, as if there is one right answer arrived at through point-of-reference reading or writing." She goes on to describe strategies for opening up the classroom conversation about literature:

> Overall, teachers conceived of the "lesson" (extending across one or many days) as including three major sections: inviting initial understandings, developing interpretations and taking a critical stance. These replaced traditional lesson segments such as vocabulary review or plot summary and provided overall structural options to include or overlook in any given lesson. (p. 208)

Inviting initial understandings simply involves asking students to describe what is presently on their minds about the piece. *Developing interpretations* calls for teachers to extend students' perspectives by posing questions to extend their thinking. Finally, *taking a critical stance* is the analysis of students' own understanding of the text and their generalizing to life. Langer endorses a sophisticated conversation about reading where the focus is on meaning. Such conversations about literature—and life— increase the sophistication with which students approach literature, engage them in thought, and create memorable experiences from their reading. For teachers to interact with students about literature, they must have significant books. Moreover, opportunities for teachers to discuss those books with another reading enthusiast—perhaps a school library media specialist—can be valuable as teachers consider what directions their conversations with students may take.

Library media specialists can support reader-response programs by discussing literary pieces with teachers and by interacting with students to emphasize the meaning and significance of what is read. In collaboration with teachers to develop thematic units for reader-response activities, the library media specialist can contribute to students' analysis beyond literal comprehension. Teachers new to thematic approaches to literature often confuse topical and thematic approaches (Donham van Deusen amd Brandt 1997). While birthdays might constitute a topic, a theme might be "Celebrations bring families or communities together and provide memories that its members can have forever." The point of a thematic approach is to elicit meaning and purpose from the reading.

FIGURE 9.1
Thematic Units

Topic	Theme	Titles
Mentors	While families have great influence on us, often a pivotal person outside our family can change our lives.	*Eleanor* by Barbara Cooney *Ben's Trumpet* by Rachel Isadora *Jip* by Katherine Paterson *The Bobbin Girl* by Emily Arnold McCully
Family	Family life includes enjoying special traditions.	*Just in Time for Christmas* by Louise Borden *Maria Molina and the Days of the Dead* by Kathleen Krull *Pablo's Tree* by Pat Mora
Generations	Family stories help to bridge generations.	*When Jo Louis Won the Title* by Belinda Rochelle *Aunt Flossie's Hats (and Crab Cakes Later)* by Elizabeth Fitzgerald Howard *Pink and Say* by Patricia Polacco *Grandaddy's Place* by Helen Griffit

Figure 9.1 shows examples of themes that develop around topics. By helping students develop a thematic statement and identify titles that provide examples of a theme applied to various settings, characters, or situations, the library media specialist is using his or her expertise in literature to add substance to classroom instruction. Similarly, library media specialists can interact with students and engage them in discussions that emphasize the meaning and significance of their reading.

Another way of supporting reader-response is to be a critical consumer of commercial literature guides. The publishing market offers a plethora of materials to assist teachers in the use of trade books. Unfortunately, too many of them reduce the reading experience to read-recall rather than to experience, enjoy, interact, and think. Questions to ask about materials designed to support teaching literature include:

- Do student questions call for analysis, synthesis, and evaluation or only literacy comprehension?
- Are activities relevant to the central theme or meaning of the work or merely cute, clever, or artistic?

- Are initiating activities helpful in focusing on the central theme or are they tangential?
- Do activities encourage the reader to respond to the text, or do they merely provide active tasks like vocabulary lists, games, crossword puzzles, or matching problems?
- Are the questions focused on higher-order thinking; for example, What do you think about . . . ? Why do you think that? How do you know that?
- Is the emphasis on the holistic view of the work rather than on isolated details?

Time to Read

Providing time to read is one more way to nurture readers. Various studies—including those of Neuman (1986), Greaney and Hegarty (1987), and Greaney (1980)—have pointed to the minimal amount of time children spend reading. Yet, in Krashen's (1993) review of research, he concludes the obvious—the more students read, the better readers they are. Also, in a carefully controlled study of 195 students in grades 5 and 6, Taylor, Frye, and Maruyama (1990) found that the amount of time spent reading during the school day contributed significantly to reading achievement. A study of middle school students found the following:

> Voluntary reading of at least one chapter in a book other than a textbook declined from 61% in sixth grade to 29% in eighth grade. In sixth grade, 32% of students reported reading for their own enjoyment almost every day; however, by eighth grade, only 20% reported doing so. (Ley 1994, p. 31)

Although there should be little argument against advocacy for time during the school day for reading—time for students to just read—the pressures of increased testing can challenge the arguments in favor of sustained silent reading (SSR) as a legitimate part of the reading program. References to the research on the effects of free reading on reading achievement must be highlighted whenever finding the time for it is challenged. SSR can be even more powerful in the development of the reading community when it extends to the entire school. SSR programs seem to work more easily at elementary schools than at secondary schools. Yet, it is often at the middle school level that reading diminishes among students. Identifying some time during the middle school day for sustained reading seems one simple solution to the hope that adolescents will continue to be readers. The schedule of the school day may require that this be a special added period, perhaps shorter than the standard class sessions, where all students and all teachers read. If reading is valued, there is a way to incorporate it into every student's daily school experience.

Choice

Choice of what to read is an important consideration for nurturing readers. Johnson and Gaskins (1992) found that the element of choice was very important to the fourth graders they studied. Even when the teacher limits the choices to a menu of titles, still the opportunity to control what one will spend time reading has a positive effect. Providing choice demands that teachers have available alternatives that will meet their goals; those alternatives may need to relate to the same theme or come from the same genre, but they must also offer some variety in tone, protagonist, and level of difficulty. The library media specialist can be instrumental in helping the teacher arrive at such alternatives.

Parental Influence

Neuman (1986) investigated the relationship between the home environment and fifth-grade students' leisure reading and identified parental encouragement as a strong correlate with children's leisure reading. She defined parental encouragement as making reading materials available in the home; providing a place for reading; encouraging the child to read books, magazines, and newspapers; and reading aloud to the children. The parents' own reading behavior was also an encouragement factor. She emphasized the importance of what parents *do* to encourage reading:

> Encouraging parents were inclined to help children relate their reading of newspapers, magazines and books to everyday events, thus making reading an integral part of daily activities. Dinner conversations offered a time to share school and social activities with other members of the family. (p. 339)

The library media specialist can help parents in this role. What a local school's parents need will vary with the nature of the population.

It may be that parents need to become aware of their own importance in their child's potential as a reader. Perhaps they need to learn about good books, or perhaps they need help in reading aloud to their children, such as strategies for reading aloud and guides to selecting books that are especially suited to reading aloud. Perhaps they need ideas for how to support reading at home. Perhaps they need help in becoming readers themselves. Principals are often seeking topics for parent nights; "helping your child be a reader" may be a very attractive topic. Sending home frequent suggestions of good books for "family reads" or reading suggestions for children can help parents. Designing reading events at school that involve parents can be another way of making them aware of their importance: a read-along-with-parents project might be an example of this. A small collection of books to help parents support their children's reading (housed as a special collection in the library media center and available for parent checkout) may be attractive in some settings. Neuman (1995) describes a community-supported parent tutoring program in Philadelphia where parents volunteered to work as a tutor/mentor with one or two children at a time. The heart of this program is the training that these parent volunteers receive—it undoubtedly also influences the way they will encourage their own children's reading at home. The library media specialist can find allies among parents to help nurture readers. Clearly, outreach to children from less supportive families is another important concern. Library media specialists may need to take a more active interest in the reading activities of children whom they identify as having little reading support at home. This can take the form of regular formal or informal reading conferences with identified children.

Social Book Discussion Clubs

Book clubs and book discussion groups have enjoyed a resurgence in popularity among adults in recent years, prompted in part by television-based book clubs. Middle schools and high schools are experiencing considerable success with such groups also. Lunch-hour meetings, after-school gatherings, and summer discussion groups are all variations, but the essential element is young people, with the guidance of an adult, coming together in a social context to discuss books (Jaeger and Demetriadis 2002). Among the advantages of the book club is the removal of grade pressure so often associated with reading. Moreover, the book club creates a more lifelike setting for readers. Young people enjoy social engagement, and book discussion groups give them the opportunity to have "civilized conversations" about literature (Frank, Dixon, and Brandts 2001). Book clubs provide opportunities for young people to practice roles and relationships that differ from the classroom—there is no hand raising or turn taking. Instead, the conversation flows and participants learn to listen actively and to formulate their comments and interject them in socially conscious ways.

More relevant to the concerns about literacy, book discussion clubs engage students in discussion of books they choose to read, and allow them to shape their responses around the books in ways that matter to them. Book discussion clubs can create a literacy culture within the school that brings attention to reading and gives readers opportunities for a sense of belonging which is so important to young people. Chandler (1997) describes her experience with a summer book discussion club she organized for high school students. In many locales, summer vacation means more social isolation for students than adults might realize; a summer book discussion club offers a meaningful way to get together socially and to sustain reading. Often, it is possible to find service organizations or local businesses that will support book discussion groups to purchase paperback copies for the participants. Book ownership can be an enticing enhancement to the book discussion group experience. In some locales, youth librarians at public libraries are eager to partner with schools to develop after-school or summer book discussion groups.

Literature Circles

The social aspect of reading is acknowledged in the literature circle, a classroom construct common in middle and elementary schools. This structure brings students together to talk about a book with their peers. Unlike many typical "reading groups" in classrooms, literature circles feature student leadership. Literature circles typically have four to six members and roles rotate among the members. These roles include discussion leader, vocabulary enricher, illustrator, and character captain (Blum, Lipsett, and Yocum 2002). These roles can be defined within an individual classroom to suit the needs of the students involved—the reading selection may influence the roles appropriate for a given circle. The roles provide a sort of scaffolding for students so that they can prepare with confidence and come to the circle with something specific to share. Ideally, students choose the title they want to read and discuss, and the circles are formed accordingly. Often the teacher has preselected texts that focus on a theme or a genre. What is most important is that readers build conversational skills for talking about texts in personal and thoughtful ways (Brabham and Villaume 2000). The library media specialist can serve as an important advisor to teachers setting up literature circles by identifying titles that will provoke deep reflection, questioning, and discussion, and that represent the variety of reading competency found within a given classroom. It may, in fact, be appropriate for the library media specialist to present brief book talks on the available selections to help students determine what text will interest them most. In addition, of course, is the opportunity to return to the circle to answer the students who ask, "What might I like to read next?"

Reading Incentive Programs

Incentive programs that feature rewards or prizes for reading are very common. They range from a simple sticker for reading a book to elaborate accumulations of points that are applied toward grander prizes. The fundamental questions are, "Do these incentive programs work— for the long run?" and "Is there a better way to encourage reading?" Alfie Kohn (1993) argues against the use of extrinsic rewards to encourage reading—or any other desirable behaviors. One of his major arguments is that rewards work as long as the rewards last, but when the rewards end, so does the behavior. He suggests that offering an extrinsic reward for a behavior immediately devalues the desired behavior; in short, if reading is so wonderful, why are prizes necessary to get people to do it?

Kohn further makes the point that rewards may indeed work for the short term. Indeed, many reading incentive programs are judged successful by the number of books the participants read during the event—while rewards are available. Rewards do work! At least they are effective at producing temporary compliance. However, the more important question is whether these participants in reading incentive programs extend their behavior beyond the duration of the incentive, or do they regress to their old behaviors—will those who were readers continue to read, and will those who were not discontinue? Some believe that extrinsically motivated exposure to the enjoyment of reading may jump-start the internal desire to be a reader. However, Kohn cites a considerable body of research to say that "any contingent payment system tends to undermine intrinsic motivation" (p. 140). The focus on the reward effectively turns the activity into nothing more than the means to an end. He suggests, in fact, that offering such extrinsic rewards can easily result in students doing less than they might have done without the reward system (for example, choosing easier books or reading fewer pages)—doing just enough to get the reward. To nurture readers, is the purpose temporary compliance or is it a lifelong behavior?

The notion of offering rewards as a means of teaching young people to be readers is counter to what constructivists profess about the way people learn. A reward system places the control of behavior on the person or agency holding the prize until such time as the student is deemed worthy to receive it. The locus of control is external to the student. Consistent with a constructivist view of learning would be developing an intrinsic enjoyment of reading. Ley (1994) identifies several research-supported ways to develop in students an intrinsic value for reading: surround students with materials about topics of interest to them, provide a nonthreatening situation for reading, give them opportunities to share with peers their reactions to what they have read, and read aloud to students. Nowhere in the list is the idea of giving students extrinsic rewards for reading.

Often reading incentive plans that make use of extrinsic rewards are justified on the basis that they improve reading achievement. One study that investigated the effect of an extrinsic reward system on sixth graders' reading achievement scores found no statistically significant differences between students who were offered pizzas as rewards and students who were simply encouraged to read more without extrinsic rewards (Adler et al. 1989).

The term *token economy* describes a system for assigning value to specific tasks and "paying" students with tokens (prizes or privileges) for performing those tasks. One of the most extensive and expensive token economies intended to encourage reading is a system of computerized tests on trade books, with accumulated points to be applied toward purchase of a wide range of prizes. What are the messages that such programs send? We read books, not to discuss them, not to enjoy them, not to appreciate them, not to see ourselves in others' lives, but to pass a literal comprehension quiz, to earn points, and to "buy" trinkets. Documentation of enormous increases in library circulation support such programs (Chenowith 2001). However, one must continue to ask whether the long-term effect of such programs will be to instill a love of reading. Will students for whom reading the last page of a story means taking a quiz to collect points embrace reading as a pleasure unto itself? Perhaps not! Donna Pool Miller (1995) puts it succinctly:

Would you really enjoy reading or want to read many books if you had to boot up the computer and answer 20 questions before you were allowed to read another one? Further, how would you like it if someone else totally dictated what you could read? (p. 22)

Carter (1996) points out that often rewards act as incentives for performing less-than-desirable tasks. She suggests that computer-based reading incentive programs like the Accelerated Reader devalue reading. She suggests that by offering points for reading, these programs place reading among the ranks of lawn mowing and taking out the garbage. Carter has monitored children's reading selections and has found that children choose not to read books they would probably enjoy if they are not on the program's list. Carter also contends that reading to take a factual test places children immediately at the efferent end of Rosenblatt's continuum. Yet, she states that lifetime readers read aesthetically. One can infer that computer-based programs detract from aesthetic reading and perhaps from the likelihood of lifetime reading. In fact, in a study of 1,500 seventh graders in ten middle schools, Pavonetti, Brimmer, and Cipielewski (2002) found that although participating students had read more books with Accelerated Reader, once the program was over they read no more than before and in fact the researchers found a negative effect in some schools. Krashen (2002) examined existing research related to the Accelerated Reader program and found clear evidence in favor of providing access to books and increasing the amount of students' reading. However, he finds nothing in the research literature to support the benefit of testing on reading or on offering rewards.

There is documentation that booktalks have a positive impact on circulation. Bodart (1986) reports highly significant increases in book circulation after students heard booktalks in a high school. In her study, the effect of the booktalks persisted through the school year as the books featured continued to have high circulation; the booktalks occurred in October and circulation was monitored through May.

One type of reading program that merits consideration is summer reading. Malach and Rutter (2003) summarize a century of research on the "summer effect" by stating that student learning declines or remains the same and the magnitude of change varies with socioeconomic status. Sustaining students' reading during the summer can help them maintain their reading skills. The state of Illinois has been particularly strong in supporting summer programs through public libraries. A study of a public library summer reading program demonstrated that children who participated indeed improved their reading skills over the summer, when compared with children who did not participate (Carter 1988). Of course, there are other factors to be considered; those students who participated were likely to have more family support for learning and reading than those who did not, and the importance of family support for reading has been discussed earlier. Still, summer programs can help keep children active in reading. More challenging, yet, is to find ways to support reading among children whose families are less likely to frequent the public library. One step is summer hours in school libraries in neighborhoods where families do not visit the public library. By making the school library accessible to children and providing even a limited level of programming, these children may be less likely to pass the entire summer without books in their lives.

In the end, the library media specialist strives to engender enthusiasm for reading for the sake of reading—whether for aesthetic purposes, the pleasure of the moment, or the efferent purpose of reading for information. The question to ask is, "Will this activity create an *enduring* enthusiasm for the power of reading?"

ACTION STRATEGIES

Learning and Teaching

- Meet with groups of students for book discussions in cooperation with reading or social studies units taught in the classroom.
- Hold individual reading conferences to discuss books with target students who need support to become readers.

Information Access and Delivery

- Market books to students by doing booktalks. School library media specialists who are constrained by having weekly classes can make use of those weekly times to do booktalks. In addition, make booktalks a standard part of the beginning of social studies units. Consider the possibilities as history classes begin study of the Civil War, World War II, and the westward movement, or as area studies of the Middle East or women's studies begin.
- Market books to teachers. Use five minutes of faculty or team meet-

ings to promote some of the latest, best books for youth—or an occasional book for adults!

Program Administration

- Bring authors to the school to speak to students. Seek support from local businesses to underwrite the event and then give it—and your sponsor—as much press as possible.
- Support and encourage providing time during the school day for students to read.
- Provide parent programs about reading to engender support for reading at home.
- Encourage read-aloud programs. Some schools have all-school thematic oral literature programs that create a community spirit centered on reading (Boothroy and Donham 1981).
- Cooperate with the local public library to encourage participation in summer reading programs. Encourage staff from the public library to come to the school to market programs and to sign up students for library cards.
- Collaborate with the public library year round to design, implement, and publicize programs and events to support reading.
- Start a book discussion club for faculty. Discussion can focus on books for the students—to help teachers learn about new books their students might enjoy. Alternatively, discussion might focus on reading materials for adults.

SCENARIO FOR DISCUSSION

In a relatively new elementary school, the media center has an excellent and "fresh" collection. Reading is a high priority in the school, which is known for having proficient readers and writers. The overall population includes many professional families with two incomes and a high level of education. Although the building teaching staff includes a wide variety of ages and experience, there are several new, inexperienced teachers. It is common practice that classroom teachers come to the library media center and select books to provide a room collection for students to use for sustained silent reading (SSR) and independent reading. Primary classrooms need to have a wide range of selections, as their readers span preprimer to advanced readers. A first-year teacher in the primary grades unit selects her books without consulting the library media specialist. One of her very independent readers takes one of the *Alice* novels by Phyllis Reynolds Naylor. Typically, upper elementary or middle school girls would read these novels. When the student's parents read the book, they are enraged that their daughter would be reading such a terrible book. They discuss their concern with the teacher, the librarian, and the principal, and then take it to the PTA. In addition, it is clear that they are telling everyone at the ball games and church that the school library is filled with pornography. What does the librarian need to do for the inexperienced teacher? How should the parents be approached? What is the school's role in self-selection?

REFERENCES

Adler, J. et al. (1989, October). "A Middle School Experiment: Can a Token Economy Improve Reading Achievement Scores." Paper presented at the annual meeting of the Midwestern Educational Research Association, Chicago, Illinois, October 19–21. ERIC document ED 312 620.

Association of American Publishers (2003, March 4). *Industry Statistics*. Retrieved November 2, 2003, from www.publishers.org/industry/index.cfm.

Berglund, R. et al. (1991, July). *Developing a Love of Reading: What Helps, What Hurts*. Literacy Research Report, CMS 15.145 No. 7. Dekalb, IL: Northern Illinois University Reading Clinic. ERIC document 332 168.

Blum, H. T., L. R. Lipsett, and D. J. Yocom (2002, March/April). "Literature Circles." *Remedial and Special Education 23* (2): 99–108.

Bodart, J. (1986, June). "Booktalks Do Work: The Effects of Booktalking on Attitude and Circulation." *Illinois Libraries 68* (6): 378–381.

Boothroy, B. and J. Donham (1981, April). "Listening to Literature: An All-School Program." *Reading Teacher 34* (7): 772–774.

Brabham, E. G. and S. K. Villaume (2000, November). "Continuing Conversations About Literature Circles." *Reading Teacher 54* (3): 278–280.

Carter, B. (1996, October). "Hold the Applause! Do *Accelerated Reader* and *-Electronic Bookshelf* Send the Right Message?" *School Library Journal 42* (10): 22–25.

Carter, B. (2000, July). "Formula for Failure." *School Library Journal 46* (7): 34–37.

Carter, V. (1988, January). "The Effect of Summer Reading Program Participation on the Retention of Reading Skills." *Illinois Libraries 70:* 56–60.

Chandler, K. (1997). "The Beach Book Club: Literacy in the 'Lazy Days of Summer.'" *Journal of Adolescent and Adult Literacy 41* (2): 104–116.

Chenowith, K. (2001, September). "Keeping Score." *School Library Journal 47* (9): 48–51.

Clarke, M. (1987, April). "Don't Blame the System: Constraints on 'Whole Language' Reform." *Language Arts 64* (4): 384–396.

Donham van Deusen, J. and P. Brandt (1997, September/October). "Designing Thematic Literature Units." *Emergency Librarian* 25 (1): 21–24.

Donham van Deusen, J. and Langhorne, M. (1997, January 1). "Iowa City Reads! The Reading Event Worth Shouting About." *School Library Journal* 43 (5): 32–34.

Eeds, M. and D. Wells (1989, February). "Grand Conversations: An Exploration of Meaning Construction in Literature Study Groups." *Research in the Teaching of English* 23 (1): 4–29.

Frank, C. R., C. N. Dixon, and L. R. Brandts (2001, February). "Bears, Trolls, and Pagemasters: Learning About Learners in Book Clubs." *Reading Teacher* 54 (5): 448–463.

Greaney, V. (1980). "Factors Related to Amount and Type of Leisure Reading." *Reading Research Quarterly* 15 (3): 337–357.

Greaney, V. and M. Hegarty (1987, February). "Correlates of Leisure-Time Reading." *Journal of Research in Reading* 10 (1): 3–20.

Huck, C. S. (1992, Summer). "Developing Lifetime Readers." *Journal of Youth Services in Libraries* 5 (4): 371–382.

Jaeger, L. and S. N. Demetriadis (2002, March). "Book Club on a Budget." *School Library Journal* 48 (3): 47.

Johnson C. and J. Gaskins (1992, Summer). "Reading Attitude: Types of Materials and Specific Strategies." *Journal of Reading Improvement* 29: 133–139.

Kohn, A. (1993). *Punished by Rewards; The Trouble with Gold Stars, Incentive Plans, A's, Praise and Other Bribes*. New York: Houghton Mifflin.

Krashen, S. (1993). *The Power of Reading*. Littleton, CO: Libraries Unlimited.

Krashen, S. (2002). "Accelerated Reader: Does It Work? If So, Why?" *School Libraries in Canada* 22 (2): 22–26+.

Langer, J. (1994, March). "A Response-Based Approach to Reading Literature." *Language Arts* 71 (3): 203–211.

Ley, T. C. (1994, January–March). "Longitudinal Study of the Reading Attitudes and Behaviors of Middle School Students." *Reading Psychology* 15 (1): 11–38.

Malach, D. A. and R. A. Rutter (2003, September). "For Nine Months Kids Go to School, But in Summer This School Goes to Kids." *Reading Teacher* 57 (1): 50–54.

Manning, G. and M. Manning (1984, May). "What Models of Recreational Reading Make a Difference?" *Reading World* 23 (4): 375–380.

Marzano, R. J. (1991). "Language, the Language Arts, and Thinking." In J. Flood et al, eds., *Handbook of Research in the English Language Arts* (pp. 559–586). New York: Macmillan.

McKenna, M. C., D. J. Kear, and R. A. Ellsworth (1995, October/November/December). "Children's Attitudes Toward Reading: A National Survey." *Reading Research Quarterly* 30 (4): 934–956.

Miall, D. S. and D. Kuiken (1995, February). "Aspects of Literary Response: A New Questionnaire." *Research in the Teaching of English* 29 (1): 37–58.

Miller, D. P. (1995, November). "Computerized Carrots—Are They Truly Reading Motivators?" *Technology Connection* 2 (7): 21–22.

Moss, B. and J. Hendershot (2002, September). "Exploring Sixth Graders' Selection of Nonfiction Trade Books." *Reading Teacher* 56 (1): 6–18.

National Center for Educational Statistics (1997, April). *Use of Public Library Services by Households in the United States: 1996*. Retrieved November 2, 2003, from http://nces.ed.gov/pubs/97446.html.

Neuman, S. (1986, January). "The Home Environment and Fifth-Grade Students' Leisure Reading." *Elementary School Journal 86* (3): 334–343.

Neuman, S. (1995, October). "Reading Together: A Community-Supported Parent Tutoring Program." *Reading Teacher 49* (2): 120–129.

Pavonetti, L. M., K. M. Brimmer, and J. F. Cipielewski (2002, December). "Accelerated Reader: What Are the Lasting Effects on the Reading Habits of Middle School Students Exposed to Accelerated Reader in Elementary Grades?" *Journal of Adolescent and Adult Literacy 46* (4): 300–311.

Pearson, P. D., L. R. Roehler, A. J. Dole, and G. G. Duffy (1992). "Developing Expertise in Reading Comprehension." In S. J. Samuels and A. Farstrup, eds., *What Research Has To Say About Reading Instruction*, 2d ed. (pp. 145–199. Newark, DE: International Reading Association.

Rosenblatt, L. (1978). *The Reader, the Text, the Poem: The Transactional Theory of the Literary Work*. Carbondale, IL: Southern Illinois Press.

Taylor, B. M., B. J. Frye, and G. M. Maruyama (1990, Summer). "Time Spent Reading and Reading Growth." *American Educational Research Journal 27* (2): 351–362.

Venezky, R. L. (2000). "The Origins of the Present Day Chasm Between Adult Literacy Needs and School Literacy Instruction." *Scientific Studies of Reading 4* (1): 19.

Wigfield, A. and J. T. Guthrie (1997). "Relations of Children's Motivation for Reading to the Amount and Breadth of Their Reading." *Journal of Educational Psychology 89* (3): 420–432.

Chapter 10

Technology

This chapter:

- examines criteria for determining how technology is used
- identifies three categories of powerful technology uses: information access, productivity, and communication
- explores the school library media specialist's roles as technology advocate, coordinator, manager, policymaker, trainer, and teacher
- considers software selection in the context of beliefs about teaching and learning
- discusses the impact of the World Wide Web on the school library media program
- examines planning for technology within a school, and the school library media program
- identifies action strategies related to technology

Information technologies (such as online catalogs, automated circulation systems, and electronic references), productivity applications (such as word processing, databases, wikis, and multimedia production), instructional technologies (such as simulations, WebQuests, and tutorials), and telecommunications (such as blogs, e-mail, and chat) are central to the work of the library media specialist in teaching, providing information, and consulting with teachers. Integrating technology into the school context involves leadership and informed decision making. It requires understanding the educational goals and philosophy of the school. It requires knowing how technology can improve teaching and learning. The school library media specialist can facilitate technology infusion by guiding decision making so that technology enhances creative and analytical work.

Because of its cost and the media attention that technology receives, the public holds high expectations for technology's impact on education. This chapter begins with guidelines for careful decision making and proceeds through technology program planning and implementation to help meet those demands.

TECHNOLOGY APPLICATIONS

The ways schools can use technology are numerous and rapidly changing. Clearly, schools cannot afford to "buy into" every application on the market—nor should they want to. Before investing in any technology application, educators must examine such questions as:

- Is this technology consistent with our beliefs about what needs to be learned and how learning occurs?
- Will this technology enable students to do something of significance that is otherwise essentially impossible or impractical?
- Will this technology enable students to do something of significance substantially better than they could otherwise?
- Why are we attracted to this technology? For its performance? For its "glitz"? Because everyone is talking about it? Because other districts or schools have it? Because it will empower our students to function at higher cognitive levels? Because it will advance us toward an important educational goal?

In-school access to computers and the Internet has improved dramatically in recent years, especially since the introduction of the E-rate, officially known as the Schools and Libraries Universal Service Program, created as part of the Telecommunications Act of 1996. This program applies fees from the telecommunications industry to fund discounts on local area networking, Internet service, and telecommunications services. Before the E-rate, several studies had investigated the differences in technology use based on the socioeconomic status of schools. King (1987), who researched 141 schools in North Carolina, found that "affluent students are thus learning to tell the computer what to do, while less affluent students are learning to do what the computer tells them" (p. 12).

Looking at students from the perspective of ability, Sayers (1995) reported "the more exciting programs are reserved for the students in the upper tracks; when lower track and minority students do get access they are much more likely to be assigned to drill and practice than to problem-solving activities" (p. 768). Piller (1992) summarizes the dramatic inequities he observed in his visits to schools when he says, "In most cases, computers simply perpetuate a two-tier system of education for rich and poor" (p. 221). An underlying assumption in these studies is that the number of computers available in schools may be no more important than the applications for which they are used. Still, in 2006, Hall (2006) asserts that many schools have the mistaken notion that providing more access to technology will bridge the digital divide. Such a notion ignores the sophistication of expert technology users over novices, as well as the distinction between using technology for entertainment and using it for information.

Other differences still remain along socioeconomic and demographic lines. The quality of connectivity both at home and at school still varies. For example, according to a Pew Internet and American Life Report (Horrigan 2006), at the end of 2005, a lower percentage of Internet households had broadband connections in rural areas (24 percent) than in urban areas (39 percent). In a 2004 Department of Commerce Report, families with incomes below $35,000 were far more likely to have dial-up access rather than high-speed access (U.S. Department of Commerce 2004). The digital divide has not entirely disappeared. Those schools serving less-advantaged children tend to have Internet available only in limited-access areas (such as computer labs), whereas in more advantaged schools, Internet use is part of the way of "doing business" and local area networking tends to provide access in classrooms, library media centers, and labs throughout the school. Vail (2003) asserts that while we have narrowed the gap in access to technology in schools, there are still serious discrepancies in teacher training and knowledge, home computer access, and technology support. Clearly, the library media specialist has a crucial role to play—in advocating for Internet access as well as providing teacher training—so that students can take greatest advantage from whatever access is available.

Roschelle and colleagues (2000) conducted an extensive review of the literature examining effective educational applications of computer-based technology. In summary, the findings indicate that identifiable dimensions characterize effective educational use of technology:

- Active engagement: Productivity applications for problem solving, data analysis and presentation, multimedia production, and simulation are likely to support subject matter understanding. These applications involve students in using technology as a tool for their own productivity. Students, not the computers, are in charge.
- Collaborative learning: Internet and digital video technologies promote collaborative activities, even among geographically distant students.
- Frequent and immediate feedback: Educational software can provide individualized academic support and feedback. For example, teachers can use e-mail to send students feedback.

One way to classify technology uses is to consider whether the application is grounded in a behaviorist or a constructivist approach to learning. Behaviorist applications place the locus of control with the computer or the teacher. For example, most drill-and-practice software gives feedback, and often rewards, when students give correct answers. The computer determines what will happen next. Students look for a single right answer, usually a factual response. Their learning is perhaps rote—particularly if speed is a factor. At best, it is at the knowledge or comprehension level. A computer-based test bank like the *Accelerated Reader* is another example of a behaviorist use of the computer, where students respond to literal comprehension questions. When students use electronic books and click on graphic elements on the screen, so that doors open or monkeys squeak, they are at best entertaining themselves, but they are not creating significant meaning. In fact, sometimes the gimmicks may distract them from the story line. Regardless of the software, when the computer is a reward for finishing work or for good behavior, the approach is clearly behaviorist. In this case, the locus of control lies with the teacher who decides when a student has earned the reward. These computer uses may support low-level student learning, but they are as expensive as many more empowering ways to use computers.

A constructivist would prefer to see students use a computer to create, whether it is a report, a spreadsheet, a Web page, or a multimedia production. Giving students a set of raw data is one way to design constructivist learning. For example, when students take facts about family size, infant mortality rates, level of education, and other demographic data for various countries, enter the information into a database, and sort or select to observe patterns in the data, they begin to create their own understanding of relationships among factors and draw generalizations. The very process of constructing the database causes them to analyze and synthesize as they generate their own understanding rather than recall someone else's. Desktop publishing, the word processor, graphing software, databases and spreadsheets, well-conceived WebQuests, collaborative tools like wikis or blogs, and well-designed simulations are all examples of applications students use for constructing meaning.

Integrating technology into a program requires a substantial investment in infrastructure, hardware, software, space, and staff time. Because schools have limited resources—human and fiscal—for technology, it is irresponsible not to set high expectations for its impact on learning. Applying stringent criteria for technology represents accountability to the public trust and to the educational future of students. The National Council of Teachers of Mathematics (1989) has been at the forefront in development of its curriculum standards. In describing how calculators and computers can enhance mathematics learning, the standards state:

> These devices and formats free students from tedious computations and allow them to concentrate on problem solving and other important content. They also give them new means to explore content. (p. 19)

The standards recommend, for example, graphing utilities and graphing calculators to extend student productivity.

Likewise, in their standards document, the National Council for the Social Studies (1994) describes "powerful" social studies teaching and learning; this description covers several dimensions of teaching, including the use of technology. The council's recommendation includes references to information, productivity, and telecommunications applications:

> Integrated social studies teaching and learning include effective use of technology that can add important dimensions to students' learning. . . . If students have access to computerized databases, they can search these for relevant research information. If they can communicate with peers in other states or nations, they can engage in personalized cultural exchanges or compare parallel data collected in geographically or culturally diverse locations. (p. 165)

Essentially, there are three categories of technology applications that offer particular power in schools: information access, productivity, and communication. Each of these categories has several important characteristics:

- The student is "in control," not the computer.
- The computer is perceived as a tool—an extension of the student's mind.
- The student uses the computer to produce, create, or generate.
- Cognitive levels of students using these applications are beyond recall and comprehension as they engage in application, analysis, synthesis, and evaluation.

Information Access

Availability of information in electronic resources just keeps increasing. Online references and databases are standard tools in school library media centers. Various search engines appear as bookmarks or short-cuts on school library media Web sites. Students need to know what criteria to apply as they select information for reliability and relevance. Students need to learn to differentiate between free and fee sources of information. They must also develop habits of evaluating information on the basis of authority of the source, currency, bias, scope, and accuracy when using Web-based information sources.

The expectations for a WebQuest are not unlike those for any good authentic assignment: that it be designed so that students do more than merely report information findings, and that students instead synthesize findings and integrate those findings into a response that represents application, synthesis, and evaluation of information. A common caveat about WebQuests is to ensure that the expectations for students go beyond reporting findings—a task that can be accomplished through copy-and-paste. Done well, WebQuests can engage students in high-order thinking as they take advantage of the expanded capabilities that technology offers.

Productivity

A wide variety of productivity software is available: authoring software like KidPix (Brøderbund) or iMovies (Apple) for visual productions; Kidspiration (Inspiration) for concept mapping; PhotoShop Elements

(Adobe), PowerPoint (Microsoft), or Keynote (Apple) for presentations; Pages (Apple) or Publisher (Microsoft) for print publication layout, word processing software, and database and spreadsheet software for problem solving. With each of these applications, students demonstrate or synthesize their learning and revise the documents they create, thereby meeting a higher performance standard than they might otherwise have set for themselves.

Web 2.0

Opportunities for cooperative work, for publication, and for online communication abound among the Web 2.0 applications. The library media specialist can be a clearinghouse for watching to see which of these applications have real learning potential in the school setting. For example, Google Docs allows students to work collaboratively and share documents as well as collaborate in real time online. Similarly, wikis offer an interesting opportunity for cooperative work in classrooms where students can develop collaborative knowledge bases about topics being studied. Using an application like Wetpaint (www.wetpaint. com) enables class wikis. Create Survey is a free application for developing and distributing online surveys, a data collection tool for student researchers. Ning (www.ning.com) provides the opportunity to create a social network within a class, a school, or a small working group. These are a few of the multitude of opportunities for technology to enhance learning opportunities in the Web 2.0 environment.

PLANNING FOR TECHNOLOGY

> Planning is a set of formal and rational activities that seeks to anticipate conditions, directions and challenges at some future point for the purposes of enhancing the readiness of personnel and the organization to perform more effectively and to attain relevant objectives by optimal means. (Knezevich 1984, p. 88)

There are several key concepts in this definition. First, planning is formal and rational. Technology costs are too high for schools and school districts not to take a formal approach to the planning process. The word "rational" emphasizes gathering information and making reasonable and informed decisions. Technology is an area in which it is easy to fall prey

---

ENHANCEMENT IN ACTION: USING BLOGS

A blog can take the form of a diary, a newsletter, or a journal. Blogs can be created through specialized services such as Class Blog (http://classblogmeister.com/). Essentially, this online writing form provides a medium for students to organize their thoughts and information, to reflect, or to publish (Oravec 2002). Unlike personal Web pages, a blog is primarily text, although it is not uncommon to include links to relevant Web sites. Blogs provide students with a sense of audience as they write, and they create a collaborative environment where students can exchange feedback for one another as writers (Kennedy 2003). Among the activities that blogs facilitate is one called "nutshelling" (Kajder and Bull 2003). Using this strategy, students extract a line from a text and paste it into the body of a new posting. They begin their new writing from there. This technique gives hesitant writers a starting point. Three challenges that blogs raise are privacy, appropriateness of content, and server space. A school must establish policies regarding the use of blogs in order to protect student identity and to ensure responsible content. Password protected access may be an appropriate consideration if local rather than worldwide publication serves the needs of the class. Used well, blogs can provide an authentic writing venue for students.

---

to the "covet thy neighbor" syndrome, in which schools buy hardware or software for no reason except that others are doing so. A rational approach to planning calls for analyzing the school's goals and technology's capabilities and then identifying the intersections where technology can substantively improve goal attainment. Another key concept in this definition is readiness of the personnel and the organization, that is, staff involvement and careful consideration of the organizational context. A final key term is optimal means. Planning involves looking for the best ways to attain the organization's objectives. Quality is important whenever considering technological innovations; the marketplace is vast and not everything in it represents "optimal means."

No school or district should be without a formal technology plan, because of the rapid change, the high costs, the range of enthusiasm

ENHANCEMENT IN ACTION:
USING WEBQUESTS FOR INFORMATION ACCESS

WebQuests can be an effective way to engage students in making use of information online. A WebQuest is "an inquiry-oriented activity in which some or all of the information that learners interact with comes from resources on the Internet" (Dodge 1997). WebQuests follow a general format of setting the stage, engaging the student in a task, providing links to a set of information sources that will help them complete the task, and guiding the process students will follow. The tasks are essentially problems that require students to select relevant information and apply it to solve a problem. Tom March maintains a Web site of effective WebQuests (www.webquest.org/). For example, in a recommended WebQuest for a middle school health curriculum, the task is introduced as follows:

> It happened in 1918, it happened in 1957, it happened in 1968, and it happened in 1977. Either a pandemic or epidemic of the flu occurred worldwide or in individual countries in those years. Hong Kong of 1996—was that a close call? As a member of a community task force, you will join three other people (Virologist, Physician, Public Health Officer, and Historian) and decide if another influenza pandemic, like 1918, can happen again. You will help the public to understand general information about influenza, its history, and its prevention and control. Questions: How can something as little as the invisible flu virus become a global killer as in 1918? Could this happen again, and if so, can the general public's awareness and vigilance be increased so a potential deadly form of influenza can be prevented or halted in its spread?

To succeed in this WebQuest, students must gather information about the flu virus, assess how it spreads, and propose how such an event could be prevented. This WebQuest meets criteria that both March and Dodge, who are pioneers in this teaching strategy, recommend. It asks students to apply the information they gather to a problem and create a product with which they transfer their learning to a defined audience.

from zealous to resistant, the importance of broad-based ownership, and the complexity of integration into the instructional program. An effective external incentive for comprehensive technology planning is the E-rate discount. Participation in the E-rate Universal Service program requires a three-year plan. To qualify for a Universal Service discount, a technology plan must meet the following five criteria (www.universalservice.org/sl/applicants/step02/):

1. Establish clear goals and a realistic strategy for using telecommunications and information technology to improve education or library services.
2. Include a professional development strategy to ensure that staff members know how to use technology to improve education or library services.
3. Include an assessment of the telecommunication services, hardware, software, and other services that will be needed to improve education or library services.
4. Provide for a sufficient budget to acquire and maintain the hardware, software, professional development, and other services that will be needed to implement the strategy.
5. Implement an evaluation process that enables the school or library to monitor progress toward the specified goals and make midcourse corrections in response to new developments and opportunities as they arise.

For technology planning to be effective, some baseline work must occur. Establishing a mission for technology in teaching and learning is an important first step. Such a mission grows out of underlying assumptions about the nature of technology and learning. One such belief is that technology is a tool that allows people to extend their capabilities by working smarter or faster. Learning results when one creates new meaning by relating new experiences and prior learning. Given these two beliefs, a mission for technology might call for students to use technological tools to access, manipulate, and communicate information. What is important is that the technology mission be closely tied to its larger context—the mission for the school. Consider this example of a school district mission statement in *Teaching, Learning and Technology: Towards a Community of Life-Long Learners Iowa City Community School District Technology Plan* (www.iccsd.k12.ia.us/technology/plan.html):

The mission of the Iowa City Community School District is to ensure that all students become responsible, independent learners capable of making informed decisions in a democratic society as well as the dynamic global community; this is accomplished by challenging each student with a rigorous and creative curriculum taught by a diverse, professional, caring staff strengthened by collaborative partnerships with families and the entire community.

The technology plan for the district is closely aligned to the district's overall strategic plan; it is not an isolated entity, but is tied to its context.

A technology plan must be the product of broad-based teamwork. Key players include teachers, administrators, parents, local business people, physical plant workers, and library media professionals. Physical plant workers are likely to know secrets about buildings that can make critical differences in networking decisions. Local business people and parents may be helpful in garnering support when they understand the program; they also bring a perspective that may generate valuable ideas or insights that are different from those of educators. Each stakeholder has something to bring to the discussions about technology, and each can serve as an advocate for ideas when implementation begins.

The technology planning process is never finished. While a long-term view is important for establishing mission and goals, short-term planning is ongoing because of the constant changes in available technologies. This is not a process to occur every five years, or even every three. It is continuous. The long-term view must provide for budgeting.

Technology is a capital expenditure; without line items in the budget for technology, planning is futile. That budget must include consideration of several items:

- infrastructure: Reliability, adequacy, and security are key attributes of infrastructure necessary to support the use of technology district-wide (Johnson 2003). Network administration is a crucial aspect of infrastructure.
- new hardware
- new software
- software upgrades
- replacement hardware: After about five years, a computer needs to be reviewed for its capacity to continue in its assigned purpose. Often by that time the processor speed, the memory limitations, or

the storage capacity makes the machine less useful for a given application. At this point, a machine may need to be reassigned to a less-demanding task or retired completely. For each new computer installation, the budget five years ahead needs to include a replacement for it.

- staff development: Release time for teachers to participate in training, trainers' stipends, and the costs of facilities, equipment, software, supplies, and technology-related conference attendance are all necessary expenses.
- technical support: As more machines are acquired, maintenance and repair, either by in-house technical staff or by contractors, becomes essential. Existing employees cannot take on this additional work because it must be the highest priority of the individual. Besides, the workload will grow.

A sound technology plan should be results-driven, with a focus on how the technology will be used and what difference it will make (Jukes 1996). The Alvord Unified School District Technology Plan delineates its intended results with timelines. (See www.alvord.k12.ca.us/district/ TechPlan06.html.) McKenzie (2002) states, "We should only acquire new technologies that will improve student performance on learning tasks that match state curriculum standards or address important local learning goals" (p. 35). Such a standard needs to be considered during the planning process to ensure that resources are allocated where they will have impact—not simply to satisfy calls for "fair and equal" distribution or simply to keep up with neighboring districts.

Staff development needs to be ongoing and incremental—not a collection of one-shot events; it also cannot be a generic set of lessons, a one-size-fits-all approach. Instead, a sound staff development plan is directly relevant to what the participants will do. For example, staff development for high school mathematics teachers will focus on using the graphing calculator and relating it to specific units in algebra. Lessons on using the Web will include examples specific to the curriculum of teachers who are participating. Staff development must also be thorough; a series of lessons with time for teachers to share ideas and to practice is more appropriate than covering many topics superficially. Before teachers can feel confident to add technology to their teaching repertoire, they must feel ownership; that can occur only when they have time to experiment, collaborate, and create for themselves. Teachers need to have adequate access to computers to build confidence and skill; providing access, either by lending computers for home use or providing computers to teachers for their classrooms, is essential. Teachers are far less likely to embrace technology when they must share computer lab space with students or when they must borrow a computer for limited times at school. Effective staff development calls for a readily available support system; when teachers forget a step in the use of a program or attempt something altogether new, they need a colleague to call—a convenient, knowledgeable, supportive colleague. Such a person can certainly be the school library media specialist.

Just as staff development needs must be addressed, benchmarks for student competencies in using technology need to be clearly defined and assessed. A good example is publication of benchmarks by the Iowa City Community School District on its Web site (www.iccsd.k12.ia.us/technology/plan.html). The benchmarks are categorized as applications (such as word processing, spreadsheets), communications, tools (such as calculators, data collection instruments), and computers and society (for example, copyright, netiquette). Grade levels and content area provide accountability for integration of these competencies.

Some state departments of education provide specific guides or templates for district level technology planning. See, for example, the New Jersey Department of Education template at www.state.nj.us/education/techno/localtech/checklist.htm or the State of Washington at www.k12.wa.us/EdTech/planning.aspx.

NETS TECHNOLOGY CURRICULUM STANDARDS

The International Society for Technology in Education (ISTE) has published foundation technology standards for students that can be used to guide development of curriculum K–12 (http://cnets.iste.org/currstands/cstands-netss.html). Lessons aimed at these standards should be integrated into content area studies to provide a meaningful context. The standards fall under six categories: basic operations and concepts; social, ethical and human issues; productivity tools; communication tools; research tools; and problem-solving and decision-making tools. The ISTE Standards emphasize that students must develop basic technical competency for operating technology. In today's electronic world, it is easy to assume that students know all they need to know about technology operations; however, this standard calls for students to understand the nature and operation of technology systems. While technology grows more intuitive each year, there continue to be lessons that must be intentionally taught—how to save and organize files, an understanding of networked systems, file-sharing, uploading and downloading. Not yet do we have a student population who really understand their technology systems in ways that make them sophisticated—or even efficient—users. ISTE asserts that we must still teach these fundamentals of technology use. These standards acknowledge that while technology enhances our ability to access and manipulate information, these capabilities bring responsibilities for ethical use as well. It is crucial that students learn that not everything that technology makes possible is ethical. The ISTE standards set expectations for students to use technology to increase their productivity, to communicate, and to engage in research. Each of these types of technology applications requires that schools develop intentional lessons in meaningful contexts so that students become intelligent and skillful technology users.

THE LIBRARY MEDIA SPECIALIST'S ROLES IN TECHNOLOGY

For effectively integrating technology into a school's program, library media specialists are well suited to play several roles: coordinator, manager, technology advocate, trainer, teacher, and policymaker. Too often, administrators have considered it necessary to add a separate position of technology coordinator, either at the district or school level, and too often the qualifications for such a position call for a person who understands hardware and networking but not applications for technology in an educational environment. Library media specialists have several attributes that qualify them well for coordinating technology use in a school or a district. First, coordinating technology is akin to coordinating any other learning resource—this is already the work of the school library media specialist. What knowledge is required to provide such coordination? Clearly, a technology coordinator must be knowledgeable about what is possible to do with technology and what is worth doing. Maintaining current awareness of what is in the marketplace is a traditional part of the school library media specialist's work. More important, making judgments about quality based on explicit criteria is also a typical library media specialist's task. To coordinate technology requires knowing the curriculum, teachers' instructional styles, and the students' learning needs; this knowledge of the instructional context is essential to all effective library media programming.

Coordinator

Library media specialists supervise a facility accessible to all departments or grades; locating shared technology facilities there adds items
to the scheduling task, but does not require a new system or access point
for teachers and students. Technology demands three kinds of support:
the educational leadership that a library media professional can offer,
technical assistance for maintenance and repair, and networking expertise. Other necessary positions are a network specialist, and technicians
to maintain and repair hardware, maintain file servers, attend to wiring,
and install software and upgrades. These technical tasks are just that—
they do not require an educator's expertise. However, coordinating the
application of technology for the overall school program indeed requires
an educator's expertise, and the most appropriate educator is the library
media specialist.

Manager

One managerial responsibility of the library media specialist is super-
vising computer labs that are often located near or in the library media
center. With access to the Internet this supervision is particularly important—students must be assisted in efficient and effective searching for
information and their Internet use must be monitored. Another management task is inventory of equipment—a task easily accomplished
using the library media center's automated circulation system. Each
hardware item can be entered into the database and then "checked out"
to its location in the building. Using this already existing system for
equipment inventory means efficiency for the school. Managing software requires keeping track of licenses—an information management
problem accomplished with a simple database program, using such fields
as title, version, publisher, vendor, purchase order number, date purchased, and license terms. Physical storage and organization of software
is a task familiar to the library media specialist.

Technology Advocate

Building-level library media specialists serve as technology advocates.
It is, however, important that their advocacy be spent on those applications that make a positive difference to teaching and learning. It is not
responsible to advocate just any use of technology or to support purchase of anything electronic any more than it is responsible to spend

library media dollars on poorly written books. Leadership is an important aspect of the technology advocate role, and sometimes leadership requires challenging technology uses that may not comport with the school's beliefs about learning or that may not play out as particularly sound ideas.

An interesting example is integrated learning systems (ILS). These systems manage instruction; examples include SuccessMaker Enterprise and KnowledgeBox. Most ILSs include instruction and practice in basic school subjects. The instructional design of most systems follows behaviorist programmed instruction (Miller, DeJean, and Miller 2000). An essential feature of all ILSs is their ability to track student progress. From the system's central server, specific lessons are automatically sent to each student's computer when the student logs on. Lessons are selected for the student based on the ILS's assessment of prior performance. Students typically progress through the prescribed lesson at their own pace. To advocate installing computer-managed instruction of this sort, one must support a behaviorist approach to learning and recalling information. The software is the primary information provider, and the student's task is to take in that information. A school committed to a holistic, interdisciplinary model of learning based on constructivist principles and inquiry would have substantive philosophical differences with integrated learning systems. Advocating an ILS in such a context would not make sense because the technology use and the educational beliefs don't match.

On a smaller scale, the library media specialist can be an advocate for appropriate use of technology applications. For example, PowerPoint presentations have become pervasive in many schools and yet some would argue that this format can be overused and inappropriately used (Shaw 2003). Sometimes the complexity of a topic calls for a formal written essay rather than a glossy presentation. As advocate, the library media specialist may need to urge teachers to reflect on whether a PowerPoint presentation demands enough of students. Advocacy must be selective, and this requires analyzing the assumptions that underpin any technology use. On a smaller scale, the library media specialist can be an advocate for appropriate use of technology applications.

Beyond determining how computers should be used comes selecting software to fit the school's beliefs and goals. Materials selection is a traditional part of the school library media specialist's work, and software selection is a logical extension of that work. In recent years, collection development has tended toward a more collaborative process. There was a time when the librarian chose library books without involvement by teachers. However, as the library media collection has become more central to curriculum and instruction, selection of materials (including software) has become a more collaborative process, involving both teachers and library media specialists.

Choosing software for a school needs to be based on explicit criteria. A standardized set of criteria should guide purchase. The set of evaluation criteria should be locally generated to match local beliefs about teaching and learning. Figure 10.1 shows an example of criteria for software selection in a district committed to constructivist learning. This commitment is evident in several of the criteria. For example, under the "Media Appropriate" category are questions about the relationship between the software and the use of manipulatives or firsthand experiences. Also, under "21st Century-Aware," the program must promote critical thinking and investigative problem solving, not rote memorization. These criteria show a direct correlation between the instructional beliefs of the institution and the decision making regarding what software to use in their schools.

When a school purchases a book, there is considerable expense because books are not cheap. There are then the added costs of cataloging and processing the book, so the cost increases. After that, the book is ready to be used. Purchase of software involves more than investment in an item, and becomes more complex: How many licenses are needed for it? What staff development will be necessary for its implementation? Where will it be accessed? Is the hardware available adequate for it? Such complexity calls for careful decision making because the cost goes well beyond the sticker price.

Students with special needs make unique demands on technology. A commitment to equity of opportunity draws the library media specialist into concern for the exceptional learner. One example of an accommodation is the array of assistive devices for Web browsing—for example, Window-Eyes is a text-to-speech synthesis program and ZoomText is a screen enlargement program. Awareness of students' needs and exploration into technological solutions is part of the role of the library media specialist (Selverstone 2003). Advocacy for technology also requires understanding the change process and having skill at helping teachers accept new ideas. For some teachers, integrating technologies into their curricula may require substantial changes in educational philosophy, classroom management, and curricular goals. After

FIGURE 10.1
Software Evaluation Criteria

Instructional Design

Quality Content
___ The content is well researched, based on sound learning theory, and up to date.
___ The program addresses skills and concepts central to teaching objectives.
___ The program supports and enhances the curriculum.
___ The program offers cross-curricular applications.
___ The program is process-oriented.
___ The program does not involve skill drilling.
___ The program promotes active learning.

Media Appropriate
___ The instructional task is appropriate to the medium.
___ The task could not be accomplished effectively with different media.
___ The program complements and extends the use of manipulatives.
___ The program appropriately provides unavailable firsthand experiences.

21st Century-Aware
___ The software promotes independent thinking, critical thinking, and investigative problem solving rather than stressing skills such as rote thinking and out-of-context memorization.

Instructionally Consistent
___ The software is consistently developmentally appropriate for the target audience (i.e., necessary reading levels do not vary greatly, subject matter is appropriate to the intended age group).

Stimulates Curiosity
___ The software engages student interest.

Challenging
___ The program has a low entry/high ceiling.
___ Students feel a sense of accomplishment.

Student Control
___ Students can use the program independently.
___ The program is open-ended.
___ Students can create their own pathways rather than merely respond to prompts.

Adaptive
___ The program suits different learning styles.
___ Students with limited English-speaking abilities can use the program.
___ The program offers special education options.

Software Design

You-Are-Here Design
___ Students can determine where they are in the program without feeling lost.
___ Students can quickly begin to use the program with minimal prompting from an adult.

Transparent Interface
___ Students' efforts are devoted to using the program, not learning how to use the program.

Describe how this program can be appropriately used for learning.

Excerpted from the form used by the Iowa City Community School District, Iowa City, Iowa.

observing implementation of technology in public schools as a part of a longitudinal study in 14 states, Foa, Schwab, and Johnson (1996) conclude:

> For technologies to be used effectively, teachers must be comfortable with a constructivist or project-based, problem-solving approach to learning; they must be willing to tolerate students progressing independently at widely varying paces; they must trust students to know more than they do about certain subjects and techniques, and in fact to take on the role of expert teacher at various times; they must be comfortable about not having complete control over what resources the student accesses or what the student learns and they must be flexible enough to change directions when technical glitches occur. For some teachers these practices are all second nature. More often, however, we are asking teachers to integrate dramatically new philosophies of education, curricular goals, classroom management techniques, and ideas about interdisciplinary and individualized education into their daily practice. No wonder the introduction of technologies is often perceived as threatening. (p. 56)

Sensitivity to teachers is nothing new to the library media specialist whose very curriculum is dependent on collaboration.

Hall and Hord (2001) describe the concerns-based adoption model (CBAM), a sequence of concerns that innovation raises. The sequence begins with "information concerns," the need for introductory information about the innovation. The library media specialist, as technology advocate, simply makes teachers aware of a new use for technology—either hardware or software—that has potential to enhance or expand the current way of learning. People resist innovation when they perceive that there is no need; a technology innovation must promise a substantial improvement in the learning experience before teachers, beyond the zealots, will have enough interest to adopt it. In short, there must be some incentive to undertake the change, and ideally that incentive needs to be the intrinsic value of the technology. Before advocating for a technology implementation, the library media specialist must have confidence that it is worth doing.

Next come "personal concerns" where the novice wonders how an innovation will affect him or her: What will I need to learn? How will I have to change to adopt this idea? Fear of failure contributes to resistance to change. This anxiety typically calls for support and encouragement. Once personal concerns are alleviated, "management concerns" emerge: How will I make this work in my classroom or schedule? It is natural to want a sense of control; teachers are accustomed to being in control of the content and flow of events in their classrooms, and innovations perceived as potentially eroding their control of instruction or their students are likely to bring resistance (Hartzell 1996). Beyond management are "consequence concerns": What difference will this make for my students? Sharing testimony of successful adopters of a technology can help teachers see the potential benefits for their own students. Next, the CBAM model suggests that needs for "collaborating" and "refocusing" emerge; at this point, teachers need to work with someone else to fit the technology precisely to their situation—an opportunity for the library media specialist and teacher(s) to work together. If library media specialists are aware of these concerns when adopting an innovation, they can more easily appreciate the teacher's viewpoint.

Trainer

Trainer is another that role library media specialists play. Experienced teachers and novices alike need to learn about technology applications that can be helpful to them and their students. Gradually, teachers entering the profession should bring increasingly sophisticated technology skills with them, but for a time, some teachers will require training in these basic skills. Yet, how can technology begin to affect student learning until teachers use and value it? Library media specialists who stay at the forefront of technology in their schools can readily offer in-service teacher training. General staff in-service training in basic technology skills is one component of such staff development. Some school districts have established minimum competencies for all teachers and ask library media specialists to assist teachers in attaining those competencies. One example is Lexington, South Carolina, where the district has established "Teacher Technology Competencies" (Lexington County School District One 2004). Their expectations are basic, but call for all teachers to have some fundamental computer skills. Among those skills are the following examples:

- Basics:
  - —Operate computer system and peripherals
  - —Navigate documents
  - —Launch an application and create a file from district-supported software
  - —Manage files
  - —Open and work with more than one application simultaneously
  - —Save files to portable devices as well as the district-provided network folder
- Social, ethical, and human issues
  - —Comply with copyright and educational fair use laws
  - —Abide by the district's Acceptable Use Policy
  - —Practice appropriate netiquette
  - —Apply safe use of the Internet with students
- Technology communications tools
  - —Use a file server
  - —Understand Wide Area Network, access rights, and security passwords
  - —Use e-mail
  - —Use Web browser and search engine
  - —Publish a Web page
- Technology research tools
  - —Use electronic encyclopedias, online library catalog, and databases
  - —Know appropriate bibliographic format for citing electronic sources
- Technology productivity tools
  - —Use word processing
  - —Create and use a spreadsheet
  - —Use a database
  - —Produce electronic slides
  - —Use a digital camera and a scanner
- Technology problem-solving
  - —Determine when technology is useful and select appropriate tools
  - —Use a technology application for problem solving

This district's staff development plan, which includes online tutorials, helps teachers become successful in gaining these minimum competencies, and library media specialists serve as trainers for some applications as well.

A train-the-trainer model is one way library media specialists can achieve staff development efficiently. In the Iowa City (Iowa) Community Schools, each library media specialist trains a cadre of teachers within a school to be trainers and mentors for teachers in using technology. The cadre in elementary schools may include teacher-trainers from each team or grade level, and in a secondary school they represent various departments. The train-the-trainer model facilitates tailoring training to the context where it will be used—an important consideration.

The need for training will continue as software is upgraded and new applications for technology are identified. The library media specialist will always need to be the "crow's nester," knowing what is on the horizon and what is worth considering within the context of the school and its students.

Teacher

Besides training teachers, library media specialists have a substantial role to play in teaching students about information technology. Specific skills to be taught are discussed in Chapter 11. It is important to keep this role in mind, however, and to consider these questions regarding new technology: What implications does this technology have for teaching? How can this technology be integrated with the information skills curriculum? What ethical questions arise?

The library's Web site plays a prominent role in teaching students with and about technology. Increasingly, the library's Web site is a device for delivering information and providing instructional tools and guides. Many well-designed school Web sites can be found online. A few exemplars are:

- New Trier High School Library (Illinois). www.newtrier.k12.il.us/library/. The home page design is clean and attractive with straightforward links to its primary resources: the library catalog, databases, selected Web-based references, audiovisual services, reading and literature guides, class links, and the style manual. The class links provide carefully selected resources for specific courses in the high school. The style manual link includes the high school's own research guide, but also links to a citation-making Web site.

In short, the student researcher is well served at this Web site in a well-conceived, well-organized framework.

- Anderson High School (Indiana). www.ahslibrary.net/. A resource-intense Web site, there are links for students to selected Web resources for subject areas as well as pathfinders for specific courses. A teacher resource link provides ideas for curriculum, lesson plans especially for integrating technology, teaching ideas by subject area, and additional resources to help teachers.
- Birchwood Elementary School, Niskayuna School District (New York). www.nisk.k12.ny.us/birchwood/index.shtml. Web sites for elementary school library media centers require careful attention to age-appropriate content. It is particularly challenging to locate Web resources that are not too text-intensive for younger children. Birchwood links to a number of external resources, and seems to take care to find sites that will pique the curiosity of elementary school children.

As Web sites are designed, the various audiences of the school library media program must be kept in mind. In addition, basic design principles that utilize the screen and technical capabilities of Web page construction are important. Significant features of particular value in school library home pages are portals for various constituents—parents, teachers, students; clean design so that the Web site does not overwhelm the visitor; careful use of color and contrast; organization designed with the end user in mind; regular maintenance to avoid dead links. Keeping at hand a good Web designer guide like Steve Krug's *Don't Make Me Think: A Commonsense Approach to Web Usability* (Krug 2006) makes sense.

Policymaker

Library media specialists provide leadership in developing a wide array of policies that provide access to constitutionally protected material, protect students, support appropriate use of technology, support provisions of copyright law, and offer equitable opportunities for use of technology.

CIPA (the Children's Internet Protection Act) has created a challenging requirement for schools in that the Supreme Court's 2003 decision upheld the constitutionality of the use of Internet filters, yet the court ruled that libraries may override the filter if it is blocking access to constitutionally protected material. How this override provision will be practically carried out is unclear. CIPA compliance is required when using funds from three federal programs: E-rate, ESEA Title II D, and LSTA. A related act known as the Neighborhood Children's Internet Protection Act (NCIPA) sets what is to be included in a school's Internet safety policy. The CIPA legislation has two basic requirements (Boss 2004):

1. A school or library must have filtering technology on all of its computers that provide access to the Internet. Both patron and staff computers are affected. The technology must protect against access to visual depictions described as obscene, child pornography, or harmful to minors in the Act. CIPA does not require the blocking or filtering of text. The law does not address the question of laptops brought in by staff and patrons, but a consensus has emerged that these need not be blocked or filtered.
2. A school or library must have an Internet safety policy and hold a public meeting to review the policy.

Traditionally, selection policies have provided guidelines for what schools buy. However, access to the Web reduces the control educators have. This more open access to information has generated action to protect students and limit access. The best response is informing students of what will constitute acceptable use of network resources in the school. Principles of intellectual freedom challenge the notion of schools censoring what will be accessible to students. Establishing that school-related information searching is the purpose for network resources seems an appropriate approach. Many schools have developed an "Acceptable Use Policy" to define parameters for using network resources. Figure 10.2 contains the text of one acceptable use policy. The policy commits students to appropriate resource utilization.

Copyright of electronic resources is a complex issue. A primary purpose of copyright is to ensure ongoing creation. Those who create must have some means of having their creation protected and, ideally, gaining some compensation for it. This purpose must be balanced against dissemination of ideas necessary for continuing intellectual and creative progress. The fair use doctrine allows certain uses of copyrighted material (for example, criticism, reporting, teaching, and scholarship) that would otherwise be copyright infringements. Four factors determine fair use:

FIGURE 10.2
Student Internet Use Agreement—
Iowa City Community School District

Internet access is coordinated through a complex association of agencies, regional and state networks, and commercial organizations. To ensure smooth operation of the network, end users must adhere to established guidelines regarding proper conduct and efficient, ethical, and legal usage. The signatures at the end of this document are legally binding. Signing this document indicates that you have read and agree to abide by its terms and conditions.

1. **Acceptable Use.** The use of your account must be in support of education and research and consistent with the ICCSD Strategic Plan and educational objectives. Use of other organizations' networks or computing resources must comply with the rules appropriate for those networks. Transmissions that violate any district, state, or U.S. regulations are prohibited. These transmissions include but are not limited to copyrighted material, threatening or obscene material, and material protected by trade secret. Use for commercial activities, product advertisement, or political lobbying is prohibited.

2. **Privileges.** The use of the Internet is a privilege, not a right, and inappropriate use will result in a cancellation of those privileges.

3. **Netiquette.** You are expected to abide by the generally accepted rules of network etiquette. These include but are not limited to the following:
   a. Be polite. Do not be abusive in your messages to others.
   b. Use appropriate language. Do not swear, or use vulgarities or any other inappropriate language.
   c. Do not reveal your own personal address or phone number or those of students or colleagues.
   d. Note that electronic mail is not guaranteed to be private. People who operate the system do have access to all mail. Messages relating to or in support of illegal activities may be reported to authorities.
   e. Do not engage in illegal activities. This includes but is not limited to, threats, harassment, stalking, and fraud.
   f. Do not use the network in such a way that you would disrupt the use of the network by other users.

FIGURE 10.2 (Cont.)

g. Assume that all communications and information accessible via the network are private property.

h. Respect intellectual property of others by crediting sources and respecting all copyright laws. Users will accept the responsibility of keeping copyrighted software from entering the local area network.

4. **No warranties.** ICCSD makes no warranties of any kind, expressed or implied, for the information or services provided through the network. ICCSD will not be responsible for any damages. This could include loss of data or service interruptions.

5. **Security.** Security on any computer system is a high priority, especially when the system involves many users. Do not use another individual's account without written permission from that individual. Attempts to log on as a system operator will result in cancellation of user privileges. Any user identified as a security risk may be denied access to the district's computer resource.

6. **Vandalism.** Vandalism will result in cancellation of privileges. Vandalism is defined as any malicious attempt to harm or destroy hardware, software, or data of another user or any of the above listed agencies or other networks. This includes but is not limited to uploading or creating computer viruses, or breaching security measures.

For students: I understand and will abide by the Internet Use Agreement. I further understand that any violation of the regulations above is unethical and may constitute a criminal offense. Should I commit any violation, my access privileges may be revoked, school disciplinary action may be taken, and/or appropriate legal action may be taken.

For parent or guardian: I have read the Internet Use Agreement. I understand that this access is designed for educational purposes. The ICCSD has taken precautions to eliminate controversial material. However, I recognize it is impossible for the ICCSD to restrict access to all controversial materials and I will not hold the district responsible for materials acquired on the network. Furthermore, I accept full responsibility for supervision when student use is not in a school setting.

- The purpose or character of the use: Use in the regular course of one's educational activities usually satisfies the requirement that the use be for nonprofit educational purposes rather than for commercial purposes.
- The nature of the copyrighted work: The fair use doctrine is more likely to apply to factual works or works intended for the educational market than to fictional or creative expression.
- The amount and substantiality of the portion: Generally, the fair use doctrine requires the least possible use of an original work. The substantiality test means that the essence of the work (for example, the theme of a musical score) is not used.
- The effect upon the potential market: Fair use should not adversely affect the original author's economic opportunities.

Multimedia copyright guidelines were agreed to and released in 1997, the result of lengthy discussion between representatives of copyright holders and educators led by the Consortium of College and University Media Centers (Simpson 1997). While these guidelines are not law, they represent an agreement on limits of use. The guidelines permit students to create multimedia works and retain them in portfolios for job interviews. Teachers may create and use copyrighted material in their multimedia productions in face-to-face instruction and may assign students to look at them independently. Teachers may also display their productions at conferences, when using copyrighted material under the limits set by the guidelines. Quantitative limits set in the guidelines of how much can be used from a copyrighted work include the following:

- Motion media (film/video): up to 10 percent or 3 minutes, whichever is less, of an individual program
- Text: up to 10 percent or 1,000 words, whichever is less; complete short poems; three poems per poet or five poems per anthology
- Music: up to 10 percent but not more than 30 seconds
- Illustrations: no more than 5 images per artist; not more than 10 percent or 16 images from a single collective work

Library media specialists need to encourage students and teachers to be aware of copyright and its protective purposes. Students must learn that access to works on the Web does not automatically mean that these materials can be reproduced and reused without permission or royalty payment; also, some copyrighted works may have been posted without authorization of the copyright holder. According to Fair Use Guidelines for Educational Multimedia, when creating multimedia projects, students should include a statement on the opening screen noting that certain materials are included under the fair use exemption of the copyright law (Consortium of College and University Media Centers 1996). These same guidelines suggest that if student work will be disseminated over the World Wide Web, then it is advisable to obtain permission for all copyrighted portions. Students also need to credit sources for works included in multimedia productions.

Technology has caused dramatic changes in how users deal with copyright. Reproduction has become simpler. Because of personal access to technologies, the locus of infringement has moved from a public activity to private or semiprivate contexts, raising enforcement problems. Perhaps most significantly, technology is creating an expectation for immediate access to information. Advancements in what is possible technologically increase the difficulty in protecting the interests of creators. The library media specialist needs to instill in students an understanding of why copyright exists. Adherence to copyright legislation should be a provision in the acceptable use policy.

Cyber safety is a growing concern and calls for policymaking, staff development, and parent education. Topics of concern include pedophiles, online dating, cyber bullying, confidentiality of personal information, hoaxes, online purchasing, pornography, online gambling, and addiction. The acceptable Internet use policy for the school district should incorporate guidelines that preclude using the Internet for illegal or unsafe activity. The library media specialist can provide leadership in staff development related to cyber safety with in-service sessions and links to resources for teachers. Topics for teachers can include teaching ethical online behavior, staff development, using the news about Internet crime and misbehavior to create teachable moments in the classroom, creating Internet scenarios for classroom instruction, and creating basic awareness of safe practices for self-protection. Parent education is an opportunity for library media specialists to step up and share their expertise. Key issues for parents include (1) acknowledging the value of the Internet as a source of information and entertainment, (2) raising parental awareness of cyber safety issues, and (3) recommending age-appropriate interventions and guidelines for Internet use at home—e.g., setting limits for Internet use or maintaining communication with young people about their Internet use. Online parent resources like "Child Safety on the Information Highway" at www.safekids.com or "Don't Believe the Type" at http://tcs.cybertipline.com are becoming increasingly easy to locate.

EVALUATION

There is no one simple evaluation tool for examining technology's impact. Chapter 13 includes a set of rubrics for use in program evaluation. The dimensions under technology include technology use, integration into the curriculum, the planning process, staff development, budget, hardware, software, and policy. Periodic evaluation of the technology program should consider all of these aspects.

Besides an overall review of the technology program, implementation of each technology application in a school needs to be evaluated. What is the expected impact of the technology? Does it meet the expectation? For example, adding an online database should result in students identifying more information sources of higher quality. An increase in magazine use, or an increase in magazine citations in student work should be evidence of its success. More important, improved content in students' projects because of increased access to quality literature use would be an even better indicator of its success. For each staff development activity, follow-up on how the staff member has implemented newly acquired skills is appropriate. Data to be collected for evaluation can vary; examples include statistical measures (such as circulation), anecdotal reports from teachers or students, sample documents or projects created by students or staff, or time-use analyses. These data need to be collected, analyzed, and shared with decision makers and funders so that technology's impact can be seen. Where results show minimal impact, the reasons need to be investigated. In response to negative findings, some applications will need to be abandoned, some will need to be improved. Potential problems may be a lack of critical mass of equipment to match the need, inadequate staff development, an inappropriate technology application, or software shortcomings. Where results show positive effects, those results need to be shared so that others can see their benefits and so that decision makers can see the outcome of their investment.

ACTION STRATEGIES

Learning and Teaching

- Teach information technologies as part of the information skills curriculum.
- Provide staff development opportunities.
- Participate in staff development planning at the building and/or district level.

Information Access

- Facilitate access to technology for teachers and students by reducing barriers:
  —Consider home checkout.
  —Purchase laptops or handheld devices to expand access to computers (Norris and Soloway 2003).
  —Pursue special teacher computer-purchase plans: some school districts have worked with local vendors to make special purchase plans available, with cooperation from local banks for low-interest loans and the school district business office for payment by payroll deduction.
  —Maintain awareness of the needs of exceptional learners and technologies that can improve their access to information. Web sites such as "Ability Hub" offer information about available technologies (www.abilityhub.com/).
  —Find creative ways to schedule staff in computer facilities so that they are accessible to students when students have time, e.g., lunch hours, before and after school.

Program Management

- Be a leader in the uses of technology for the entire school.
- Read periodicals that help maintain current awareness in the area of technology.
- Establish criteria for technology applications and software selection to promote a commitment to quality in the use of technology.
- Use the automated circulation system to manage hardware inventory.
- Serve as the school's reminder that technology must be used in the context of the instructional program, not as an add-on.

- Provide leadership in developing policies related to acceptable use of resources, cyber safety, copyright, privacy, and intellectual freedom as these relate to technology.
- Collect data to document the uses of technology and its impact; include statistics on use of equipment, facilities, and software, as well as sample documents and projects created by students to demonstrate the qualitative impact technology has had.

SCENARIO FOR DISCUSSION

Hitchcock Elementary School has a high percentage of students from lower socioeconomic backgrounds. A strong before- and after-school program (BASP) meets in the building. It benefits many students, and the new library media specialist wants to do her part to maintain a positive relationship between this program's staff and the school staff. In the past, the BASP has used the computer lab in the library media center after school. School staff members, however, have expressed concerns about problems with the lab use by this group (for example, unsupervised Internet use, inappropriate downloading, changes to the desktop, mistreatment of mouses and keyboards). The library media specialist has initiated a conversation with the BASP director about these concerns, but no changes have been observed. What next?

REFERENCES

Boss, R. (2004). "Meeting CIPA Requirements with Technology." Chicago: Public Library Association. Available: http://www.ala.org/ala/pla/plapubs/technotes/internetfiltering.cfm.

Consortium of College and University Media Centers (1996, March 28). *CCUMC Fair Use Multimedia Guidelines.* Retrieved July 27, 2004, from www.ccumc.org/copyright/mmfairuse.html.

Dodge, B. (1997, May 5). "Some Thoughts about WebQuests," *The WebQuest Page.* Retrieved December 26, 2003, from http://webquest.sdsu.edu/.

Foa, L., R. Schwab, and M. Johnson (1996, May 1). "Upgrading School Technology." *Educational Week 15* (32): 52.

Hall, D. (2006) "Bridging the Gap: Strategies for Creating Equitable Learning Opportunities." *Learning and Leading with Technology 33* (7): 15–18.

Hall, G. E. and S. M. Hord (2001). *Implementing Change: Patterns, Principles, and Potholes.* Boston: Allyn and Bacon.

Hartzell , G. (1996). "Wrestling with Resistance." *Technology Connection 3* (3): 10–12.

Horrigan, J. (2006). "Pew Internet and American Life." Accessed March 22, 2008, at www.pewinternet.org.

Johnson, D. (2003). "Maslow and Motherboards: Taking a Hierarchical View of Technology Planning." *MultiMedia Schools 10* (1): 26–33.

Jukes, I. (1996) "The Essential Steps of Technology Planning." *The School Administrator 53* (4): 8–14.

Kajder, S. and G. Bull (2003). "Scaffolding for Struggling Students: Reading and Writing with Blogs." *Learning & Leading with Technology 31* (2): 32–35.

Kennedy, K. (2003). "Writing with Web Logs." *Teaching & Learning 7* (11): 11–13.

King, R. A. (1987, April). "Rethinking Equity in Computer Access and Use." *Educational Technology 27:* 12–18.

Knezevitch, S. (1984) *Administration of Public Education.* New York: Harper & Row.

Krug, S. (2006). *Don't Make Me Think: A Commonsense Approach to Web Usability.* Berkeley, CA: New Riders.

Lexington County School District One (2004). "Instructional Technology: Teacher Technology Competency Assessment (TTCA)." Lexington, SC: Lexington County School District. Available: www.lexington1.net/technology/?page=instruct/ttca.htm#competencies.

March, T. *Best WebQuests.* Retrieved March 21, 2008, from www.bestwebquests.com.

McKenzie, J. (2002). "Tech Smart: Making Discerning Technology Choices." *Multimedia Schools 9* (2): 34–39.

Miller, L., J. DeJean, and R. Miller (2000). "The Literacy Curriculum and Use of an Integrated Learning System." *Journal of Research in Reading 23* (2): 123–135.

National Council for the Social Studies (1994). *Expectations of Excellence: Curriculum Standards for Social Studies.* Washington, DC: National Council for Social Studies.

National Council of Teachers of Mathematics (1989). *Curriculum and Evaluation Standards for Mathematics.* Reston, VA: National Council of Teachers of Mathematics.

Norris, C. A. and E. M. Soloway (2003). "The Viable Alternative: Handhelds." *School Administrator 60* (4): 26–28.

Oravec, J. (2002). "Bookmarking the World: Weblog Applications in Education." *Journal of Adolescent & Adult Literacy 45* (7): 616–621.

Piller, C. (1992). "Separate Realities." *MacWorld 9* (9): 218–230.

Roschelle, J. M., R. D. Pea, C. M. Hoadley, D. N. Gordin, and B. M. Means (2000). "Changing How and What Children Learn in School with Computer-Based Technology." *Future of Children 10* (2): 76–101.

Sayers, D. (1995). "Educational Equity Issues in an Information Age." *Teachers College Record 96* (4): 767–774.

Selverstone, H. (2003). "Tech for Kids with Disabilities." *School Library Journal 49* (6): 36–37.

Shaw, T. (2003). "Dodging the Bullets: The Danger of Reductionism in PowerPoint Presentations." *MultiMedia Schools* 10 (5): 46–47.

Simpson C. (1997) "How Much, How Many, and When: Copyright and Multimedia." *Technology Connection* 4 (1): 10–12.

Universal Service Administration Company (2008). "Step 2: Develop a Technology Plan." Washington, DC: Universal Service Administration Company. Available: www.universalservice.org/sl/applicants/step02/.

U.S. Department of Commerce (2004). *A Nation Online: Entering the Broadband Age*. Accessed March 21, 2008, at www.ntia.doc.gov/reports/anol/index.html.

Vail, K. (2003, July). "Next Generation Divide." *American School Board Journal* 190 (7): 23–25.

Chapter 11

Information Literacy

This chapter:

- examines information skills to be taught
- considers responsibilities and dispositions as aspects of information literacy
- describes assignments and activities that challenge students to work at high cognitive levels
- proposes self-assessment as a significant component of information literacy
- explores mental models of information process as they influence students' performance
- describes the ways that information technology—especially the library Web site—support the development of information literacy
- compares college standards for information literacy to American Association of School Librarians standards
- identifies action strategies for information skills instruction

There was a time when a canon of information was the central focus of a curriculum. However, the learning environment of the twenty-first century is vastly different and demands a more process-oriented curriculum. Students must leave our schools with skills to access, evaluate, and use information with efficiency and sophistication. The modes for information delivery are changing in scope, media, and organization. New tools for managing and communicating information emerge with ever increasing frequency. Succeeding in an environment of rapid change demands skills to function effectively. In addition, it will be essential that students leave our schools with the appropriate dispositions for continuing to learn—dispositions of curiosity, open-mindedness, investigative enthusiasm. Third, they must accept responsibilities. In eras long past, information belonged to the few, the elite. Now information is broadly accessible, but it must be used in a framework of ethics and responsibility. Finally, the ability to self-assess one's information work is inherent in independent learning. All these dimensions come together to define information literacy, and all must be considered in designing the instruction and the context for information literacy programs.

INFORMATION LITERACY SKILLS AND KNOWLEDGE

The skills and knowledge dimensions of the American Association of School Librarian's (AASL) *Standards for the 21st Century Learner* outline the competencies necessary to engage effectively in the research process. These are delineated in 29 discrete skills summarized in Figure 11.1. For the complete list of skills, see www.ala.org/aasl/standards (American Association of School Librarians 2007).

Examining the research process provides insight into how best to teach these skills. Several models for the research process are available in the literature, including those of Eisenberg and Berkowitz (1990), Pappas and Tepe (Zimmerman, Pappas, and Tepe 2002), Kuhlthau (2004), Stripling (1988), and others. All incorporate these basic elements: posing an information question, locating potential sources of information, examining and selecting relevant information, synthesizing, and communicating results. All models acknowledge that information processing is not a simple linear task, but instead is recursive in nature; as students explore a topic, their research question may change. As they examine information and identify gaps, they return to the task of locating information. A school does well to adopt an information search model to provide a theoretical substructure to its information literacy curriculum. Adoption of an information process model serves to:

- Break down the research process so that educators can design lessons to teach that process
- Provide a common lexicon for communication among library media specialists, teachers, and students
- Guide students in the research process

FIGURE 11.1
Summary of Information Literacy Skills from AASL's
Standards for the 21st Century Learner

Standard	Summary of Skills
Inquire, think critically, and gain knowledge	• Follow an inquiry process • Develop and refine questions • Find, evaluate, and select appropriate sources • Evaluate information • Make sense of information gathered • Make use of technology tools • Collaborate with others to broaden and deepen understanding
Draw conclusions, make informed decisions, apply knowledge to new situations, and create new knowledge	• Apply critical thinking skills to construct new understandings, draw conclusions, and create new knowledge • Analyze and organize knowledge, making use of technology tools • Collaborate with others to exchange ideas
Share knowledge and participate ethically and productively as members of our democratic society	• Use the writing process, visual literacy, and technology tools to express new understandings • Use information and technology ethically and responsibly
Pursue personal and aesthetic growth	• Read, view, and listen for pleasure and personal growth • Respond to creative expression of ideas • Seek information for personal learning • Organize personal knowledge • Use social networks to gather and share information • Use creative forms for expression

- Help educators monitor what is taught and determine how well students are learning (Donham, Bishop, Kuhlthau, and Oberg 2001, p. 16)

Foremost among researchers who have examined information processes is Carol Kuhlthau, who has closely monitored students working in libraries and has analyzed her observations in an effort to understand the process and appreciate students' needs. Only when the information process is explicitly considered can library media specialists know what students need in order to be successful.

After extensive research, Kuhlthau (2004) identified common patterns in students' information work. She describes that process in six stages (initiation, selection, exploration, formulation, collection, and presentation), each with its own typical tasks as well as feelings, as summarized in Figure 11.2. Throughout her work, Kuhlthau emphasizes that movement from task to task is not necessarily a sequential process, but

FIGURE 11.2 Kuhlthau's Stages of the Information Search Process	
Intellectual Tasks	Feelings
Initiation • Recognize the need for information *Selection* • Decide on a topic for study *Exploration* • Search for information to become familiar with the topic *Formulation* • Focus the perspective on the topic	*Anxiety* *Uncertainty* *Optimism* *Confusion* *Frustration* *Doubt* *Clarity* *Interest*
Collection • Gather information	*Confidence*
Presentation • Organize information • Communicate results	*Satisfaction* *Relief* *Disappointment*

rather one of moving forward and backward as the results of one part of the process require the student to clarify or expand on a previous task. Kuhlthau's information process model provides a sound guideline for developing an information skills curriculum.

The library media specialist has several tasks to accomplish in implementing an effective information skills curriculum:

- Identify the strategies to be taught (Figure 11.3 provides a starting point).
- Consult with teachers to determine how to relate the teaching of these information strategies to classroom curriculum.
- Plan with teachers for the development of these skills.
- Teach lessons and mini-lessons on specific strategies in the context of students' assignments; provide aids such as pathfinders, Web bookmarks, annotated bibliographies, or models of bibliographic format.

At initiation, the student must recognize the need for information; this stage is often characterized by some feeling of anxiety. During selection the student must decide on a topic for study. This is a time of intellectual testing to set a direction for exploration, based on assignment requirements, information available, or other criteria. Commonly, this preliminary work gets too little time or attention. At the initiation and selection stages, if students brainstorm with others about possible topics or tap into their own prior knowledge about a topic they can develop a more meaningful research question. Too often, because the topic decision is rushed, students pose a rather low-level, fact-based research question. One activity often overlooked in this pre-search stage is background-building. Students need to spend time just gaining background about a topic before they begin to generate their research question. This may involve watching a video, reading in general reference sources, taking a field trip, or browsing on the World Wide Web. Whatever the medium, the task is to become knowledgeable enough about the topic to be able to pose significant questions. In this way, the research question can go beyond simple fact finding, because students will have already accomplished this during their background building work. Giving more time to the pre-search stage may make the difference between a research question that asks, "What is chemical warfare?" and one that asks, "What are the technical, social, and political barriers to controlling chemical warfare and can they be overcome?"

FIGURE 11.3
Sample Strategies for Information Processing

Determining the information need
- Brainstorming
- Free writing
- KWL (know, want, learn)

Exploring
- Webbing or concept mapping
- Browsing
- Background reading in encyclopedias or general reference or non-fiction materials (for young children, this may mean the teacher or library media specialist will read a book to students)
- Watching a video and extracting information from it

Focusing
- Generating a research question

Accessing information
- Using a prepared pathfinder
- Setting and using bookmarks for Web sites
- Using keyword searching, including Boolean logic
- Using advanced search options
- Using truncation
- Using navigational features of print and electronic resources, e.g., headings, "find" commands, cross references, bookmarks
- Evaluating resources (e.g., appropriateness, availability, relevance, suitability, currency, authority, reliability)

Using and interpreting information
- Using tables, charts, maps within articles
- Using headings and typography to efficiently locate information
- Skimming and scanning
- Note taking
- Downloading
- Identifying patterns or trends
- Developing a thesis statement
- Determining relationships, e.g., comparison/contrast, cause/effect
- Outlining

Communication information
- Creating a product or presentation
- Sharing findings

In exploration, the KWL strategy (derived from the phrases "What I **Know**," "What I **Want** to find out, and "What I **Learned**") encourages pre-search thinking. The library media specialist must encourage teachers to allocate adequate time to this stage. Activities like background reading without detailed note taking (a good time for general reference sources, such as encyclopedias), brainstorming, browsing, and KWL activities will provide the foundation needed for students to enter into the next stages adequately prepared. Browsing is useful to help students move toward a personally interesting focused investigation (Pappas 1995). Students can browse by using an electronic encyclopedia, choosing a broad topic like baseball and examining the article titles that emerge. (One might find a specific personality like George Steinbrenner or Connie Mack of interest, or the National Baseball Hall of Fame, or Gambling in Baseball, or the Negro Baseball Leagues may emerge as potential topics after browsing such a list.) Students can browse topics and subtopics in an online catalog or an electronic database to generate ideas for focusing their topic. Browsing print sources (for example, perusing tables of contents or bookshelves) can help in the exploration stage as well. All this background work is aimed at stimulating curiosity in the student so that an authentic question can emerge. Remember that initiation, selection, and exploration are interwoven and occur recursively as students refine their understanding of the topic.

A particularly crucial aspect of information work is generating a research question that will lead to new understandings and insights— not merely to a summary of what the published literature says. Dahlgren and Öberg (2001) provide a taxonomy of questions that may be useful in encouraging students to generate a promising research query. They suggest five categories of questions:

- *Encyclopedic questions*: These are the general factual questions student might pose that would lead them to write a report analogous to an encyclopedia article. Examples: What is feminism? What is causing global warming? Too often this is the kind of question students imagine as they begin an assignment. This kind of question that will yield a report, but not a research paper; it will yield information but rarely insight.
- *Meaning-oriented*: These questions require students to construct meaning of a concept or phenomenon, often within a given context of time or place or events. Examples: What is the significance

of feminism in the context of today's increasing emphasis on "family values"? What are the international issues of acid rain?

- *Relational*: These questions require the researcher to explore the relationship between or among phenomena. Examples: What factors have influenced women's opportunities from pre–women's movement of the 1960s to today? What is the effect of climate change on polar bears?
- *Value-oriented*: These questions require the researcher to interpret events or phenomena in the context of a value system; this may be religious, political, social, gender, racial, or other social values. Examples: What has been the impact of the women's movement on men's family roles? What is the importance of animals being identified as endangered species?
- *Solution-oriented*: These questions require the researcher to examine a problem and seek solutions to that problem. Example: How can the remaining barriers that continue to impose a glass ceiling for professional women be removed? How can the coral reefs be protected from further loss?

School library media specialists can give students this taxonomy of questions or recommend a specific type of question for a particular assignment. These categories of questions help to articulate the purpose of the research and help the student researcher set a direction for his or her work. Teaching these categories to students can help them understand the nature of inquiry.

Sometimes teachers focus the topic for students because of their course objectives. In those cases, the library media specialist can encourage teachers to develop topics that move students beyond simple answer seeking toward higher cognitive levels. For example, the common animal research assignment that requires students to choose an animal and determine what it eats, where it lives, and who its enemies are offers little challenge beyond transferring information from the source to their own paper. Library media specialists can suggest to teachers that this kind of "research" gives students too little intellectual challenge; instead they can offer an alternative assignment that meets the teacher's content area objective, yet also extends the cognitive level at which students must work. For example, instead of the traditional fact-finding animal report, in one elementary school the teacher asks children to choose an animal about which they will write a story. The story must show the animal behaving in ways that characterize its true nature and the setting must be the natural habitat of the animal. This assignment creates a very different challenge for students from simply reading and reporting. Another example of a more challenging assignment is for students to design a zoo exhibit for the animal studied; their product might be a diorama of the exhibit, accompanied by detailed building instructions. Whether the teacher provides the focus or the student identifies it, the exploration stage is a time of particular uneasiness when the topic is still general—and it may sometimes seem confusing or overwhelming. At this time, the student may be particularly inarticulate about his or her information needs.

In the formulation stage there is a focused perspective on the topic. The student knows what to look for and then needs efficient strategies for searching. Kuhlthau (2004) describes this as "the turning point of the search process," when the focus of the information quest becomes clear. Increased confidence may characterize this stage. Collection involves gathering information; now the student can specify his or her needs more clearly and can better select relevant information. At the collection stage, students need to know how to access information sources. They will appreciate a pathfinder from the library media specialist (see Figure 11.4). Pathfinders give students suggestions of where to look along with helpful hints. Besides aids of this sort, students need search strategies.

Here library media specialists teach lessons on choosing keywords, using Boolean operators and truncation, skimming and scanning in either print or electronic formats, using a database thesaurus and controlled vocabulary, downloading, note taking (using "notepad" features of electronic resources as well as paper-based note taking and highlighting), and organizing findings. Important in this stage is the processing of information. Too often, students move from collecting to reporting too quickly. Activities that stimulate students to process often include substantive conversation with others about their findings or reflection on their findings. For example, after reviewing information they have found, students can be asked to engage in a free writing exercise to describe what information they have discovered that surprised them or what questions have remained unanswered. Or students can be grouped together to share their findings with others and challenged to pose questions to one another to stimulate personal responses to their findings. For young people, it is important to provide intentional opportunities for them to think about their findings, to engage intellectually, and to challenge themselves to think critically. These are not intuitive behaviors for young students, so it is important to structure opportunities for them.

FIGURE 11.4	
Pathfinder Template	
Not every pathfinder will have all categories of sources; the students' assignment will determine which are most appropriate.	
Source	Hints
Reference Collection	Identify briefly titles that would apply to the topic being investigated; give a brief annotation indicating what kind of information would be provided, location, and call number.
General Collection	Suggest keywords or combinations of keywords that might be used in searching for the topic; include useful search hints.
Magazines	Suggest keywords or combinations of keywords that might be used in searching for the topic; include useful search hints. Indicate how to get the document itself once the citation has been found.
Specialized Electronic Resources	Identify any specialized CD-ROM resources that might relate to the topic and suggest keywords or combinations of keywords that might be used in searching for the topic; include useful search hints.
World Wide Web	Give brief instructions on how to approach the topic via an appropriate search engine. See Debbie Abilock's page for assistance in choosing an appropriate engine: www.noodletools.com/debbie/literacies/information/5locate/adviceengine.html
Knowledgeable Individuals	Suggest arranging a time to interview an expert on the topic. Advise students about preparing questions in advance and either taking notes or recording the interview.
Outside Source	Suggest other libraries or resources and give steps for accessing them (Internet access, telephone numbers, addresses, hours, etc.)

Finally, at the presentation stage, students begin to synthesize what they have learned and apply their findings to the research question. As they work in this stage, it is not uncommon for them to return to earlier stages to collect additional information or even adjust their focus. Here students will need skill in creating a product or presentation to communicate what they have discovered. The specific media they use will determine what presentation skills they need. Library media specialists can offer suggestions of various forms for presentation (for example, debates, letters and journals, multimedia projects, speeches, posters, printed brochures, case studies, or video). Whatever the format, the library media program must be ready to provide the resources and guidance for students to create quality products. Suggesting formats for presentation should occur at the beginning of the process, since the chosen format will influence the kinds of material students seek during the collection stage.

Information work takes time. Quality work demands that teachers allocate enough time for students to move methodically through all tasks, to reflect on what they are learning as they collect information, and to create an effective way to present what they have learned. Advocacy for time—particularly time in the library media center—is an important responsibility for the library media specialist. Another critical concern is teaching. The information process grows more complex as more information is available and as search tools expand in number and complexity. It is never appropriate to say that students no longer need direct instruction as well as one-on-one help. At least brief mini-lessons (for example, demonstrating the idiosyncrasies of a specific search tool, introducing specialized print sources on a relevant topic, or presenting ways to determine a resource's authority) will be appropriate throughout high school. Such lessons, at all grade levels, are best taught at the point of need (that is, when students are engaged in a task that will require use of these sources).

INFORMATION LITERACY DISPOSITIONS

AASL's *Standards for the 21st Century Learner* goes beyond skills. Dispositions constitute another dimension of these standards—the attitudes the student brings to the learning process. By underscoring the importance of dispositions, this document acknowledges that information work requires a stance characterized by readiness to learn. We might expect that students who bring the disposition of a learner to the research process will engage more deeply, be more likely to generate authentic questions, and be more likely to arrive at new understandings or insights—the ultimate purpose of the research process.

When Ron Ritchhart (2001) explores an alternative view of intelligence, he synthesizes the dispositions of learning. The library media program contributes toward developing learner dispositions:

- *Be open-minded*. A foundation principle for library collections is the provision of multiple perspectives. A school library media center is an environment that fosters acceptance of diverse viewpoints.
- *Be curious*. By providing an array of resources that can pique interests of students, the school library media center can serve as the stimulus for curiosity. While essential, a collection of current and high-quality resources alone will not be enough to engender curiosity. School library media specialists can serve as mediators between students and the collection. In that role, they can model curiosity as they help students consider what questions they could pursue and guide them to resources in that pursuit.
- *Be metacognitive*. When students engage in any sort of library research, it is important for them to learn to ask and answer the questions "When do I have enough information?" and "Is my information of high enough quality?" and "Am I pursuing a worthwhile question?" "Have I investigated various perspectives?" A disposition of self-assessment can readily be taught in the context of the library media program. For example, at the Web site of the San Benito High School in Hollister, California, Achterman and Campbell (2005) offer a research guide featuring variety of ways to assist student in their research process. A "checkpoint" strategy encourages students to self-assess their research process (Achterman and Campbell 2005).
- *Be strategic*. The library media center provides an excellent laboratory for strategic thinking. To begin, students must have an appropriate mental model of the information search process—they must see it as a process of authentic inquiry, not a process of assembly or transfer of information from a source to their end product. The library media program needs to help students learn to be planful as they pursue interests of their own.

- *Be investigative*. School library media specialists can help students focus their investigations narrowly enough that they can examine questions in depth and arrive at findings and insights of significance. At the Springfield Township High School Virtual Library, Joyce Valenza (accessed 2008) offers a tool called "Question Brainstormer." School library media specialists can use tools like this to help students generate substantive questions that require them to explore and investigate in depth. Too often students are rushed through this early stage of their work out of eagerness to move on to the subsequent stages of their research.
- *Reason.* The library media center offers a reasoning playground. When a teacher librarian and a classroom teacher plan together, they can create meaningful opportunities for students to develop their abilities to reason. The role for the teacher librarian is to challenge students' assumptions, question their assertions, point out fallacious reasoning, and insist on adequate evidence and evaluation of sources of information. Engaging students in conversations—whether these are informal or scheduled—is productive and gratifying.
- *Use evidence*. By searching for information in the library media center, students can develop an appreciation for the use of evidence to support an argument or to make a decision. Teaching students to seek verification and to reconcile differences between sources of information are the kinds of critical thinking skills that can be taught when students are working with information from an array of resources.

INFORMATION LITERACY RESPONSIBILITIES

Citizens in a free society appreciate the opportunities to access information freely. Like any right or freedom, this opportunity is accompanied by responsibilities, and the AASL (2007) *Standards for the 21st Century Learner* explicates responsibilities that emerge from central principles of the information professions:

- respect copyright and intellectual property;
- seek divergent perspectives;
- contribute to the exchange of ideas in a community;

- use information technology responsibly; and
- use valid information and reasoned conclusions.

School library media specialists can model and encourage students in these responsibilities. Indeed, library media specialists can encourage teachers to expect students' adherence to copyright law and guidelines. Instruction can guide students in appropriate attribution and citation, as well as discriminating to select valid information and logical argument. Collections in library media centers should encourage divergent perspectives. Policies support the responsible use of information technology. While these responsibilities may not be as concrete or measurable as information literacy skills, they constitute as important a place in the information literacy program as citizenship responsibilities hold in the government curriculum.

INFORMATION LITERACY SELF-ASSESSMENT STRATEGIES

Lifelong learning is the heart of the mission of information literacy curricula. The long-term intent is for students to leave school knowing how to continue to learn. To achieve independence as a learner, students must develop the ability to self-assess or self-monitor as they are seeking new knowledge. Critical in self-assessment in this context is the ability to monitor one's information seeking. To develop independence, school library media specialists and teachers can work together to develop habits that cause students to reflect on their work. Repeatedly asking students to pose questions of themselves is one way to develop a habit of self-assessment; questions to practice with students to help them develop appropriate self-monitoring habits might include: (1) Do I have enough information to meet my needs? (2) Are the sources of my information authoritative? (3) What other points of view should I consider? (4) Have I critiqued findings to differentiate between fact and opinion and to examine evidence and conclusions for faulty reasoning? (5) Have I accurately represented facts in my expression of findings?

INFORMATION TECHNOLOGY AND INFORMATION SKILLS

Information technologies support all aspects of information literacy. A prominent technology role is access to information—whether the information appears in physical resources within the library media center or is delivered electronically. Clearly, the Internet provides information across such a wide range of authority and quality that demands students learn to be astute consumers of information. To evaluate information critically, students will find the following criteria:

- *Relevance*: Is this source of information directly relevant to my focused topic? If not, how can I change my search strategy to find more relevant sources? Is the information too specific or too general?
- *Suitability*: Does the information make sense to me? Can I easily paraphrase what I am reading?
- *Currency*: How important is copyright date for my topic? Is it likely that newer information would affect accuracy?
- *Authority*: Is the author knowledgeable and the source reputable? Is there an authoritative organization supporting this information? Is there potential for bias?
- *Reliability*: Is the information based on fact or is it simply opinion? Can I find sources to verify information?

Information technology extends beyond sources of information. Other information technologies include tools for:

- *Information management*. Technology can assist students in keeping track of information they have gathered. For example, Del.icio.us (http://del.icio.us/) is a Web-based tool for managing Web site bookmarks, allowing the user to create tags for entries to develop an organization scheme.
- *Concept mapping*. Inspiration is an example of a highly intuitive software application for generating graphic organizers and concept maps to help students organize ideas and information.
- *Collaboration*. Google Docs, for example, affords students the opportunity to share files for group work. Stixy (http://stixy.com/) functions like an online bulletin board, allowing users to post notes, photos, calendars, or lists, just as one would use a bulletin board.
- *Citation*. For citing information sources, students can use an application like the Citation Machine (http://citationmachine.net/). Ready availability of a tool to generate citations following conventions of a specific style affords students a convenient way to be responsible users of information.

- *Communication.* A wide array of tools facilitate communication, including wikis, blogs, and presentation tools like SlideRocket (http://www.sliderocket.com), an open source tool for creating online sharable/portable presentations.

Becoming information literate requires competency in using information technologies for all stages of the information process, not just the search for information.

The library's Web site is a valuable tool for information literacy support for students. Of particular value is the development of unit or assignment pages that provide point-of-need guidance online for students. Tailored to specific assignments, these pages can provide such assistance as (1) exploratory pages to help student gain background as they seem a focus for their research; (2) resource pages that provide information for research—both Web and library resources; (3) links to concept mapping software to develop graphic organizers for projects; (4) links to collaborative software when students are required to do group work; (5) guides for citing resources; (6) templates for products such as pamphlets or newsletters or templates for note taking—in short, the information resources for all stages of work required to meet the teacher's assignment expectations. These assignment or unit pages can be posted to the library Web site for 24/7 access by students.

ASSIGNMENTS FOR TEACHING INFORMATION LITERACY

A key element for students to develop information literacy is the type of assignments teachers give them. Assignments can demand nothing more than fact finding, or they can demand analyzing and applying information. Library media specialists need to consult with teachers about the nature of their expectations and keep at the forefront the cognitive demands of assignments. Indeed, Gordon (1999) admonishes educators when she asserts, "Implicit in the typical report assignment is an underestimation of what students can do, sending a clear message to them that they are passive recipients of information" (Gordon 1999, paragraph 5).

Consider the Civil War as an example. Middle school students can be assigned to write a report about a specific battle or a specific personality from the Civil War era. Either of these tasks can quickly become an encyclopedia article in style and content. More important, the process for completing the assignment can simply be transfer of information from a print or electronic source to the student's paper or screen. Alternatives to this assignment can challenge students to do more than rewrite the information they find. Some possibilities include:

- *Letter*: Read about the conditions of soldiers during the Civil War. Write a letter as a Civil War soldier describing life in a camp, or a battle, or a prison camp, or as an African American soldier in the Colored Troops. Criteria for evaluation will include how specific and accurate your details are and how authentic the writing is to the personality you created.
- *Editorial*: Read about slavery from both the Union and Confederate points of view. Write two newspaper editorials, one for a Southern newspaper and one from the Abolitionist viewpoint. Criteria for evaluation will include how specific and accurate the supporting details are and how effectively you develop the argument for each side.
- *News story:* Read about a specific battle. Write a newspaper article or create a television news report about it as if you were an on-the-scene reporter. Criteria for evaluation will include how specific and accurate the details of your report are, how well you adapt the facts to a news-reporting style, and how well you match your reporting to the target audience (North or South).

What attributes of these assignment options set them apart from simply reporting the facts? First, these students are seeking information to apply to a larger problem—a letter, an editorial, a news story. They will not simply rewrite the facts, but rather they will incorporate the facts into meaningful communication. The first attribute is that the assignment goes beyond fact finding. These assignments demand careful attention as students select information; relevance is crucial because they are not merely reporting a list of facts, but must choose information that exactly suits the end product—the news story, the editorial, or the letter.

Learning to select information that really matters makes students critical information consumers. These students have considerable latitude in choosing what they will do. Choice often results in increased commitment—and ultimately engagement in the task at hand. Not only do students have choice among the three options, but also within each option there is still opportunity for the student to focus the task. So, the second attribute is student choice. Because these options all take a human-interest approach to the assignment, students are not writing and thinking in the manner of a textbook writer. This human-interest approach makes history become a story of real life, not merely a collection of facts. The third attribute, then, is that these assignments offer students a sense of personal interest. Elliot Eisner (1994) has observed that affective and cognitive processes are interdependent strands that lead to a unified understanding. By incorporating a personal, affective aspect to the assignments, these two domains interact, creating a more meaningful experience for students. Finally, these options are open-ended. There is not one right answer for any of the assignments; rather, there are criteria for determining quality. Questions demand analysis, synthesis, and evaluation. This moves the information process well beyond fact finding and incorporates creativity. Students can gather their information in a variety of ways—reading historical fiction, watching a video, or examining primary and secondary sources. The presentation of their findings invites creativity—a likely way to engender interest in the task. In short, four factors should characterize assignments: assignments should go beyond fact-finding, they should offer students choices, they should provide a sense of personal interest, and they should be open-ended (that is, seeking answers should require thinking at higher levels of Bloom's Taxonomy), requiring application, analysis, synthesis, and/or evaluation (Bloom 1956).

Technology has increased the options for the final product that students create as a result of their research. While such options offer better opportunities to meet the various learning styles of students, an important caveat is to avoid overemphasizing the form or product to the detriment of the research process itself. Besides rewarding the attractive end product, one must also acknowledge such aspects of the assignment as framing the research questions, selecting and integrating authoritative information sources, and choosing the most appropriate mode of presentation for a given audience (Callison 2000).

Designing challenging and engaging assignments can make it possible to teach an information skills curriculum that ensures that students are effective users of information and ideas. Without intellectually demanding and personally engaging assignments, students will not move beyond the lowest levels of information work (such as the mechanics of information searching and fact collection). While there are times when locating a single fact solves an information need, it remains important that students develop skill in critically assessing information and in applying it to more complex problems as well.

MENTAL MODELS OF INFORMATION PROCESSING

A mental model is an intellectual framework created by integrating what one knows or has experienced within a given concept or activity. Learning is the process of putting new information into an existing context, framework, or mental model by reorganizing ideas (assimilating) or by reconstructing an old framework until the new ideas or experiences fit (accommodating) and a new mental model emerges (Stripling 1995). Pitts (1995) investigated the effects of mental models on students' information work. Her findings offer insight into students' library use. She classified learners, based on their mental models of information processing, as either novices or experts. She describes the novice as one who has little prior knowledge in the topic; his or her personal understandings are fragmentary, based on a limited perspective. The expert has more connected understandings and a more global perspective. Pitts (1995) examined the work of a high school class where the assignment was to create a video documentary on a topic related to marine biology. For this project, there was no direct instruction related to either the process or the content of the assignment. Pitts's assessment of the students' information processing was that they used very little information from libraries and that they were often unsuccessful in their search for information. She identified several reasons for their unsuccessful use of libraries. First, she suggested that students had incomplete subject-matter mental models and that this led to incomplete identification of their information needs. Her analysis of student searching revealed that most searches were very general in nature. In addition, she observed that students had limited mental models for information-seeking and information-use systems (that is, they had no mental framework for the organization of information in libraries). They nearly always looked in only one place, the electronic catalog. If they did go beyond the electronic catalog, they showed little understanding of which other resources would be likely to provide what they sought. A final problem she identified was the inaccurate mental models that adults had of the students' subject expertise or of their information skills. Adults tended to provide locational advice only, assuming either that the student could identify the most appropriate resource or overestimating the student's expertise in the topic.

Pitts's (1995) findings have some powerful implications for schools. First, library media specialists can help students develop a framework for information processing by giving students a model of the information process and the tasks associated with it as well as a framework for the organization of information. Models like this can help students approach information work with an appropriate frame of reference. In addition, teachers can provide students with a framework for the discipline within which they are working. Finally, adult support throughout the information process—not just at the beginning or at the end—will help students maintain a sense of direction about their work. Various strategies can guide students during the process (Stripling 1995):

- *Encapsulation*: At the end of a work session, students briefly record their understanding of the information they gathered.
- *Research log*: Students maintain a research log throughout the process, recording each day what they have learned, what questions they now have, and what they need to do next.
- *Conferencing*: Library media specialists and teachers confer with individuals or small groups at the end of a work session to discuss their reflections on their work so far.
- *Reflection:* Teachers and library media specialists pose questions for students to ask themselves along the way: Am I really interested in this topic? Do my research questions go beyond collecting information to interpreting or evaluating? Do I have support for all of my conclusions?
- *Rubrics:* Library media specialists and teachers develop rubrics for the information-processing tasks and refer students to them during each work session.

Overall, the instructional goals of the library media program link directly to the work students bring to the library media center from the classroom. Collaboration between the library media specialist and the teacher is essential to achieve library media instructional goals. Library media specialists bring to that collaboration a set of processes and strategies for students to learn while the classroom teacher has instructional goals related to the content area. By creating challenging assignments and providing instruction, support, and adequate time, this team can provide students with the tools needed to be critical information consumers.

INFORMATION LITERACY STANDARDS FOR HIGHER EDUCATION

The Association of College and Research Libraries (2000) has followed the example of the American Association of School Librarians by developing and publishing standards for information literacy to be met by college students. These standards are:

- Determine the extent of information needed.
- Access the needed information effectively and efficiently.
- Evaluate information and its sources critically.
- Incorporate selected information into one's knowledge base.
- Use information effectively to accomplish a specific purpose.
- Understand the economic, legal, and social issues surrounding the use of information, and access and use information ethically and legally.

High school library media specialists may find it particularly appropriate to share these standards with students and teachers to lend credence to the importance of these competencies for their college-bound students. The common concern for information literacy from kindergarten through college should encourage school librarians and librarians in higher education to communicate with one another.

Library media specialists in high schools may want to give their students a preview of the kind of assignments they are likely to encounter in college courses. Gordon (2002) suggests that students can anticipate the expectations that await them if they view examples of college assignments. It might be appropriate for high school librarians working with college-bound seniors to introduce students to examples of collegiate syllabi for institutions where local students tend to go. Assignments are often available on Web-published college syllabi. Examination of assignments may raise such questions as the following:

- Do students appreciate fully the difference between the Internet and subscription databases?
- Do they apply criteria to assess the authority of information from Web sites?
- Does the term "peer-reviewed" have meaning for them?
- Do they know how to integrate cited information into their own writing?

- Do they know what a hypothesis is? A thesis?
- Can they formulate a researchable question?
- Do they know how to analyze and present data?

While academic librarians are increasing their efforts at promoting and teaching information literacy, college faculty are still likely to make assumptions about the abilities of their incoming students—they may or may not anticipate the need to arrange for library instruction for their students. As students arrive at college doors, they will benefit from having had a sound foundation for information literacy in high school. Since college librarians are not consistently brought into the classroom as students engage in research, one aspect of that foundation is knowing the value of seeking help from a librarian.

BEYOND REPORTING

Students need to develop information literacy competency, not only to be successful in school but also to be capable lifelong learners. An intended outcome for learning is the discovery of new insights as one processes information, by interpreting and integrating findings from a variety of sources, including one's prior knowledge. An insight is a clear and deep understanding of a complicated problem, phenomenon, or situation. An important word in this definition is the word "deep." Deep understanding calls for students to "own" the ideas and information they take from their information searching. Wiggins and McTighe (1998) use the term "enduring understanding" to describe the important "big ideas" that educators want students to retain after they have forgotten many of the details (p. 10). Students must have engaged themselves fully enough in their research to be conversant with the ideas and facts they have uncovered, and be able to apply those ideas to situations, problems, or decisions. This is the way adult information seekers work— they seek and gather information in order to apply it to situations or problems. These big ideas often result from insightful thinking.

For students to develop the ability to arrive at insights in a way that will be useful for lifelong learning, schools must provide experiences that challenge students not only to collect and report information but also to go beyond reporting to analyze, evaluate, and synthesize. Five aspects of an information literacy program can take students beyond collecting information to reaching insight. These aspects are summarized in Figure 11.5.

When teachers direct the questions that students will explore, students take on the role of answer seeker. They look for information to respond to the teacher's query—period. However, they do not own the inquiry, nor are they likely to reflect on their findings in ways that will lead them to insights. When students can direct their own inquiry, they are likely to be more vested in their quest, and subsequently more likely to push themselves to ask the "so what?" questions that can lead them to insight. Similarly, when students respond to fact-oriented assignments, they are again collecting information to respond to largely closed-ended rather than open-ended queries. To the extent that assignments expect students to respond at the conceptual rather than the factual level or to address issues rather than information, students are more likely to arrive at insights. Authenticity is an important attribute for tasks that will engage students and lead them to be reflective and insightful. When students perceive that their work is aimed only at communicating with the teacher or pleasing the teacher, the likelihood of that engagement diminishes. When students can identify a more authentic audience for their work, it takes on new meaning and sets them up for thinking

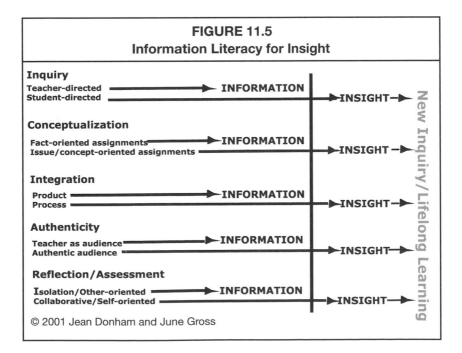

FIGURE 11.5
Information Literacy for Insight

© 2001 Jean Donham and June Gross

insightfully. Finally, when the assessment of student work is collabora-tive, students feel more ownership in the results. If at the end of an in-formation quest, students turn in a product to the teacher and the teacher does nothing more than return it to them with a score or grade, the work is merely an exercise. When teacher and students review the work to-gether, the discussion is likely to bring students to a level of insight that might have been lost without the interchange of a collaborative assess-ment process. The teacher can pose questions that give students oppor-tunities to think reflectively and to consider what they might pursue further to enhance the work they have just completed.

These five attributes of information literacy programs—student-di-rected inquiry, concept-oriented assignments, integration of the research process (as well as the end product) into the instruction, an authentic audience, and collaborative assessment—increase the meaningfulness of the research experience for students and help them develop the intel-lectual processes that will make them insightful information consumers as adults.

ACTION STRATEGIES

Learning and Teaching

- Review models of information processing skills and identify or adapt one to be the basis for your information skills curriculum.
- Review assignments with teachers to assess what level of Bloom's Taxonomy is necessary to accomplish the tasks.
- Collaborate with faculty to design Web pages to support assign-ments or units that serve as specific resource guides for all aspects of information literacy related to a specific unit or assignment.
- Teach specific strategies or skills in information processing when classes come to the library media center. This is appropriate at all grade levels. Often there is an assumption that high school stu-dents do not need instruction; however, as their assignments grow more complex, their search skills need to become more sophisti-cated—strategies they learned in middle school may not help them at this level.

Information Access

- Work with classroom teachers to develop a map or matrix to organize where information process skills fit for each grade level. Skills can be matched to specific classroom assignments. Be certain that specific skills appear more than once so that students apply them in different contexts and at increasing levels of sophistication.

Program Management

- Reach out to community college, college, or university librarians to exchange teaching strategies and resources for meeting the information literacy standards.
- Analyze how best to schedule library media center access so that students have access to expertise and resources when they have the need. This is likely to include not only school-day times, but also before and after school.

SCENARIO FOR DISCUSSION

The Big Hollow Elementary School library media program has made great strides in teaching to the AASL's *Standards for the 21st Century Learner.* The library media specialist is particularly proud of efforts toward Standard 4, which calls for learners to "use skills, resources, and tools to pursue personal and aesthetic growth."

Instruction has focused on helping students learn to select and locate books for independent reading that are appropriate in level of difficulty and interest. The population of Big Hollow Elementary has changed somewhat in the past five years. More students are coming from homes characterized as lower socioeconomic status (more free-lunch families, more transient families, more single-parent families). Throughout the school there is widespread concern about developing both skills and habits as readers. A fourth-grade teacher attends the state's International Reading Association (IRA) meeting where she visits with some teachers from Des Moines. As they commiserate with her about Big Hollow Elementary's demographics, they tell her about their reading initiative: the Accelerated Reader (AR) program. She returns to Big Hollow Elementary full of enthusiasm because of the excellent results experienced in Des Moines. At the next faculty meeting, she brings up the AR program and suggests that the upper unit (grades four through six) adopt it. She suggests that the library put all the AR books in a special section. The library media specialist is concerned about how this change will affect her instruction for Standards 4 and 5. What should the library media specialist do?

REFERENCES

Achterman, D. and R. Campbell (2005). "Check Point 1." Hollister, CA: San Benito High School District. Available: www.sbhsd.k12.ca.us/sbhslib/research/11checkpt1.htm.

American Association of School Librarians (2007). *Standards for the 21st Century Learner*. Chicago: American Library Association. Available: www.ala.org/aasl/standards.

Association of College and Research Libraries (2000). *Information Literacy Competency Standards for Higher Education*. Chicago: American Library Association.

Bloom, B. S. (1956). *Taxonomy of Educational Objectives: The Classification of Educational Goals*. New York: Longmans.

Callison, D. (2000). "Assignment." *School Library Media Activities Monthly* 17 (1): 39–43.

Dahlgren, A. and G. Öberg (2001). "Questioning to Learn and Learning to Question: Structure and Function of Problem-Based Learning Scenarios in Environmental Science Education." *Higher Education* 41 (3): 263–282.

Donham, J., K. Bishop, C. C. Kuhlthau, and D. Oberg (2001). *Inquiry-Based Learning: Lessons from Library Power*. Worthington, OH: Linworth Publishing.

Eisenberg M. B. and R. E. Berkowitz (1990). *Information Problem-Solving: The Big Six Skills Approach to Library and Information Skills Instruction*. Norwood, NJ: Ablex.

Eisner E. (1994). *Cognition and Curriculum Reconsidered*. New York: Teachers College Press.

Gordon, C. (1999). "Students as Authentic Researchers: A New Prescription for the High School Research Assignment." *School Library Media Research Online* 2. Available: www.pla.org/ala/aasl/aaslpubsandjournals/slmrb/slmrcontents/volume21999/vol2gordon.cfm.

Gordon, C. (2002). "A Room with a View: Looking at School Library Instruction from a Higher Education Perspective." *Knowledge Quest* 30 (4): 16–21.

Kuhlthau, C. C. (2004). *Seeking Meaning: A Process Approach to Library and Information Services*. Westport, CT: Libraries Unlimited.

Pappas M. (1995). "Information Skills for Electronic Resources." *School Library Media Activities Monthly* 11 (8): 39–40.

Pitts, J. M., edited by J. H. McGregor and B. Stripling (1995). "Mental Models of Information: the 1993–94 AASL/Highsmith Research Award Study." *School Library Media Quarterly* 23 (3): 177–184.

Ritchhart, R. (2001). From IQ to IC: A Dispositional View of Intelligence. *Roeper Review 23* (3): 143–150.

Stripling, B. K. (1988). *Brainstorms and Blueprints: Teaching Library Research as a Thinking Process.* Engelwood, CO: Libraries Unlimited.

Stripling, B. (1995). "Learning-Centered Libraries: Implications from Research." *School Library Media Quarterly 23* (3): 163–170.

Valenza, J. "Question Brainstormer." Retrieved April 10, 2008, from www.sdst.org/shs/library/questbrain.html.

Wiggins, G. and J. McTighe (1998). *Understanding by Design.* Alexandria, VA: Association for Supervision and Curriculum Development.

Zimmerman, M., M. Pappas, and A. Tepe (2002). "Pappas and Tepe's Pathways to Knowledge Model." *School Library Media Activities Monthly 19* (3): 24–27.

Chapter 12

Assessment of Student Work

This chapter:

- defines assessment and clarifies its purposes
- applies performance assessment to information literacy
- discusses rubrics and the benefits they offer in defining and assessing the information literacy curriculum
- discusses how rubrics help define the information literacy curriculum
- discusses self-assessment
- describes other assessment tools
- identifies action strategies for assessment

ASSESSMENT DEFINED

Assessment and evaluation are easily confused. Examining their etymologies helps to clarify the critical differences between them. Assess(us) is the past participle of the Latin verb *assidere*; the prefix is the preposition *ad* meaning near and the root is the verb *sidere* meaning to sit. The visual image of assessment then is sitting down beside someone. It is a cooperative task. It has come to mean careful examination based on the close observation that comes from sitting together. Evaluation, on the other hand, carries a connotation of judgment, as it means ascribing value to something. Its visual image is of something being done to, rather than done with, someone. Nothing in the etymology of evaluation suggests that it is a collaborative process. Its meaning suggests that its primary purpose is to make a judgment about the value of something.

Assessment serves four purposes, two for teachers and two for students (Donham 1998). These purposes are illustrated in Figure 12.1. First, and perhaps most important for the students, assessment is a means of monitoring progress in order to improve their performance. The basic question is, "How is the student progressing on the established criteria?" When students know how their work compares to a standard, they can then set appropriate goals for themselves and they can focus on what needs to be improved. Assessment contributes to student evaluation—its second purpose. Periodically, at conference time, report card time, or the end of a school year, student progress is synthesized into a grade or a narrative. The purpose is to recognize accomplishment; this feedback also informs the student. Assessment provides information for the teacher as well, and thus contributes to instructional decisions. The basic question is, "How can I use the evidence provided by assessment to improve my teaching so that these students do better?" Finally, the results of assessment can inform the teacher about how well the instructional program is working and what needs to be modified or improved so that future students will perform more successfully. In summary, assessment serves these four purposes. Two are formative (that is, they inform the teaching and learning process and suggest ways to correct the course), and two are summative (they indicate the degree of success in both learning and teaching):

Formative:
- Improve student achievement by giving feedback on student progress
- Improve the instruction by giving feedback on its effectiveness

Summative:
- Evaluate student performance
- Redesign instructional programs by monitoring student achievement

Assessment is not a single event, but rather a part of the learning experience. Some would say that observers should not be able to distinguish immediately between teaching and assessing because the two processes are so integrated.

Authentic assessment suggests that assessments should engage stu-

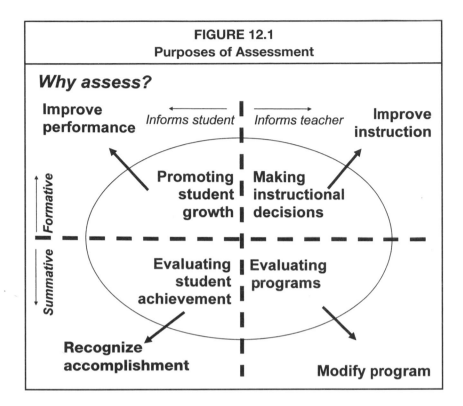

FIGURE 12.1
Purposes of Assessment

Why assess?

Improve performance — *Informs student* | *Informs teacher* — Improve instruction

Formative | Summative

Promoting student growth | Making instructional decisions

Evaluating student achievement | Evaluating programs

Recognize accomplishment

Modify program

dents in applying knowledge and skills in the same way they are used in the real world. When a student researches a local solid-waste disposal problem and proposes real solutions by writing a letter or making a presentation to the city council, there is an opportunity for authentic assessment. While there is clearly value in authenticity, it is not crucial to the task of using assessment as a teaching strategy.

Performance assessment refers to students demonstrating their understanding with a tangible product or observable performance. Performance assessments have been a part of the arts programs for years as solo festivals, concerts, and plays; the assessments occur when the judge applies criteria for good performance to review a student's performance. Performance assessments are, of course, a part of athletics when the coach reviews the players' performance in the game. In these situations, what the students do demonstrates what the students have learned.

To envision assessment in the library media center is to see the library media specialist moving among students as they work, sitting down beside individual students, and comparing their processes and products to a set of expectations. Sometimes a checklist encapsulates the expectations. If a fourth-grade student is researching an animal for life science, the checklist might be a list of the possible sources: an encyclopedia, the online catalog, selected Web sites, for example.

Sometimes a simple checklist may not be adequate to help students be successful; in those cases they may need a more descriptive guide that defines for them what excellence looks like, both in process and in product. One form for such a descriptive guide is a rubric.

RUBRICS

Rubric derives from the Latin adjective for "red." Rubrics in a liturgical context are directions for conduct of religious services, written in prayer books in red ink. In education, rubrics are intended to direct students. An assessment rubric is an ordered set of criteria that clearly describes for the student and the teacher what the range of acceptable and unacceptable performance looks like. This definition has several key words, the first of which is "ordered." A rubric sets out to describe a continuum of performance from expert to novice. Descriptions occur at points along the continuum, and these descriptions are ordered from high to low. Each rubric describes levels or degrees of performance. "Criteria" is the next key word in the definition. A rubric provides criteria for excellence in performance in order to compare a student's performance to criteria, not to the performance of other students. The next key word is "describes," for a rubric creates a visual image of what excellent performance looks like as well as a description of the degrees of excellence along the continuum. Descriptive language is a key to the rubric; for example, we can say that a student took notes effectively. This does not describe the note taking; it labels it as effective. In a well-written rubric we might instead say, "A student paraphrased the essential relevant information from the source." Or, to describe delivery in public speaking, one might state: "The rate of speaking and the voice quality varied so that major points were emphasized." Such a description creates a mental model for the student because the performance is described, not merely labeled as "Rate: Excellent."

The range of performance portrayed by a rubric is another key idea in the definition. A rubric describes a range of performance descriptions so that students can gauge themselves along a performance continuum.

Most often, students improve their performance incrementally. Descriptions of stages toward excellence guide such incremental growth. Usually rubrics have three or four levels of performance. Sometimes each of these levels of performance is assigned a score (4 = highest level, 1 = lowest level). Using words, rather than numbers, to identify those levels of performance helps give students a sense of the progressive nature of rubrics. For example: novice, apprentice, competent, expert.

These identifiers suggest that the student can progress toward the expert level, whereas assigning numbers suggests that they have attained a score that has permanence. The words "novice" and "apprentice" suggest that the student is on the path toward expert, but simply isn't there yet. Such language connotes more confidence in the student's ability to succeed than does the label of a 0 or F. Rubrics should offer a guide so that students know what it takes to be an expert. Reducing the rubric's information to a number nullifies it.

Another way to envision a rubric is to consider it a road map to success for students. Of course, road maps are examined at the beginning of trips, and so with rubrics, it is crucial that they be given to students in advance and then used throughout the task to gauge where students are and to nudge them up the performance continuum. When, for example, students "get lost" in a project spending too much time creating a beautiful cover, the rubric is useful to refocus their efforts. Students can know how to be successful when they know at the outset what success looks like.

Creating Rubrics

Rubrics represent a carefully articulated description of performance across a continuum of quality or sophistication—a continuum from novice to exemplary performance. To create such a description requires careful analysis of the desired performance. One of the best ways to generate rubrics is to begin by observing closely a range of products or performances. If the topic is to generate a thesis statement for a research paper—a part of the task-definition phase of research—then observing products created by a variety of students will yield a range of quality and sophistication. Consider, for example, a high school research paper assignment for which students write a thesis statement that represents a position taken on an issue. The following examples might emerge from students:

- This paper is about chemical warfare.
- There are many examples of the use of chemical warfare in twentieth-century history.
- Control of chemical warfare is complex.
- It is impossible to control chemical warfare today because of scientific, tactical, and political factors.

By analyzing examples of students' thesis statements, the critical attributes of an exemplary statement become clearer: the thesis statement reveals what the student believes about a topic. The thesis statement includes the topic and a debatable position statement. Three critical attributes are sought: statement of topic, statement of position, and the potential for the position to be argued.

The rubric becomes a description of progress toward a goal like the one displayed in Figure 12.2, where the three critical attributes or dimensions of writing a thesis statement are identified and then levels of performance about each are described.

Steps for writing a rubric include:

- Identifying attributes or dimensions of good performance: for example, in writing a rubric about note taking, the first question is, "What are the critical attributes or dimensions of good note taking? What should students be conscious of?" Answers might be use of paraphrasing, organization, and relevance.
- Organizing the attributes into a range of descriptions: the range most often will have three or four distinct points.
- Describing performances of graduated degrees of quality or sophistication: one way is to envision good performance and poor performance; another is to observe performance or examine products.

In the example in Figure 12.2, the attributes of a thesis statement were statement of the topic, statement of a position, and the potential for the position to be argued. In the note-taking example, one asks, "What does exemplary use of paraphrasing look like? What does poor use of paraphrasing look like?" At the end of such a process, a rubric provides both teacher and student with descriptions of what good performances look like—a veritable road map for students to follow. It describes where they are in their performance toward improved quality. Students then

FIGURE 12.2 Writing the Thesis Statement			
	Expert	**Apprentice**	**Novice**
Topic statement	The topic is narrowly focused.	The topic is too broad.	The topic is unclear.
Arguable position	The position taken in the statement could have a counter statement written in opposition to it.	The position taken is a statement of opinion but there is little or no argument against it.	The position taken is a statement of fact.
Position statement	The thesis statement includes a statement of opinion about the topic.	The thesis statement describes the topic, but takes no stand.	The thesis statement is too general.

have information about what they need to do to improve and the teacher has information about what students need to learn. A useful rubric contains ordered positions along a continuum. Whether the continuum includes three levels of performance or four, it is important that each level be distinguishable from those on either side of it. The Rubricator, a computer software program, assists in development of rubrics. Information is available at www.rubrics.com.

A common error in designing rubrics is to describe performance with such adverbs as "frequently," "sometimes," or "always." Rubrics are more often used to assess a single performance. These modifiers suggest that the assessment relates to multiple performances; as such, they are appropriate for summative, but not formative, evaluation. Other adverbs to avoid are words like "effectively," "well," and "poorly." These words judge, but don't describe. Be aware that rubrics are intended to describe quality, not quantity, in performance. Avoid developing rubrics where better performance is only more—for example, instead of "uses more library resources," the description should be "uses more relevant resources" (Wiggins 1996). One way to guide development of rubrics is to use one. Figure 12.3 provides a rubric for rubrics. Using it as a guide can help to improve the quality of rubric writing.

FIGURE 12.3 Assessment of a Rubric	
Content	
Expert	The rubric identifies the critical attributes or dimensions of performance
Proficient	The rubric addresses a skill or concept, but not that which is crucial to success
Apprentice	The focus of the rubric is fuzzy
Novice	The rubric focuses attention on an inappropriate attribute or dimension
Language	
Expert	The rubric describes in specific language various qualities of performance, including action verbs that help direct a quality performance
Proficient	The rubric is descriptive, but lacks specificity so that it is difficult to improve performance
Apprentice	The rubric uses comparative language to describe levels of quality, e.g., *more, less, sometimes,* shifting the emphasis from quality to quantity
Novice	The rubric uses evaluative language to rate various qualities of performance, e.g., *good, excellent, exemplary,* with a risk of subjectivity or personal judgment rather than qualitative description
Range	
Expert	The "cut point" between *acceptable* and *not acceptable* is clear, and the "top point" describes excellence
Proficient	The "cut point" between *acceptable* and *not acceptable* is clear, but the top point only describes acceptable performance, not excellence
Apprentice	Marginal performances could arbitrarily land on either side of the "cut point"
Novice	The student cannot tell where the "cut point" is

Types of Rubrics

Rubrics can be written in at least two forms: holistic and analytic. A holistic rubric has only one general descriptor for performance as a whole, whereas an analytic rubric includes multiple rubrics organized according to the dimensions of the performance being assessed. To assess a student's writing by listing the qualities that make it excellent, good, or "not there yet" is to look at it holistically. This type of rubric is most useful at the summative stages of assessment when overall performance is at issue. For a pianist, the feedback at the end of the recital may indeed be a holistic view, interrelating tone, expression, time, posture, and volume into a complex rubric called "style." An advantage of analytic rubrics is that they describe the discrete elements or dimensions of the performance separately. In Figure 12.4, the rubric breaks down the criteria for note taking so that attention focuses on use of relevance, comprehension, and organization—three specific qualities of concern in the note-taking process.

Rubrics for Assessing Student Performance in the Library Media Program

Rubrics offer a structure for assessing student performance both at the formative and summative stages. In the formative stages, using rubrics is a teaching strategy. An example of such a rubric is the one used for the U.S. history assignment described in the shaded box (see also Figure 12.5). Note that this rubric does not address every aspect of work that students will do to accomplish this task. Instead, the focus of the rubric is those aspects that the teacher and library media specialist feel deserve emphasis. This rubric guides individual students—as well as teachers and library media specialists—as students work. Traditionally, a library media specialist might approach a table where students are working and say, "How are you doing?" and receive a response, "Okay," and then proceed to the next table. Instead, using a rubric to guide assessment as teaching, the library media specialist would say, "Let's look at how you are doing. Look at the rubric for note taking and look at your notes. Where are you on the continuum?" Assessing where students are while the work is in progress may result in a correction of their information seeking that will save them time and improve the quality of their process and their end product. That is, after all, the intention of assessment. Likewise, as students go through other aspects of the assignment, other dimensions of the rubric can be applied.

FIGURE 12.4 Rubric: Note Taking	
Relevance	
Expert	The information in my notes relates directly to my research question(s).
Proficient	My notes have some information related to my topic but not to my research question(s).
Novice	The information in my notes does not answer my research question and doesn't quite fit my topic.
Comprehension	
Expert	I understand everything I have written in my notes; there are no words that I cannot define.
Proficient	There are words or ideas in my notes that I cannot explain myself, but I can get more information so that they make sense to me.
Novice	My notes are copied from my sources and I don't really understand them.
Organization	
Expert	My notes are grouped according to each research question or subtopic.
Proficient	My notes are grouped according to the source where I found the information.
Apprentice	My notes are organized according to when I took them.
Novice	My notes are written as one list of information.

To use a rubric, first analyze the assignment to determine what process skills will be most important for the task. Generate rubrics for those process skills in language appropriate to the level of the students. Distribute the rubrics when the assignment is given to the students. Depending on the age and the style of interaction, the rubrics can be reviewed as a group, or students can be encouraged to review them individually. Most important, as students work on the assignment they should have the rubrics in front of them. As teachers and library media

---

ENHANCEMENT IN ACTION:
EVALUATING AN ASSIGNMENT

Assume that high school students have this assignment: Choose a decade in twentieth-century U.S. history and create an iMovie about it. Your production should create an informative portrayal of the decade, including economic, political, and social aspects. You should develop essential questions about each aspect (that is, questions that lead to the essence of the decade); your questions should help frame your inquiry so that you effectively portray the character of the decade. You may need to do some background reading before you develop your questions. The information included in your product should represent responses to those essential questions. The presentation should exhibit effective use of iMovie's capabilities. For an assignment such as this one, the teacher and library media specialist might work together to develop a rubric-based assessment instrument to distribute to students at the beginning of the project. An important benefit of using rubrics in teaching information literacy in the library media program is that rubrics describe processes in ways that are meaningful to classroom teachers as well. They become a way of defining the information literacy curriculum not only for the library media specialist and the students, but also for the teachers.

---

specialists approach students to monitor progress, the rubrics are the focus of conversation:

> Let's take a look at your notes so far: our rubric for organization suggests that notes be organized in some way. Which statement from the rubric describes how your notes are organized? What does the description at the next level up say? Can you follow that method and get your notes organized in that way? I think it will make the writing a lot easier.

There are some crucial conditions for using rubrics as a teaching strategy. First, students must have the rubrics before they begin the task. The idea is for these to be guidelines to success, so they are not kept

Figure 12.5
Rubric: Studying a Decade

Task definition: Formulating a focus

Expert	I chose information that answered my essential questions about the decade
Proficient	I chose information that was relevant to the portrayal of the decade
Apprentice	I chose information that presented interesting information about the decade
Novice	I chose information that was irrelevant, trivial or unimportant to a portrayal of the decade

Organizing information from multiple sources

Expert	I organized information according to topics and subtopics which I created
Proficient	I based my organization on one source and added some details or examples from other sources
Apprentice	I summarized information from individual sources but did not relate information from one source to that from another
Novice	I used a single source for the majority of information

Producing a multimedia presentation Organization/design of stack

Expert	I created a logical organization for the stack and the cards
Proficient	I planned the cards within stack clearly, but the navigation between cards is sometimes confusing
Apprentice	I used some elements in ways that distract from the message, e.g., too many different transitions, too many or too few graphics, irrelevant sounds or graphics
Novice	My screens are too cluttered or too sparse so that the user might have difficulty navigating

Multimedia elements

Expert	My stack has text elements that are balanced with relevant visual or sound elements
Proficient	My stack has text, graphics and sound, but they are not always directly related to one another
Apprentice	My stack has too little text or too few graphics
Novice	My stack is all text or all graphics

secret until grading time. Students receive the rubrics at the time of the assignment. Second, one-time use of a rubric is unproductive. If the intent is to improve performance, then students need multiple opportunities to continue their progress. If students receive a rubric for note taking along with an assignment, it should reappear with future assignments so that students gain from their previous learning and extend their skills.

In addition to being a guide to student work, rubrics can be useful for end-of-term or end-of-unit assessment of student work. At the summative stage, assessment becomes evaluation, yet the rubric format can still be useful for describing to students the qualities of their work and the qualities of exemplary work so that they can see how close or far they are from it. A grade labels the student achievement, but provides no specific information to help the student improve performance; it says "good enough" or "not good enough" when what is needed is a specific description of what "good enough" represents and how to reach that level. In this way, the rubric justifies the grade. While students may argue with a B, it is harder to argue when the B is supported by a rubric that describes the student's performance. Finally, using rubrics in summative assessment can contribute to consistency; the more defined the criteria are, the easier it becomes to apply the criteria evenly among students and across performances.

Rubrics for Defining the Information Literacy Curriculum

While rubrics are usually considered important for the part they play in student assessment, they also have an important place in helping to define curriculum. Writing a rubric requires examination of the outcome—a performance or a product—to determine what constitutes success. By such examination, one can analyze what students need to learn to be successful. The rubric essentially provides a structure for task analysis. For example, when introducing children to keyword searching, one task is to identify the keywords or key concepts in the research question. Observing students doing keyword searches will quickly reveal what they need to know. How often do students make one attempt in an online catalog, find nothing based on that keyword search, and declare that the library has nothing on their topic? A rubric for keyword searching may help analyze what must be taught and may guide students beyond that first trial-and-error effort. The task at hand is to examine the question and determine what to enter as a keyword. If the question is, "What are the beliefs about life after death among Confucians?" the novice is likely to look for a word in the question and type that word in as the keyword. However, Confucians may not result in any hits. Students should progress from finding a keyword in the research question toward identifying a list of relevant terms. The more sophisticated searcher distinguishes between broader and narrower terms, identifies synonyms, and uses truncation. The rubric format helps clarify what may need explicit teaching—in this case, creating a list of alternative terms to search and using truncation.

Whenever students begin an assignment, an assessment instrument is created, and rubrics for relevant information literacy skills are incorporated drawing from the curriculum guide. A K–12 information literacy curriculum might have a list of information skills and accompanying rubrics for the following aspects of information work:

Defining the task:
- Selecting a topic
- Formulating a focus
- Generating an open-ended research question

Seeking information:
- Identifying keywords and key concepts in the research question
- Filtering sources (e.g., distinguishing fact and fiction, skimming, scanning, and applying such criteria as relevancy, authority, accuracy, and currency)

Accessing information:
- Searching by keyword (e.g., using synonyms, truncation, Boolean logic)
- Using an index

Using information:
- Taking notes
- Interviewing
- Paraphrasing

Synthesizing information:
- Organizing information from multiple sources
- Eetermining patterns or trends
- Creating comparisons or contrasts
- Relating information to the research focus

Presenting information:
- Presenting information in an appropriate format (e.g., written report, multimedia presentation, speech, exhibit)
- Creating a bibliography

To translate this curriculum guide into practice, the rubrics will be a reference for the development of specific assessment instruments for student assignments. The rubric in Figure 12.5 would derive from rubrics in such a curriculum guide. Activities would include:

- Having brief, informal conferences with students as they proceed through an assignment and/or as they complete it: this is what the library media specialist does when classes are working in the center.
- Communicating with teachers about student progress: this is probably the brief conversation at the end of the period, or the quick note written on the rubric sheet and sent to the teacher via e-mail or in-house mail. The message is, "Here is where I see students having difficulty, based on specific rubric points."
- Reviewing curriculum and lessons based on student assessment: this is the evaluation of how things went, ideally carried out with the teacher at the end of the unit, with notes for change in what is done for next time.

These activities relate to the purposes of assessment: give feedback to students to improve their progress and to acknowledge quality, inform teachers so that necessary teaching occurs to improve student performance, and inform teachers about the instructional program so that it can be revised to better meet student needs.

Some people find rubrics too constraining for the student or the teacher. At times it seems that the highest level of performance is not high enough for some students. One solution to this concern is to add a column at the high end of the rubric, label it "Legendary Performance" and ask the student to write the description of what he or she does beyond the highest level (Lockett 1996). Another concern is that students may work hard at moving to the next level of performance on a rubric but narrowly fail to reach it. Again, the consultant suggests simply adding "skinny columns," that is, lines drawn between labeled points where a performance falls between levels to indicate to a student that he or she is progressing and is almost there.

A final concern about rubrics is that library media specialists might focus too tightly on details and lose sight of information literacy overall. Writing a rubric about finding the index at the back of a book is probably unnecessary. More important is using the index to access the needed information, so the rubrics for index use need to be related to choosing search terms, using pagination information, and using cross references and subheadings. The point is that, like task analysis, rubric development can be taken to an unnecessary extreme. Consider the processes that need teaching, reteaching, and repeated practice, and consider the processes for which there are levels of sophistication in performance—these are the processes for which rubrics can be helpful. A key question may be: Is this something one either does or does not do, or are there degrees of quality? If there are degrees of quality, then a rubric may help students move to higher and higher levels of performance.

Rubrics for Self-Assessment

The AASL *Standards for the 21st Century Learner* include self-assessment strategies aimed at engaging students in reflection of their own learning. Self-assessment is indeed an important skill for lifelong learning. The key question for self-assessment is whether students can examine their own performances and use their own observations to identify how to improve. Golfers continue to improve their game by analyzing and monitoring their own performance; when a ball falls short of its intended mark, they review the backswing, the follow-through, the stance, to determine what went wrong and how to improve. This same self-assessment behavior will help students continue to use information resources effectively as adults.

When an online search about buying a used car yields too much information, searchers can consider what they have done wrong and how best to correct it. The key for the golfer or the consumer is to have criteria on which to base their self-assessment. What should the good swing look like? How can the keyword search be modified?

By developing in students the practice of assessing their work, the focus shifts from the task to the process. The use of specific criteria for assessing the process gives students practice at thinking about criteria for high-quality performance. While journaling and other narrative techniques are also useful self-assessment strategies, they lack the structure of criteria-based assessment found in rubrics. Without some guidance, students may not focus their assessment on what matters most in a process. Developing skill in applying criteria can help students look at their own work more objectively. When rubrics are provided, students should be encouraged to identify which level best describes their own work before a teacher identifies where they are on the continuum. If the teacher disagrees, then a conversation can begin to justify that position. However, if independence is a goal, then the first attempt at assessment needs to belong to the learner. For rubrics to work effectively for self-assessment, there are three critical attributes:

- Explicit criteria: The criteria provide enough description that students know what successful performance looks like.
- Structured feedback: The criteria are ordered to show students how close to excellence they are. Feedback is not hit-or-miss; all students get feedback.
- Front-end information: The criteria for success are provided as the student begins the work, not at the end.

OTHER ASSESSMENT TOOLS

Performance assessment is based on observable activity. Clearly, some intellectual processes cannot be observed directly. One can only make assumptions about those processes based on outward actions by the student. This means that some thought processes will be difficult to assess based on performance or product. Other assessment strategies are available to help students analyze their work. Two examples of narrative methods are the I-Search process, advocated by Macrorie (1988) and described by Joyce and Tallman (1996), and student research journaling.

In the I-Search process, students report their research as a personal narrative describing not only what information they have found but also how they found it. By explicitly describing their process, students reveal their research strategies and they self-assess what worked and what didn't. When their self-assessment is coupled with feedback from teachers, students gain further insight into what works and what doesn't.

Student journaling is another strategy for student's self-analysis in the research process. Here, students step back from their work, periodically, and make journal entries about their progress, their frustrations, and their successes. Careful monitoring of the journal can inform teachers of what students need to learn. In a case study, Tallman (1998) found that through journaling, educators can challenge students to reexamine

---

ENHANCEMENT IN ACTION: RUBRIC FOR SELF-ASSESSMENT

Just as teaching information literacy is a challenge faced in both K–12 settings and in higher education, so is the matter of assessment of student performance a topic of interest in both venues. For example, Dr. Shannon Whalen at Adelphi University developed a rubric for her Contemporary Health Issues course. The rubric described the desired end product, and Whalen provided it with her course syllabus so that students knew from the beginning what her expectations were. Figure 12.6 shows an adaptation of one of her rubrics that can serve as a model for research papers not only at the collegiate level, but in high school as well. Three dimensions set this rubric apart from many others: transfer of knowledge, depth of discussion, and cohesion. These three dimensions, however, focus attention on the essence of the research paper—the learning that students demonstrate as a result of their information searching. By providing this rubric at the beginning of her course, Whalen enables students to monitor or assess their work as they proceed. Clear descriptions of her expectations help students know how to judge their own work.

---

their research and engage in higher-order thinking as they make judgments about their work.

Harada (2002) describes the use of journaling with elementary school students and emphasizes that in the early stages of journaling, students made a high proportion of nonspecific comments. Later, however, their entries exhibited more specificity and depth as they described both their activities and their feelings at each stage of research. Such progress speaks for the power of journaling as a strategy for helping students gain understanding of the research process. Harada and Yoshina (2005) emphasize that qualitative assessment tools like logs or journals provide deep insights into the development of information literacy. Furthermore, these reflective assessment exercises provide opportunities for metacognition so that students can begin to understand their own processes.

Both journaling and the I-Search process engage students and teachers in a dialogue about their information work. These strategies are open-ended; therefore they demand some sophistication about the informa-

FIGURE 12.6
Research Paper Rubric

Criterion	Expert	Proficient	Apprentice	Novice
Transfer of Knowledge	The paper demonstrates that the writer fully understands and has applied concepts learned in class.	The paper demonstrates that the writer, for the most part, understands and has applied class concepts.	The paper demonstrates that the author, to a limited extent, understands and has applied class concepts.	The paper does not include any concepts from class.
Depth of discussion	In-depth support and elaboration in all sections of the paper.	In-depth support and elaboration in most sections of the paper.	Brief discussion in all the sections of the paper or in-depth discussion in only a few sections.	Brief discussion and/or limited support for ideas
Cohesion	Ties together information from all sources. Paper flows from one issue to the next. Author's writing demonstrates understanding of the relationship among material obtained from all sources.	For the most part, ties together information from varied sources. Paper flows, but with some disjointedness. Author's writing demonstrates understanding of the relationship among material obtained from all sources.	Sometimes ties together information from all sources. Paper does not flow—lacks transitions.	Does not tie together information. Paper does not flow and appears created from disparate sources. Writing does not explain relationships between "chunks" of information.

FIGURE 12.6 (Cont.)

Criterion	Expert	Proficient	Apprentice	Novice
Spelling and Grammar	No spelling and/or grammar mistakes.	Minimal spelling and/or grammar mistakes.	Noticeable spelling and grammar mistakes.	Unacceptable number of spelling/grammar mistakes.
Sources	More than 7 current relevant, authoritative sources. All Web sites used are credible (e.g., from .org or .gov). Special interests acknowledged as such. Includes at least one general background source.	Cites 7 current relevant sources. Popular magazine articles used are acknowledged as such. All Web sites are credible, i.e., from professional or government organizations.	Fewer than 7 current sources; some sources are from popular publications, but not noted as such. Not all Web sites utilized are credible and/or sources are not current.	Fewer than 7 current sources. Popular sources not distinguished from scholarly. Web sites utilized lack authority.
Bibliography Page	The bibliography page reflects all sources utilized in text. No mistakes in format. Additional sources utilized are attached.	The bibliography page reflects sources utilized and discussed in text.	The bibliography page is incomplete.	Does not include bibliography page.
Appearance	Clean, neat and well organized. Standard format and font. Looks professional.	Clean, neat and well organized. Standard font and format.	Different fonts and formats. Somewhat "tattered and tired" looking.	Unorganized, varied fonts, unprofessional looking.

Source: Adapted from Shannon Whalen, Adelphi University (*http://academics.adelphi.edu/edu/hpe/healthstudies/whalen*).

tion processes in students, or they require some specific prompting from teachers to focus students' remarks. Prompts like "Write an entry in your journal today about organizing your note cards" or "Write an entry in your journal today about the problems with searching in the database" may give students enough of a cue to reflect on what they know about the process and may reveal enough about their frustrations to cue the library media specialist about what they need to learn. Such information becomes a point of departure for either individual conversation with students or mini-lessons for whole classes to facilitate their progress. A comprehensive program will use various assessment strategies over time, based at least in part on the sophistication of students' understanding, their propensity for writing, the preferences of the teacher, and the character of the information work.

A checklist may be an appropriate assessment instrument, if, for example, one needs to determine whether a student accomplished a step in a process or included a component of a product. For a travel brochure completed for a geography class, the checklist might include:

Content:
- Name of country
- Weather
- Sightseeing
- Transportation

Presentation:
- Graphics: picture or map
- Readable text

End-of-unit interviews are another way to assess students. Brief, structured interviews can provide insight into what the students know about the information literacy. The teacher and library media specialist can share responsibility for brief interviews with students at the end of a unit involving intensive research. Questions to ask might be:

Tell me about your project.

How do you find your information?

Did you ever get stuck? What did you do then? What was hard about doing research?

How could you tell when you were done with research? How could you tell if you did a good job?

What did you learn from this research?

Collecting responses to these interview questions, the teacher and library media specialist can then use the data to determine what worked and what did not work in the instruction. In addition, they can identify what needs to be taught next. Finally, they can use the data to judge students' knowledge of research strategies.

TESTS

Conventional testing is a long-standing method for collecting data about what students know and can do. An important consideration in the testing environment is the purpose of assessment: is the purpose of the test to provide evidence of achievement for accountability or to improve learning? If the purpose is to improve learning, then, according to Stiggins (2002), the following strategies should accompany the testing environment:

- Inform students of the achievement targets.
- Develop classroom assessments that provide students with interim descriptive feedback (in contrast to judgmental or evaluative feedback) about their progress.
- Adjust instruction based on the results of classroom assessments.
- Engage students in frequent self-assessment, with standards held constant so that students can observe their own growth.

A testing program benefits from the complementary use of a variety of classroom assessments (such as rubrics, conferences, journals). Stiggins (2002) cites a study by Black and William who conclude that classroom formative assessment increased students' scores on standardized achievement tests; in fact, they reported effect sizes of one-half to a full standard deviation. Stiggins explains that increases of this magnitude can yield gains of 30 percentile points, two grade-equivalents, or 100 points on the SAT scale. Such results suggest that if the purpose of testing is to document student achievement for accountability, then schools do well to make use of other assessment strategies between high-stakes tests since such interim assessment appears to produce better standardized test performance.

In testing, it is crucial to ensure that the test measures what matters. Most schools use standardized tests, and many standardized tests have a subtest on using reference sources. Library media specialists do well to examine tests to know what is being asked. With this knowledge, they can either ensure that they are teaching the skills tested, or they can point out to administrators, teachers, and parents the discrepancy between what is being taught and what is being tested. Boolean logic, truncation, and evaluating sources are all topics emphasized in information literacy curricula; standardized tests currently place heavy emphasis on identifying keywords, alphabetizing, and choosing an appropriate resource for a given question. Testing services struggle to update their tests to match existing curricula; however, they tend to be conservative out of concern for equity across the nation. They worry that schools without computerized catalogs and online databases will be at a disadvantage when test items assume familiarity with resources not available to them. These are times to monitor test items carefully to observe how well the test items reflect the local resources and local teaching.

Specialized standardized tests of information literacy offer opportunities to measure student performance and document the effectiveness of the library's instructional program. Educational Testing Service (http://www.ets.org) has developed the iSkills test appropriate for high school seniors as they transition to college. The test includes items on students' abilities to define an information need, search for information from the Internet and databases, evaluate information for authority, organize their findings, draw conclusions, synthesize information, and communicate findings. Normed results provide the opportunity to compare students' scores with those of students nationally. The very availability of such a test signals a new acknowledgement of the importance of information literacy. While the ETS test has a price tag, the TRAILS (Tools for Real-Time Information Literacy Skills) online test is free (www.trails-9.org). This test, developed at Kent State with funding from the Institute for Library and Information Literacy Education, assesses student knowledge in how to develop a topic, identify potential sources, apply search strategies, evaluate sources and make ethical decisions about information use. Individual and class scores give an indication of areas of strengths and weaknesses in students' information literacy. Results can be shared with school administrators to demonstrate program effectiveness and can be shared with classroom teachers to identify areas for improvement. Overall, these tests are particularly valuable for measuring program effectiveness.

One side effect of the higher levels of accountability prompted by the No Child Left Behind legislation is less attention to process learning (such as information literacy) and more emphasis on content learning (such as reading, mathematics, or science). Such a resurgence of emphasis on content draws resources away from library media programs unless their impact on students' overall achievement can be conveyed. In such an environment, the need for advocating for the importance of information literacy as a life skill—as well as the impact of the library media program on reading and other disciplines—cannot be understated. Library media specialists will want to share results of research that shows relationships between effective library media programs and student achievement as measured by these achievement tests. Keith Curry Lance is associated with substantial efforts at measuring the relationship between library media programs and achievement in states across the nation. Results from eighteen state studies reveal findings similar to the following Wisconsin findings, which are summarized: "The Wisconsin Study demonstrated higher reading and language arts test performance across all grade/school levels in schools with higher levels of library media program staffing" (Lance 2006). While socioeconomic factors are significant influences on student performance, the Wisconsin study notes that library media program variables (staffing, time spent working with students, and resources) explained 3.4 percent of the variance in reading test performance at the elementary level. At the middle/junior high school level they explained 9.2 percent of the variance in reading performance. At the high school level, they explained 7.9 percent of the reading variance and an even higher percent, 19.0 percent, of the language arts variance. At the high school level the impact of a robust library media program was almost 7 percentage points greater than the impact of the socioeconomic variables.

The library media program can naively be considered a fringe or nonessential program under pressure for test performance in content areas, especially in settings where test results are highly valued. Therefore, these findings need to be shared with administrators and teachers to support continued library media program development.

Where testing is highly valued, development of tests that examine the processes taught in library media programs may be appropriate. Again, with the notion of "what matters gets measured," library media specialists may need to board the testing bandwagon if information literacy is to remain an important part of the instructional program in the school. If information literacy testing is to be a method of data collection in the milieu of assessment locally, it is important to construct tests that measure what matters with validity and reliability. Creating objective multiple-choice tests is difficult when one is testing process and not content learning. Library media specialists who are designing tests may want to consider writing "search story problems" (Fagan 2002). These test items are essentially information searching situations, where students are given an information problem and asked to describe the terms they would use to search a database. The library media specialist must then write the best search string and then consider what would be an acceptable answer and what would be unacceptable. Similarly, search story problems might aim for students' understanding of other aspects of the information search process, such as defining a topic by posing a question like:

> Your teacher has assigned you to write a paper about some aspect of nuclear energy. List the first five steps you will take to do this assignment.

Again, this exercise requires the library media specialist to create a list of the critical attributes to be found in the response, for example, background building ("read an encyclopedia article about nuclear energy to get some background") and focusing the topic ("narrow my topic to one aspect of nuclear energy").

As long as tests are important, the library media specialist needs to join the conversation by:

- Studying the items on standardized tests to determine how well they fit what is being taught.
- Informing colleagues about research that shows relationships between library media programs and test performance.
- Encouraging the use of alternative methods of formative assessment (such as rubrics, checklists, journals) to improve learning and teaching; emphasize the positive effect that such assessments have on summative assessment in testing.
- Considering tests as one assessment method for demonstrating students' learning in the information literacy curriculum and designing tests that assess students' research process knowledge and skill when accountability is an issue.

CONCLUSION

Rubrics, I-Searching, journaling, checklists, interviews, and tests are all assessment strategies that provide information for student evaluation and that will help educators know what needs to be taught in the future. While the summative measurement of student achievement is important for accountability, formative assessment that informs teaching and gives students a description of their performance and the target performance should continue to be an important part of the assessment activities. In fact, research supports implementing both testing and alternative forms of assessment for the best student achievement. Matching the assessment tool to the purpose calls for judgment by the library media specialist and the teacher. It is important to have a variety of assessment techniques in one's repertoire.

ACTION STRATEGIES

Learning and Teaching

- Observe students doing information work. As you observe, think in terms of the range of performance sophistication or quality, and structure your thoughts around a rubric. What do you see when a novice approaches an electronic encyclopedia to develop a search strategy? What do you see when an expert begins the same task?
- Consider a variety of methods for assessment (including checklists, interviews, rubrics, journaling, testing, and the I-Search process) in order to focus students' attention on the research process, not just the end product.
- Examine standardized test items to determine what is being asked of students. Provide information to teachers to help them interpret the match between items on the test and what is being taught.

Program Management

- Review the information literacy curriculum and identify the major skills to be taught. For those skills, develop rubrics to describe levels of performance. Share rubrics with teachers to extend their vision of information literacy.
- To help align what happens in the library media center with classroom practices, discuss with teachers the assessment methods they use.
- Share results of studies that show the relationship between student performances on standardized tests and school library media

programs. Advocate for continued support for library media programs in highly test-conscious environments.

SCENARIO FOR DISCUSSION

In Hill City, national standardized tests are administered in October each year to students in grades three through six. The library media specialist works with students—sometimes in collaboration with teachers, sometimes in isolation—throughout the year to help students learn strategies for locating and using information. However, he has been unable to persuade teachers to integrate synthesis and evaluation of information into classroom work on a regular basis. The results of the current year's standardized tests have arrived in the building. The principal makes it a point to come to the library media center and comment on how well the students performed on the test regarding use of sources of information. The library media specialist, however, regards the test as invalid for testing what he is teaching because many items on the test do not reflect the modern school library media online information resources. How should he respond to the principal?

REFERENCES

Donham, J. (1998). *Assessment of Information Processes & Products*. Professional Development Series. McHenry, IL: Follett Software Company.

Fagan, J. C. (2002). "Selecting Test Item Types to Evaluate Library Skills." *Research Strategies 18* (2): 121–132.

Harada, V. (2002). "Personalizing the Information Search Process: A Case Study of Journal Writing with Elementary-Age Students." *School Library Media Research Online 5*. Retrieved July 28, 2004, from www.ala.org/ala/aasl/aaslpubsandjournals/slmrb/slmrcontents/volume52002/harada.htm.

Harada, V and J. Yoshina (2005). *Assessing Learning: Librarians and Teachers as Partners*. Westport, CT: Libraries Unlimited.

Joyce, M. and J. I. Tallman (1996). *Making the Writing and Research Connection with the I-Search Process: A How-To-Do-It Manual for Teachers and School Librarians*. New York: Neal-Schuman.

Lance, K. C. (2006). "School Impact Studies." *Library Research Services*. Retrieved March 18, 2008, from www.lrs.org/impact.php.

Lockett, N. (1996, January 11–12). *Rubrics in the Classroom*. Iowa Success Network Workshop, Cedar Rapids, Iowa. Handout.

Macrorie, K. (1988). *The I-Search Process*. Portsmouth, NH: Heinemann Publishing.

Stiggins, R. J. (2002, June) "Assessment Crisis: The Absence of Assessment for Learning." *Phi Delta Kappan 83* (10): 758–765.

Tallman, J. (1998). "I-Search: An Inquiry-Based, Student-Centered, Research and Writing Process." *Knowledge Quest 27* (1): 20–27.

Wiggins, G. (1996, December/January). "Practicing What We Preach in Designing Authentic Assessments." *Educational Leadership 54* (4): 18–25.

Chapter 13

Program Evaluation

This chapter:

- discusses the importance and purpose of program evaluation
- discusses the importance of data collection and analysis
- examines benchmarking as a comparative strategy for evaluating and improving programs
- suggests rubrics for assessment of program components
- identifies action strategies for program evaluation

PURPOSE OF EVALUATION

"What gets measured gets done" is a familiar maxim among educators. It speaks to the importance of program evaluation. Measuring a program against a set of standards has been one typical approach to program evaluation. Accrediting organizations have set and applied standards, such as number of volumes in the collection, full-time equivalency of professional staff, number of hours of support staff, seating capacity of facility, and number of computer work stations available. These standards can be classified as inputs, that is, these are resources the program needs to function. Other measures include circulation counts, attendance counts, or number of classes scheduled into the facility; these measures can be classified as outputs, that is, they measure use of the resources. However, while these measures have value, a program is more than simple inputs and outputs. Critical questions about a library media program might be:

- What difference does it make to student learning?
- What contributions does it make toward increasing teacher effectiveness?
- What difference does it make to the intellectual atmosphere of the school?
- In what ways does it improve the coordination across grade levels and disciplines?
- How consistent is the program with its instructional context?

In many states, mandates for library media programs are either nonexistent or so very general that schools within one jurisdiction could have either a minimal program or an exemplary program and meet the guidelines. This open-endedness, especially in times of diminishing resources, can render the library media program vulnerable, and thus calls for careful accountability to decision makers.

One reason for caring about evaluation is the fact that administrators typically have little formal training about school library media programs during their career preparation (Barron 1987). Consequently, they need to learn about the library media program's potential. Everhart (2003) reports that principals typically use informal methods for evaluating library media programs. Her research suggests that principals use the following criteria to determine that a library media program is functioning appropriately:

- Active engagement of students
- Interaction between library media specialists and teachers/students
- An inviting environment
- A variety of materials
- Relevant displays
- Books being borrowed by students

While these may be useful indicators, they are at risk of being subjective and capricious. A variety of circumstances could cause these informal observations to convey an inaccurate interpretation of the effectiveness of the library media program. At the very least, such observations should be accompanied by a more definitive method of evaluation in order for the results of the evaluation to be used appropriately in decision making.

Evaluation can serve multiple purposes. Like assessment, evaluation can inform the library media specialist about what is working well and what needs improvement. Program evaluation can also inform administrators about what the program should be doing for students and teachers as well as diagnose what steps may be needed to bring the program closer to its potential. In *Operating and Evaluating School Library Media Programs: A Handbook for Administrators and Librarians,* Yesner and Jay (1997) provide a topical approach for looking at positive and negative features of programs and provide strategies for improvement. Evaluation can give parents, students, and teachers insight into ways to make better use of the library media program by making them more aware of its services.

Evaluating the library media program presents these challenges:

- Confusing evaluation of the library media specialist with evaluation of the program
- Addressing the administrators' lack of knowledge about what the program should be or do
- Applying performance standards that are primarily inputs (for example, number of volumes, computers, seats, and staff members)
- Applying performance standards that are primarily numeric outputs (for example, circulation, number of classes met) without connection to the impact they have on student learning

Three steps are important in the process of evaluating a library media program:

- *Collect and analyze data* to indicate what is happening in the library media center.
- *Involve the stakeholders* (administrators, teachers, parents, community members, and students) so that they can learn as much as possible about the program's potential.
- *Educate the stakeholders* by giving them descriptive language about the program; one possible tool for this step is a rubric.

DATA COLLECTION AND ANALYSIS

Evidence-based practice is a term common in the medical and social work literature. It suggests that problem solving and decision making are based on analysis of available evidence. Similarly data-driven or data-based decision making is the catch phrase in management literature. In either venue, the underlying premise is that we cannot make sound decisions without collecting and analyzing data. In the library media program, data can demonstrate not only that there is use of the library media center and its resources, but also the quality of that use. Typical data collected for library media program evaluation include circulation figures, class visits to the library, head counts, classes taught, collection size, Web page hits, database searches, and age of physical collection. All of these are useful measures. However, if the library media program is focusing on collaboration with faculty as well as emphasizing the program's role in the teaching and learning process, then additional aspects of the program should be tracked and reported.

An example of such data tracking is shown in Figure 13.1. Library media specialist Denise Rehmke designed this *FileMaker Pro* database to record activity in her program. Each record in the database represents a classroom unit where the library program has played a role. The fields included track several important program dimensions. The Benchmarks field lists the benchmarks that appear in the district's information literacy curriculum. By recording for each unit which benchmarks were emphasized, the library media specialist can review the year to see how much attention each benchmark is getting by grade level or by department. Similarly, the Research Tools field provides evidence for teaching the research tools available in this center. Over time, the library media specialist can determine if some have not been taught at all; this observation will call into question whether there have been missed opportunities or whether these tools are not useful in the school's curriculum. This database tracks both the information literacy and the literature models from the district's library media curriculum. Some units will focus on literature, and others may focus on the information literacy model. The Level of Involvement field tracks the degree to which the library media specialist is involved in the unit. Data collected here over the year can provide good information to the principal about how the library media specialist is involved in teaching and learning. Tracking departments can help identify those that are and are not making use of the library media program. Collecting and analyzing these data gives the library media specialist real information about the program so that he or she can answer such questions as the following:

- Which information skills are *not* being taught?
- Which departments are not making use of the library media center?

FIGURE 13.1
Database Record

FileMaker Pro - [District InfoLit 03-04]

File Edit View Insert Format Records Scripts Window Help

Information Literacy Curriculum 2003-2004 — Iowa City Community School District

Librarian: Rehmke
School: West
Teacher: Van Zante
Department: Language Arts
Course: English 10H

Unit: Author Research

Grade: ☐ K ☐ 1 ☐ 2 ☐ 3 ☐ 4 ☐ 5 ☐ 6 ☐ 7 ☐ 8 ☐ 9 ☒ 10 ☐ 11 ☐ 12

Start Date: 8-27-2003   **Length:** 4 days

Sections: 2   **Students:** 59

Level of Involvement: ☐ plan ☒ gather resources ☒ prepare materials ☒ teach lesson ☒ assist students ☐ assess

Unit Overview: Students work in groups to research 1 of 10 selected authors: biography, representative works, major influences/autobiographical aspects, reputation and criticism, stylistic...

End Product: Class presentation

Standards:
- ☐ 1 access info
- ☒ 2 evaluate info
- ☒ 3 use info
- ☐ 4 appreciate lit
- ☐ 5 personal

Info Lit Model:
- ☒ 1 define info need
- ☒ 2 locate info
- ☒ 3 process info
- ☒ 4 create/communicate
- ☐ 5 assess

Literature Model:
- ☐ nonfiction   ☐ character
- ☐ biography   ☐ setting
- ☐ historical fiction   ☐ plot
- ☐ realistic fiction   ☐ point of view
- ☐ fantasy   ☐ theme
- ☐ science fiction
- ☐ traditional lit
- ☐ poetry

Research Tools:
- ☐ Library Catalog
- ☐ Almanac
- ☐ Print Encyclopedia
- ☐ Print Reference
- ☒ Non-fiction Books
- ☒ WorldBook Online
- ☐ Britannica Online
- ☒ EBSCO
- ☐ ProQuest
- ☐ SIRS
- ☐ NewsBank
- ☐ LitFinder
- ☐ American Decades
- ☐ Gale Collection
- ☒ Wilson Biographies
- ☐ Web Search Engines

Production Tools:
- ☒ Word
- ☐ Desktop Pub
- ☐ KidPix
- ☐ Excel
- ☒ PowerPoint
- ☐ HyperStudio
- ☐ Kidspiration
- ☐ Inspiration
- ☐ iMovie
- ☐ Digital Camera
- ☐ Scanner
- ☐ Video camera
- ☐ Digital video
- ☐ Linear video

Benchmarks:
- ☐ e lib organization   ☐ print/elect reference
- ☐ e book parts   ☒ electronic indexes
- ☐ e info need   ☐ internet
- ☐ e keywords   ☐ evaluates info
- ☐ e table of contents   ☐ notetaking tech
- ☐ e index   ☐ other extraction tech
- ☐ e catalog   ☒ bibliographic citation
- ☐ e call numbers   ☐ graphic organizer
- ☐ e fact/fiction   ☐ outlining
- ☐ e main idea   ☒ creates product
- ☐ e notetaking   ☒ lit selection
- ☐ e "just right"   ☐ ethical use
- ☐ e text/visuals
- ☐ e lit type
- ☐ e lit elements
- ☐ e respects lib
- ☐ e citing sources
- ☐ e ethical tech use
- ☐ info need
- ☐ question/thesis
- ☒ possible sources
- ☒ keywords
- ☐ search strat/techniques
- ☐ operators
- ☐ navigation techniques
- ☐ catalog

10/29/2003

- How much collaboration is occurring between teachers and the library media specialist?
- What is the nature of assistance the library media specialist is providing to teachers?
- Are our scanners being used heavily? Will we need to add another one?
- Are we overusing PowerPoint and should we alert teachers to that?

Designing a database to collect and manage data about the program offers an efficient and systematic way of collecting evidence about the library media program. While a locally developed system for tracking library media activity has great advantages of tailoring to the local curriculum and local tools, a generic product can provide a useful way to collect and analyze data also. The commercial program Impact is available from LMC Source. This product provides a Microsoft Excel template for collecting data about program activity, recording it, and then reporting using a variety of charts and graphs. Whether one creates a locally designed database or adopts a commercial product, the data collected help inform goals for the next year (such as academic departments to be targeted, standards to be taught). It is difficult to imagine how one improves a program each year without collecting and analyzing data about program activity.

Besides collecting data of this sort, a brief survey at the end of a resource-based unit can provide further indication of how well the library media program is performing. Consider the following examples of survey questions:

- Were your students frustrated in searching for information for their assignment?
- What topics/questions went underresourced?
- Did your students have all the necessary information literacy skills to do their assignment?
- Did students have enough time in the library media center to complete their work?

By being involved in the evaluation of the library media program, stakeholders increase their understanding and ownership of the program. As results are analyzed, it is important that the stakeholders participate in identifying accomplishments to be recognized and in setting goals for continued improvement of the program. Participation in the analysis is the part that really provides a feeling of ownership. Finally, when stake-holders help report the results to the constituents (parent organizations, faculty, and staff, for example), they develop a sense of pride in their findings and enthusiasm for the next steps—and readily support allo-cating the resources needed to continue improvement.

The data collected to describe the library media program can func-tion for both formative and summative evaluation of the program. For-mative evaluation occurs frequently, and the findings facilitate making decisions about how to revise a program. By frequently reviewing data, the library media specialist can apply the findings to change aspects of the program. Summative evaluation is an end-point analysis of the ef-fectiveness of a program; it is the kind of process that often occurs in cycles, such as the accreditation cycle. Periodically, at summative evalu-ation points, such as accreditation or periodic district-level reviews, the accumulated data can provide a measure of the program's successes and weaknesses. By continually collecting and analyzing data, the op-portunity for continuous improvement presents itself. Too often, pro-gram performance is considered only when an event like reaccredita-tion stimulates schools to move into accountability or reporting mode. By developing a culture of continuous improvement, the library media program can make modifications frequently and respond to the needs of its clientele more readily.

BENCHMARKING

So far, evaluation has been discussed as an internal process within a school library media program. Looking beyond one's own setting can help identify growth opportunities. Benchmarking is a process of exam-ining a program internally, then searching for "best practices" in other organizations and adapting practices that promise to improve perfor-mance (Epper 1999). This strategy is grounded in the total quality man-agement movement and fits into the mode of continuous improvement. Here evaluation is not an event scheduled to occur periodically, but rather a way of operating all the time. The "other organizations" considered in benchmarking may be other similarly situated school library media pro-grams, or they might be organizations that share some aspect of the work of school library media centers. For example, Epper mentions South-west Airlines comparing notes with a pit crew of an Indy 500 race-car team to improve on-time departures. School library media specialists might look, for example, at college libraries for Web site design practices or at retail training programs for customer service excellence.

Finding "best practices" within school library media programs may also be an effective approach to benchmarking. The American Association of School Librarians (AASL) annually names "National School Library Media Programs of the Year." These programs exhibit "best practices" in school librarianship. Winners are announced each year at the American Library Association annual meeting, and information about the winners is available at the AASL Web site. Comparing the practices of these acclaimed programs to a local library media program can provide new targets or programming ideas.

Another type of comparison for benchmarking is to look at data on school library media programs as represented in survey results and compare those findings to the local program to measure status or progress. The National Center for Educational Statistics provides data from their "Schools and Staffing Survey" at its Web site (www.nces.ed.gov/surveys/libraries/school.asp). Tables in this report break out data by region, community type, school level, and enrollment to provide comparable settings for benchmarking. Increasingly, state data are becoming available and thus offer opportunities to benchmark a program. An advantage of state data is the comparability of budgeting methods and constraints within each state. Library Research Service provides links to several sets of state statistics at its Web site (www.lrs.org/School_stats.htm). Schools and school districts can compare themselves on the basis of data provided in these survey reports. One other source of comparative data is the biennial survey conducted by Marilyn Miller and published in *School Library Journal* (Miller 2001). While the sample surveyed for this report is of *School Library Journal* subscribers and so has some potential for bias, still the data can provide a benchmark against which to measure a program's own data.

Benchmarking involves looking for best practices, comparing the local program to those best practices, and identifying ways to improve local practice. It may involve comparing quantitative data or it may involve comparing practices. Either way, the results of benchmarking should be shared with stakeholders to help gain advocacy for program growth and development.

RUBRICS FOR PROGRAM EVALUATION

Program evaluation provides the opportunity to educate stakeholders about what the program is doing to support teaching and learning. Rubrics provide an excellent form for such a purpose because they describe a range of levels of quality in a performance. By providing rubrics on the various dimensions of a library media program, it becomes apparent where the strengths and weaknesses of the program are. More important, because of their descriptive nature, rubrics communicate a program's quality to those outside the library media profession. Far too many teachers, parents, and administrators have not seen the best quality in all aspects of the library media program. Rubrics can help them to extend their vision so that they can understand more clearly what the goals of the library media professional might be for the program.

In the previous chapter, rubrics are described as an effective way to assess student progress. They offer a description of good and less-than-good performance, and a scaled guide that gives a range of performance quality. For program evaluation, the rubric adds structure. The American Association of School Librarians (Adcock 1999) has published a set of rubrics based on the association's guidelines for library media programs, to guide program evaluation. These rubrics provide an excellent general profile for interpreting the association's guidelines.

Even more specific rubrics can provide guidance for evaluating a library media program. An important benefit of rubrics is their description of what a library media program could and should be, so more detailed description may be helpful, especially in settings where teachers and administrators are more naive about the potential for a program. Figure 13.2 presents rubrics for program evaluation, focused on information literacy, communication, reading, collection, technology, collaboration, scheduling, and climate. Within each of these dimensions are specific facets to be evaluated. Perhaps this set of rubrics will serve as a model and can be adapted for a program evaluation process that incorporates the priorities of other library media programs.

STAKEHOLDERS

Involving stakeholders in the library media program evaluation provides a way for the library media program to see itself as others see it and to communicate to others what the program does for the school. A

FIGURE 13.2
Rubrics for Program Evaluation

Information Literacy

Skills Curriculum	**Comprehensive.** A written curriculum guide, based on an information process model, contains a sequence of information seeking and using strategies, model lessons, and assessment strategies.	**In progress.** A written curriculum guide contains a sequence of information seeking and using strategies.	**Under development.** Plans exist for developing a formal curriculum guide.
Integration	**Integrated.** A matrix or map identifies where all information skills fit into classroom activities for introduction, elaboration, and reinforcement; lessons are taught in coordination with classroom activities.	**Ad hoc.** As teachers make assignments, information seeking and using strategies are taught in relation to the assignment.	**Isolated.** Information skills are taught sequentially without regard to classroom activities.

Communication

Principal	**Shared vision.** The principal envisions the library media program as an integral part of the school.	**Supportive.** The principal supports the library media program with resources and communications to constituencies.	**Passive.** The principal takes no action to support the library media program.
Parents	**Involved.** Parents participate in the library media program through volunteerism, committees, and programs.	**One-way.** Parents receive information from the library media program through newsletters and other communication media.	**Indirect.** Parents learn about the library media program through their children or classroom teachers.
Business	**Involved.** The library media program has active partnerships with businesses.	**Informative.** The library media program targets relevant information to local businesses, such as bookstores or electronics dealers.	**Indirect.** Businesses know about the library media program only from general school district communication.
Public Library	**Collaborative.** The school library media specialist and the public librarian communicate regularly and frequently about programs and resources.	**Informative.** The school library notifies the public library about specific programs or activities on an ad hoc basis.	**Indirect.** School and public libraries know about each other's programs and resources only through publicly disseminated communication.

FIGURE 13.2 (Cont.)

	Reading		
Classroom Support	**Integral.** The library media specialist meets with teachers as they plan and define the focus for thematic units and provides them with reading resources.	**Supportive.** The library media specialist identifies resources to support units and delivers them to teachers.	**Supplemental.** The library media specialist responds to specific requests from individual teachers by providing supplementary materials.
Materials Support	**Selective.** The library media specialist provides materials that meet exact specifications for the instructional focus, for appropriate levels of difficulty, and for high-quality standards.	**Expansive.** The library media specialist delivers whatever materials are available on the general topic of the unit.	**Self-help.** The library media specialist encourages teachers to visit the library media center and explore available materials.
Promotion	**Initiating.** The library media specialist promotes reading by initiating book talks and individualized reading guidance.	**Responsive.** The library media specialist supports students' interest in reading when asked.	**Passive.** The library media specialist sets up displays and provides book lists to support existing interest in reading.
	Continuous. Reading promotion is ongoing.	**Periodic.** Special short-term reading promotion activities occur.	**Intermittent.** Reading promotion primarily occurs as special events.
	Intrinsic. Activities to promote reading are grounded in intrinsic motivation (i.e., reading for the sake of enjoyment or information).	**Neutral.** Effort focuses on students continuing to read.	**Extrinsic.** Special reading promotions feature extrinsic rewards for students who read.

	Collection		
Collaboration	**Collaborative.** Decisions about collection priorities are made through collaboration between library media specialist and teachers.	**Consultative.** Teachers offer suggestions for collection development.	**Autocratic.** The library media specialist makes collection decisions independently.

FIGURE 13.2 (Cont.)

Curriculum Support	**Curriculum-based**. Curriculum support is a high priority for collection additions.	**Curriculum-related**. Curricular topics are considered in collection development, but not as a high priority.	**Balanced**. Balance is the highest priority in collection development.
Levels of Difficulty	**Client-based**. Level of difficulty responds to assessment of the local student clientele.	**Balanced**. A balance among easy and challenging materials is sought.	**Unheeded**. Criteria other than level of difficulty are considered.
Diversity	**Multicultural**. Cultural diversity is considered in collection development, including but not limited to cultural groups represented in the local population.	**Client-based**. Materials are selected to match those cultures represented in the school's population.	**Spontaneous** Multicultural materials are selected as they are requested but without specific planning.
Currency	**Current**. Collection is kept current by additions and weeding according to a regular schedule of review of the total collection.	**Mixed**. Some parts of the collection, particularly time-sensitive topics, are maintained by additions and weeding.	**Outdated**. Collection shows evidence of little or no weeding.
Adequacy	**Ample**. Collection has ample materials to meet the needs of its clientele.	**Adequate**. Collection can usually meet the basic needs of clientele.	**Inadequate**. Collection lacks materials for topics commonly investigated.
Quality	**Criteria-based**. Selection of materials is based on explicit criteria defined by quality, learning goals, and beliefs.	**Quality-based**. Selection is based on standards of quality defined by reviewing media.	**Demand-based**. Selection is based on what teachers and/or students request exclusively.

Technology

Technology Use	**High cognitive level**. Uses of technology cause students to work at Bloom's application level or higher.	**Low cognitive level**. Uses of technology require students to work at the knowledge or comprehension level.	**No cognitive criteria**. No criteria are applied for selection of technology uses based on cognitive level.

FIGURE 13.2 (Cont.)

Integration	**Full integration.** Uses of technology are chosen to expand existing curriculum goals.	**Aligned.** Uses of technology are connected to the curriculum.	**Isolated.** Technology applications are taught for their own sake.
Planning Process	**Formalized.** Planning for technology integration is ongoing and includes broad-based participation.	**Ad hoc.** When money is available, a planning committee convenes to decide how to spend it.	**Unilateral.** A single individual or a select few make decisions about technology.
Staff Development	**Comprehensive.** All staff members must meet a set of competencies for using technology.	**Adaptable.** Staff development includes use of applications that can be adapted to meet individual needs.	**Elective.** Staff members choose from a menu of technology training based on their own self-assessment or personal interest.
	Relevant. Staff development has direct application to the work of the staff members who participate.	**Need-driven.** Staff members seek out technology-related training as they identify a specific need.	**Basic.** Staff development focuses on the basics of how to operate equipment.
	Hands-on. Training is hands-on with modeling by instructors.	**Modeled.** Technology skills are taught by modeling.	**Theoretical.** Technology training is theoretical, without practical application opportunities.
	Ongoing. Support is readily available as staff members integrate new skills into their work.	**Intermittent.** Review sessions are offered periodically.	**One-time.** Training occurs at scheduled times and no ongoing assistance is conveniently available.
Budget	**Comprehensive.** The annual budget includes specific line items for training, new hardware, replacement hardware, hardware upgrades, repair, new software, software upgrades, supplies, and technical support staff.	**Basic.** Line items are included in the annual budget for hardware and software.	**Ad hoc.** As money becomes available, it is spent on technology.

FIGURE 13.2 (Cont.)

Hardware	**Focused critical mass.** As each technology application is recommended, the necessary critical mass of hardware is purchased.	**Scattered deployment.** Hardware is deployed to spread available resources throughout the school fairly rather than according to what critical mass is needed to meet a specific need effectively.	**Under-equipped.** Too little hardware is available to accomplish an identified goal.
Software	**Criteria-based.** Software selection is based on explicit criteria related to learning goals and beliefs.	**Quality-based.** Software selection is based on standards of quality as defined by reviewing media.	**Demand-based.** Software selection is based on what teachers and/or students request exclusively.
Policy	**Formalized.** Written policy exists for copyright, intellectual freedom in electronic environments, equity, privacy, and other technology-related concerns. These policies have Board approval and are reviewed systematically. They are communicated to all appropriate constituencies.	**Informal.** Policy decisions about technology-related issues have been discussed and agreed to, but are not formalized.	**In progress.** Policy for technology-related issues is under discussion.
Collaboration			
Team Roles	**Defined.** Members of the planning team, including the library media specialist, have clearly defined roles and expectations.	**Informal.** When a task needs to be done, whoever volunteers does it.	**Unassigned.** Conversations do not lead to assignment of tasks.
Level of Professional Complexity	**Professional.** The library media specialist collaborates with teachers to design instructional objectives, activities, and/or assessment and to identify resources.	**Supportive.** The library media specialist recommends and provides resources.	**"Go-fer."** The library media specialist provides resources requested by teachers.

FIGURE 13.2 (Cont.)

Scheduling

Integration	**Integrated**. Based on collaborative planning, classes are scheduled when activities require lessons on seeking or using information. Classes may come to the center several days in a row for information work.	**Reserved**. Each class has a block of time reserved for their use as needed.	**Fixed**. Each class comes to the library media center on a regular basis; lessons may or may not be aligned with classroom activities.
Access	**Open access**. Both library media center and classroom policies allow students to access the library media center whenever they need to.	**Controlled**. Students have regularly scheduled opportunities to access the library media center.	**Limited**. Students can access the library media center when their class is scheduled there.

Climate

Friendliness	**Inviting**. Students and staff feel welcome to use the library media center and show no hesitation to ask questions.	**Neutral**. The library media center has no affect—it is neither friendly nor unfriendly.	**Austere**. Students and staff use the library media center only when necessary; they are reluctant to seek assistance.
Productivity	**Productive**. Students are working productively at worthwhile tasks; a buzz of activity is evident as groups converse about their work.	**Silent**. Students work quietly and in isolation.	**Distracting**. Too much social activity distracts from work.
User Orientation	**Assistive**. Library media staff behaviors indicate to students and teachers that the library media center is a place for assistance and that they are important "customers."	**Passive**. Library media staff answer questions when asked, but do not initiate assistance.	**Supervisory**. Library media staff supervise behavior rather than provide information assistance.

teacher's perspective of the library media program is reminiscent of the fable of "The Blind Man and the Elephant"—each sees the program only through the filter of his or her interaction with it. As data are collected, it is instructive to share the "big picture" with faculty as well as administrators, boards, and parent groups. As others learn about the totality of the program, they become advocates to help it gain the resources it needs for development. In addition, they bring perspectives that can be constructive. In the end, program evaluation is aimed at helping the program become better at supporting the mission of the school—teaching and learning. Data collection and analysis followed by sharing and gathering observations from stakeholders is a process that can deliver the opportunity for the program to have an impact on students today and in the future.

ACTION STRATEGIES

Learning and Teaching

- Analyze students' assignments using Bloom's Taxonomy as a guide, to determine whether they are merely recalling information or instead are analyzing, synthesizing, and evaluating information.
- Maintain a file of units developed collaboratively by teachers and the library media specialist to document contributions to teaching and learning.

Program Administration

- Review a mission statement for the program.
- Review the professional literature to build background for assessing the existing program.
- Involve various constituencies (administrators, teachers, students, parents) in the evaluation process. Provide them with summaries of background information from the literature. Gather input from them using surveys, focus groups, or other input strategies.
- Design and use rubrics that describe the elements of the program in concrete language with emphasis on the program's impact on teaching and learning.
- Use a matrix or curriculum map to monitor teaching of information skills in the context of classroom curriculum.

- Collect data to profile the status of the program based on inputs (e.g., staff, facilities, access, resource collection, equipment) and outputs (e.g., circulation, classes, staff development, teacher consultation, student production) and compare them to data from other programs in the state or nation.
- Consider successful organizations beyond school library media programs—what aspects of their success might be relevant to the library media program? Adapt these "best practices" to the school library media program.
- Develop new goals for the program based on collected data and on rubric-based assessment.
- Identify needed inputs for accomplishment of new goals.

SCENARIO FOR DISCUSSION

The text suggests benchmarking as a strategy for evaluating a program, and recommends "stretching" to improve based on best practices exhibited elsewhere. List some organizations outside of the school library media programs whose best practices might be adapted to the library media program. Identify the practices worth considering. How might the library media specialist adapt these best practices to the school library media program?

REFERENCES

Adcock, D. (1999). *A Planning Guide for Information Power: Building Partnerships for Learning with School Library Media Program Rubric for the 21st Century.* Chicago: American Association of School Librarians/American Library Association.

Barron, D. D. (1987, March). "Communicating What SLM Specialists Do: The Evaluation Process." *School Library Journal 33* (7): 95–99.

Epper, R. M. (1999, November/December). "Applying Benchmarking to Higher Education: Some Lessons from Experience." *Change 31* (6): 224–231.

Everhart, N. (2003, March). "Evaluation of School Library Media Centers: Demonstrating Quality." *Library Media Connection 21* (6): 14–19.

Miller, M. (2001, October). "New Money, Old Books." *School Library Journal 47* (10): 50–60.

Yesner, B. L. and H. L. Jay (1997). *Operating and Evaluating School Library Media Programs: A Handbook for Administrators and Librarians.* New York: Neal-Schuman.

Chapter 14

Leadership

This chapter:

- defines leadership attributes for library media specialists
- discusses "leading from the middle"
- incorporates the notion of strategy into leadership
- describes the role of library media specialists in mentoring within the profession

Throughout this book, library media specialists are portrayed as playing leadership roles in their schools. They bring to the school a vision for the ways in which the library media program intersects with all aspects of the school community and curriculum. They work collegially with teachers, administrators, staff, and parents. They bring expertise in literacy, the information-seeking process, and applications of technology appropriate for their settings. It is fitting to end this book with a chapter that makes explicit the leadership characteristics of the library media profession.

LEADERSHIP ATTRIBUTES

Warren Bennis (1999) promulgates a set of traits for successful leaders in business. As shown below, these characteristics can apply also to library media specialists:

- *Technical competence:* Library media specialists have knowledge of information organization, teaching, management, and resources. Their set of skills and knowledge are unique in their schools. Technical competence evidences itself in a variety of specialized knowledge and skill sets. Certainly knowledge of information technology is foremost here; this involves current awareness of Internet resources that meet the educational and information needs of the school. It requires ability to use and teach others to use an array of hardware and software for learning and productivity. Technical knowledge also refers to knowledge about information organization and access; this reaches in various directions, including knowledge of cataloging of physical resources as well as knowledge of the structure of online databases in order to teach efficient access skills. Technical knowledge here can also include knowledge of literature and information resources and the ability to engage students with a variety of texts that will inform and inspire them.
- *Conceptual skill:* Library media specialists have considerable procedural knowledge, but they also think in terms of principles and concepts. Principles of organization, access, confidentiality, and ethical use of information guide their policymaking, while conceptual understanding of information systems informs their resource management and information dissemination. Conceptual skill extends also to the nature of inquiry—what does it mean to engage in the inquiry process and how do students develop appropriate mental models of that process?
- *People skills:* Library media specialists know they cannot be successful in isolation. Library media specialists communicate, inspire, and delegate. They establish collaborative networks within their local learning community. Teachers and principals are primary among the people with whom library media specialists must collaborate. Research consistently indicates that preservice programs for both teachers and school administrators fail to address the role of library media specialists (Roberson, Applin, and Schweinle, 2005). Hence, if they will be partners with library media specialists, they must learn about the benefits of such collaborations once they are in practice, and only library media specialists can teach them. Developing positive relationship with these colleagues will require excellent interpersonal skills characterized by initiative, careful listening, empathy, and clear communication.

- *Judgment*: As managers of substantial space and resources, library media specialists are called on to make decisions promptly, even with imperfect data. They make daily decisions regarding purchasing, resource allocation, scheduling, work assignments, and instruction. To the extent possible, these decisions are informed by data, but in their real world it is rare that data are so clear and comprehensive as to remove the need for judgment calls. Limitations on resources will routinely require choices and justification for those choices.
- *Character:* Grounded in the foundations of librarianship, library media specialists are inspired by a set of beliefs that guide behavior. These beliefs are related to principles of librarianship as well as principles of the education profession. Primary among these beliefs are commitment to open access to information, confidentiality for information users, affirmation of intellectual property rights, and equity.

Steven Covey (1990) speaks of the circle of influence as defining the limits around those things that a person can control. Within one's circle of influence are one's own thoughts and behaviors. Because library media specialists enjoy a comprehensive view of the school, it is often tempting to extend one's reach beyond that circle of influence. Leaders know and respect the limits of their circles of influence.

More important, leaders act from an internal locus of control. This orientation suggests that a person has the power to control the outcome of his or her own actions. By contrast, people whose orientation is an external locus of control frequently look outside themselves to explain their situation. Externally oriented library media specialists might contend, for example, that they cannot teach information literacy skills because the teachers will not cooperate, or the principal does not give adequate support, or the facility does not accommodate instruction, or some other external barrier prevents their success. Internally oriented library media specialists, on the other hand, will listen to teachers' concerns and find alternative ways to schedule the teaching or organize lessons to make it work for the students' sake. In other words, they will look within their circle of influence for solutions. They embrace the responsibility to make good things happen in their schools. Locus-of-control orientation is the difference between saying "I can find alternatives or compromises" and "There is nothing I can do." Leaders are can-do people who look to themselves to make programs great and inspire others to join in the enterprise.

Gary Hartzell (2000) discusses the importance of being proactive. He acknowledges that one's work environment can influence the maximal level of job performance, but he quotes J. M. Crant, a psychologist, who states:

> The notion of proactivity argues that we can intentionally and directly influence these and other elements and by doing so influence and enhance our chances of being successful in our jobs. (Crant, as cited in Hartzell 2000, p. 15)

Hartzell suggests that proactive people look for change opportunities, they anticipate and prevent problems, and they take action and tend to persevere. All of these behaviors imply an internal locus of control—a belief that the power to make things work lies within and the external environment can be influenced.

In *Good to Great*, Jim Collins (2001) analyzes why some companies "make the leap" from good companies to great companies. Library media specialists who aspire to lead "great" programs can benefit from keeping in mind two bits of advice resulting from Collins's analysis:

- Understand what you can and cannot be best at. The library media profession calls for diverse skill sets that include knowledge of the literature appropriate for the ages of students served, skill in technology applications, knowledge of information organization systems, and teaching aptitude. Clearly, each library media specialist has special strengths in some areas of expertise. Leaders will work to be the best at those areas, and strive to be as good in other areas as is reasonable. Rare is the library media specialist who is a true expert in all dimensions of the field; the challenge is to pursue to the maximum what one has aptitude for and to strive for acceptable performance in the other aspects of the field.
- Pursue what you are deeply passionate about. Passion is a word often associated with leadership. Soul searching to determine where one's passion lies is a first step toward becoming a leader—whether that passion is the gratifying feeling of seeing a student learn something new, or the effect of a literary work, or the power of technology to communicate information, or any other aspect of the profession. While the library media program is comprehensive and

embraces many dimensions, the passion for one aspect of the field will generate the intense enthusiasm to invigorate and inspire students and to keep oneself energized. This is not to say that all other aspects can be ignored, but acknowledging and pursuing one's passion can help sustain one's own energy as a leader.

A library media specialist who intends to take a leadership role must exhibit a set of critical skills and understandings that begin with a vision. Such a vision portrays the intent of the library media program in the context of the overall school curriculum. Fullan (1996) suggests three attributes for a sound vision: "sharedness" (the degree to which it is shared), "concreteness" (the degree to which people have some concrete image of what it will look like) and "clarity" (the degree to which people are skilled in carrying it out). To make that vision real requires collaborative skills that include the ability to communicate effectively with others, to listen actively, to negotiate, and to earn the professional confidence of colleagues. While these "people skills" are important for leadership, technical competence is essential as well; just getting along is not enough—expertise matters. For the library media specialist these technical skills include the ability to organize information sources effectively and to use information technology efficiently. This technical knowledge must be grounded in conceptual understandings of information access, criteria for quality in both information and literary resources, and teaching and learning theoretical constructs and their application to the local setting. These skills and understandings can be perceived as radiating from the vision, as illustrated in Figure 14.1.

LEADING FROM THE MIDDLE

Lao Tzu, a Chinese Taoist philosopher said, "When the best leader's work is done, the people say, 'We did it ourselves.'" Schools are collaborative environments and library media specialists can succeed only when they work collegially with the other educators in their organizations. A principal holds a position of ex officio leadership in the school. The position innately holds power and demands followership among the rest of the school community. However, a library media specialist leads more often through influence; the position he or she holds, while likely to be unique in the building, is collegial, not superior to the rest of the faculty.

Having influence requires establishing one's expertise, working

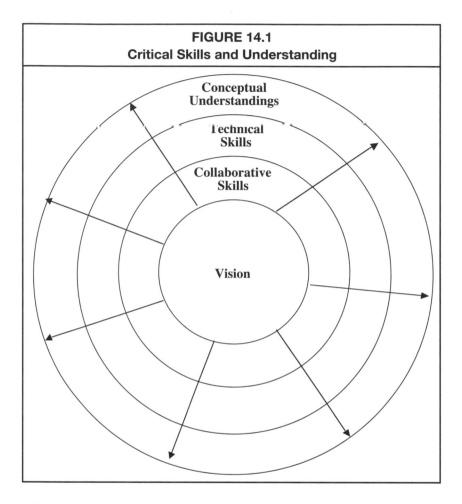

FIGURE 14.1
Critical Skills and Understanding

collegially with others, articulating one's ideas clearly, maintaining a good "say-do" ratio (one does what one says one will do), and establishing processes for continuous reflection and assessment.

To substantiate expertise, the library media specialist must demonstrate what he or she knows and can do, whether it is in the domain of literature, teaching, educational technology, or information seeking. No teachers will accept the influence of a colleague when they lack confidence in that person's expertise. Because the field of library media is diverse and changing, library media specialists must engage in constant learning. This requires reading the literature of the relevant age groups, developing new technology skills as the need emerges, keeping abreast of new information resources, and maintaining awareness of the current professional literature. Leaders are, in Covey's (1990) language, always "sharpening the saw." Library media specialists who aspire to be leaders are always looking for learning opportunities to expand and update their expertise.

Working collegially requires that library media specialists engage in active listening and seek connections between the school's mission and goals and those of the library media program. An opportunistic disposition allows the library media specialist to watch for ways to integrate the library media program into the academic program. By modeling best practices with technology or initiating conversations about new resources, library media specialists can bring their special expertise to bear on curriculum and instruction.

Clear and articulate communication is a key element in asserting leadership among colleagues. Maintaining familiarity with the language of the classroom will enhance dialogue with teachers. This requires reading in the professional literature of teachers and attending to state and national mandates that dictate the language of educational accountability.

The "say-do" ratio compares what one says and what one does. To be perceived as a leader among one's colleagues, it is essential that this ratio be high—that we can and do carry out what we promise. For example, the information literacy curriculum needs to be articulated and student performance needs to be assessed against defined benchmarks. The results of this assessment need to be reported to teachers and administrators. This level of accountability will garner the respect necessary for the library media professional to have influence.

Finally, reflection and self-assessment provide the avenue for continuous improvement. All aspects of the library media program benefit from systematic review. Library media specialists gain the respect of their colleagues when they articulate a disposition of continuously seeking to get better—whether it is improving resources, improving lessons, or improving the environment of the library media center. By adhering to the value of feedback and revision, the library media program sets a standard worthy of respect and confidence.

In order to lead from the middle, library media specialists must put themselves into influential positions. This requires, for example, volunteering to serve on curriculum committees or faculty leadership teams. The ability to articulate why the library media specialist belongs on such committees is important in many situations if no precedent exists for such leadership involvement. The library media specialist can readily point out that he or she has a unique vantage point in the school as a result of working with all students and all teachers. This vantage point can be valuable to almost any committee. Furthermore, the library media specialist's expertise in the area of technology can be a valuable asset in many situations. In addition, the library media specialist is ready to serve as "resourcer" for any group that will need information gathering. Helping the principal begin to see the benefits of library media involvement in school decision-making groups is a first step toward exerting influence and "leading from the middle."

STRATEGIC LEADERSHIP

"Strategic" is a word often used to describe military operations where the key steps are anticipating what needs to happen, devising a plan to set the course of action, and organizing resources to carry out the plan for success. Critical attributes include looking to a desirable future (vision), planning the steps for attaining that future (action planning), and assessing progress (benchmarks and outcomes). Effective library media programs are ever-changing, and setting the course for change requires strategic thinking and strategic leadership. Reeves (2002) defines strategic leadership as the simultaneous act of executing, evaluating, and reformulating strategies, and focusing organizational energy and resources on the most effective strategies. Since it is likely that teachers and administrators have not personally experienced the kind of library media program called for in national guidelines, the library media specialist must be proactive in articulating a vision for the library media program.

A vision is a clear mental picture of a desired future. A vision needs to be easily perceived and clearly communicated. A library media center might be a resource-filled center for teaching and learning. Such a vision is quite different from a storehouse of educational resources. It might be the academic center for the school; that is quite a different vision from an academic support program. The library media specialist is in the best position to articulate a vision for the program and communicate it to others. Close behind development of a vision comes the need to articulate a mission statement for the library media program. While this statement can be developed collaboratively with other educators in the school, the leadership for its development comes from the library media specialist. The mission statement will provide a focus for developing the goals and objectives of the program. Again, these goals must then align with the school's mission and goals in order to connect the library media program with its constituency.

Strategic leadership requires setting standards for performance and measuring performance against those standards. When teachers, administrators, students, and parents participate in setting direction, they are more likely to participate in carrying out the plan and helping to find the resources to make progress.

Another aspect of strategic leadership is opportunism. A strategic leader is in a state of readiness—ready to seize opportunities as they arise. Davies (2003) describes strategic leaders as having the ability to define the critical moment for moving in new directions or interventions. When a school staff begins discussion of a new curriculum initiative—character education or integrated mathematics, for example—the strategic leader is ready to assert how the library media program fits into that initiative. This requires a strategic mind-set, calling for the library media specialist to be active in committees, task forces, brainstorming sessions, leadership teams, or whatever forms idea-generating groups take within the school. A disposition to create opportunities for involvement in the larger school community characterizes leading school library media specialists. In football parlance, the winning coach or the effective leader is not bound to the playbook but is ready to go with the "audible" play or formation when the situation arises. Some people attribute success to luck or serendipity (Blanchard and Shula 2002). The school of strategic leadership would say, however, that people create their own luck or seize the opportunities that serendipity offers.

REFLECTION

Effective leaders reflect periodically on progress made and goals yet to be met. At least once a year it is worthwhile to ask three questions:

1. What will I do differently from what I did last year?
2. What will I stop doing that I did last year?
3. How and when will I know that I am making progress?

Journaling is a strategy that helps sustain the energy that leadership demands. It requires discipline to journal daily, but as with physical workouts, once one establishes the habit, it simply becomes a part of the daily routine and it becomes hard to imagine a day without the ritual. To get started, a leadership journal entry might simply ask each day:

- What did I learn today?
- Whom did I nurture today?
- What challenge did I confront today?
- How did I make a positive difference today?

MENTORING

The field of library media offers many opportunities to challenge one-self. It is important that library media professionals share their enthusiasm for their chosen field with others and encourage excellent teachers to consider joining the profession. Similarly, library media specialists can mentor their own students toward the information professions by showing enthusiasm for what they do, and by encouraging students to consider the career opportunities the field offers in schools and in other settings as well. For the field to flourish, it must attract bright newcomers, and those working in the profession are best positioned to encourage them.

NATIONAL BOARD FOR PROFESSIONAL TEACHING STANDARDS

Established in 1987, the National Board for Professional Teaching Standards (NBPTS) offers National Board Certification that attests to a teacher's high-level skills and ability to satisfy rigorous professional teaching standards. NBPTS has established a set of standards for earning designation as a board certified library media specialist. The standards are organized around what library media specialists know, what they do, and how they grow as professionals. Candidates are required to provide evidence of their work within each of these areas of the standards. The process is rigorous, but the result is certification as a professional leader in a context well respected throughout the education profession. Details are available at (National Board for Professional Teaching Standards, accessed 2008).

While board certification is holistically aimed at leadership, in addition, the standards have a focus area in Standard X related to leadership as well. Here a library media specialist is described as an instructional leader who "forge[s] greater opportunities for learners" (National Board for Professional Teaching Standards, accessed 2008, p. 43). Indeed, such a description summarizes the role of library media specialists. Library media specialists carry out that role by taking initiative, partnering with other educators, reflecting on professional practices, and assessing and evaluating. They communicate with stakeholders in their community, manage staff and resources, and use research to support programs for which they advocate. These are the behaviors of leaders in the library media profession. The NBPTS certification process is a voluntary opportunity for an experienced library media specialist to take the challenge of examining his or her professional practice, measuring it against rigorous standards, and attaining affirmation as a professional leader.

ACTION STRATEGIES

Learning and Teaching

- Identify your special expertise—e.g., literature, technology, information searching—and "play" to that strength in developing the library media program to establish your expertise with teachers. Develop your less dominant areas of expertise to fit the needs of your constituencies.

Information Access

- Increase the visibility of the library with an easily navigable library home Web page; include the library media program's vision and mission statement on the page. Advocate high-profile linking from the school's home page to the library page.

Program Management

- Involve stakeholders in strategic planning for the library media program.
- Add information about careers in librarianship to the library's home page.
- Volunteer to be on building-wide committees—school improvement plan team, faculty council, technology team, parent advisory

committee, curriculum council. Then, be an active participant. Listen well, and volunteer to be the note taker/reporter. Write up and distribute the minutes promptly. Whatever the actual work of the committee (drafting/writing goals, conducting surveys, putting together slides, etc.), volunteer to do it. Thoughtfully offer up your viewpoint—which is slightly more global than that of most classroom teachers. Don't be self-serving. Make everything look good (professional). Taking on extra work shows that you care about the school, not just your library media program.

SCENARIO FOR DISCUSSION

At the Ford Elementary School, classroom teachers are concerned about their students selecting books at their own reading level. The library media specialist teaches students various strategies for selecting books at the appropriate level. One example is the "five finger test" (reading the first two pages of the book and putting up a finger each time they encounter a word they do not know). However, the teachers want the books in the library media center to be marked with their reading levels according to a readability test so that they can direct a student to choose a book at a specific level. The library media specialist has some concerns about this strategy—she has reservations about the reliability of readability level, she is concerned that this approach will limit selection, and she wants students to learn to make independent decisions as they select books. The text addresses the fact that library media specialists "lead from the middle" with influence rather than authority in many situations. How can the library media specialist influence this situation and maintain a good working relationship with teachers?

REFERENCES

Bennis, W. (1999, Spring). "The Leadership Advantage." *Leader to Leader*. Retrieved April 1, 2004, from www.pfdf.org/leaderbooks/l2l/spring99/bennis.html.

Blanchard, K. and D. Shula (2002). *The Little Book of Coaching*. New York: HarperBusiness.

Collins, J. (2001). *Good to Great: Why Some Companies Make the Leap and Others Don't*. New York: Harper Collins.

Covey, S. (1990). *The Seven Habits of Highly Effective People.* New York: Simon and Schuster.

Davies, B. (2003). "Rethinking Strategy and Strategic Leadership in Schools." *Educational Management & Administration 31* (3): 295–312.

Fullan, M. (1996). "Professional Culture and Educational Change." *School Psychology Review 25* (4): 496–500.

Hartzell, G. (2000, March/April). "Being Proactive," *Book Report 18* (5): 14–19.

National Board for Professional Teaching Standards. *Library Media/Early Childhood Through Young Adulthood.* Accessed February 19, 2008, at www.nbpts.org/for_candidates/certificate_areas1?ID=19&x=43&y=12.

Reeves, D. B. (2002) *The Daily Discipline of Leadership: How to Improve Students' Achievement, Staff Motivation, and Personal Organization.* San Francisco: Jossey-Bass.

Roberson, T., M. Applin, and W. Schweinle (2005). "School Libraries Impact Upon Students Achievement and School Professionals' Attitudes That Influence Use of Library Programs." *Research for Educational Reform 10* (1): 45–52.

For Further Reading

This list is a selective compilation of books for enriching the professional collection of the school library media center. The resources were selected specifically to facilitate the connection between the library media program and its educational community.

STUDENTS

Goslin, David A. (2003). *Engaging Minds: Motivation & Learning in America's Schools.* **Lanham, MD: Scarecrow.** Analysis of the characteristics of life for today's youth and the implications for motivating them to invest and sustain the effort that learning requires.

Immroth, B. and de la Peña McCook, K. (2000). *Library Services to Youth of Hispanic Heritage.* **Jefferson, NC: McFarland.** Discusses demographics outstanding literature, information needs of migrant workers, and workshops and services for parents, teens, and children.

Kohn, A. (1993). *Punished by Rewards: The Trouble with Gold Stars, Incentive Plans, A's, Praise, and Other Bribes.* **New York: Houghton Mifflin.** Discussion of the dangers of extrinsic rewards.

Wesson, C. and Keefe, M. J., eds. (1995). *Serving Special Needs Students in the School Library Media Center.* **Westport, CT: Greenwood Press.** Organized according to the three roles of the library media specialist: teacher, information specialist, and consultant, strategies for supporting students with special needs are described.

CURRICULUM AND INSTRUCTION

Kohn, A. (1999). *The Schools Our Children Deserve.* **New York: Houghton Mifflin.** Well researched, this book makes the case for applying what researchers know about learning in contrast to political rhetoric about what is best for American education.

Wiggins, G. and McTighe, J. (1998). *Understanding by Design.* **Alexandria, VA: Association for Supervision and Curriculum Development.** Raises important questions about the design of curriculum such as: How do we pose essential questions that lead to deep learning? How can we design curriculum to engage students in the facets of understanding: explanation, interpretation, application, perspective, empathy, and self-knowledge?

PRINCIPAL

Farmer, L. (2007). *Collaborating with Administrators and Educational Support Staff.* **New York: Neal-Schuman.** Recommendations for ways of working with administrators at all levels as well as specialized staff in technology, special education, and curriculum leaders.

Wilson P. P. and Lyders, J. A. (2001). *Leadership for Today's School Library: A Handbook for the Library Media Specialist and the School Principal.* **Westport, CT: Greenwood Press.** Topics included are building rapport, communication, assessing/evaluating, working with teachers, strategic planning, technology decisions, and community involvement.

COMMUNITY

Jones, P. and Shoemaker, J. (2001). *Do It Right! Best Practices for Serving Young Adults in School and Public Libraries.* **New York: Neal-Schuman.** In the first half of the book, Shoemaker concentrates on the school library media center, while in the second half Jones addresses working with young adults in the public library.

Lukenbill, W. B. (2004). *Community Resources in the School Library Media Center.* **Westport, CT: Libraries Unlimited.** Step-by-step guidance for integrating community resources into the school library media program.

COLLABORATION

Buzzeo, T. (2002). *Collaborating to Meet Standards: Teacher/Librarian Partnerships for 7–12* . **Worthington, OH: Linworth.** Describes the ideals of collaboration and some of the variations found in schools. A template for use in planning collaborative units is included as well as 19 collaborative units, including samples of task analysis activities for students, interviewing guides, and rubrics.

Kearney, Carol A. (2000). *Curriculum Partner: Redefining the Role of the Library Media Specialist.* **Westport, CT: Greenwood Press.** Examines how the library media specialist works as a curriculum partner with teachers and administrators.

Miller, D. (2004). *The Standards-Based Integrated Library: A Collaborative Approach for Aligning the Library Program with the Classroom Curriculum,* **2nd Edition. Worthington, OH: Linworth.** Presents the library media specialist and teacher working as full teaching partners to create a collaborative atmosphere for student success. Incorporates information literacy and content standards and helps to create multidisciplinary lessons that are inquiry-based and interactive.

SCHEDULING

Ohlrich, K. B. (2001). *Making Flexible Access and Flexible Scheduling Work Today.* **Englewood, CO: Libraries Unlimited.** Provides justification for this type of scheduling with study results and statistics, and outlines ways to plan and implement such programs.

Shaw, M. K. (1999). *Block Scheduling and Its Impact on the School Library Media Center.* **Westport, CT: Greenwood Press.** A comprehensive guide for library media specialists moving to block scheduling. Includes experiences of twelve secondary school libraries that have moved to block scheduling. Discusses planning, networking, curriculum and instruction, professional development, technology, and assessment.

COLLECTION

Lowe, Karen (2001). *Resource Alignment: Providing Curriculum Support in the School Library Media Center.* **Millers Creek, NC: Bea-**

con Consulting. Steps and strategies for honing a collection that is aligned with curriculum standards.

Kerby, Mona (2006). *Collection Development for the School Library Media Program: A Beginner's Guide*. Chicago: American Library Association. Practical and relevant information about collection development issues such as policies, selection criteria and sources, ordering, weeding, and evaluation.

LITERACY

Bush, Gail (2005). *Every Student Reads: Collaboration and Reading to Learn Reading*. Chicago: American Library Association. Reading strategies geared for elementary and secondary students.

Day, J. P., ed. (2002). *Moving Forward with Literature Circles: How to Plan, Manage, and Evaluate Literature Circles That Deepen Understanding and Foster a Love of Reading*. New York: Scholastic Professional Books. Provides advice on how to plan, manage, and evaluate literature circles as well as relating the practice to what we know about developing literacy.

McCabe, J. (2003). *The Wasted Years: American Youth, Race, and the Literacy Gap*. Lanham, MD: Scarecrow Press. Includes the voices of practitioners and researchers in an attempt to identify the factors that are perpetuating the literacy gap in American secondary schools.

Pitcher, S. and Mackey, B. (2004). *Collaborating for Real Literacy: Librarian, Teacher, and Principal*. Worthington, OH: Linworth. Provides a definition of literacy and explores scaffolding. Includes multicultural issues, comprehensive instruction, integration of reading and writing, and assessment.

TECHNOLOGY

Hopkins, J. (2004). *Assistive Technology: An Introductory Guide for K–12 Library Media Specialists*. Worthington, OH: Linworth. Explains how to make your library readily available to every student, from using the accessibility features built into Microsoft Windows, to purchasing a wide range of the newest assistive technologies.

Schrock, K. (2000). *The Technology Connection: Building a Successful Library Media Program*. Worthington, OH: Linworth. Includes guidelines for evaluating Web pages, rubrics for scoring multimedia projects, using the Internet, building influence in the school library, technology integration, and copyright issues.

INFORMATION LITERACY

Conley, D. (2005). *College Knowledge.* San Fancisco: Jossey-Bass. Aimed at high school students and teachers, this book provides standards for student success in higher education in English, mathematics, natural sciences, social sciences, second languages, and the arts. The English and social sciences include research skills for those areas.

Donham, J., Kuhlthau, C. C., Bishop, K., and Oberg, D. (2001). *Inquiry-Based Learning.* Worthington, OH: Linworth. Explores strategies for placing emphasis on student-directed inquiry in classroom-generated research activities.

Kuhlthau, Carl C., Maniotes, L. K., and Caspari, A . K. (2007). *Guided Inquiry: Learning in the 21st Century.* Westport, CT: Libraries Unlimited. Kuhlthau's model in the context of constructivism and inquiry-based learning.

ASSESSMENT

Harada, V. and Yoshina. J. (2005). *Assessing Learning: Librarians and Teachers as Partners.* Westport, CT: Libraries Unlimited. A practical guide that describes a variety of assessment tools and their appropriate applications to information literacy learning.

Joyce, M. and Tallman, J. (1996). *Making the Writing and Research Connection with the I-Search Process: A How-To-Do-It Manual for Teachers and School Librarians.* New York: Neal-Schuman. Strategies for using the I-Search process and incorporating it into the information literacy curriculum.

Marzano, R. J., Pickering, D., and McTighe, J. (1993). *Assessing Student Outcomes: Performance Assessment Using the Dimensions of Learning Model.* Alexandria, VA: Association for Supervision and Curriculum Development. A summary of the use of rubrics for assessing students' performances. Includes model sets of rubrics for such dimensions as complex thinking and information processing.

PROGRAM EVALUATION

Bradburn, F. B. (1999). *Output Measures for School Library Media Programs*. New York: Neal-Schuman. Quantitative measures for gathering evidence for evaluation of the library media program. Suggestions for ways to use data to gain program support.

Church, A. P. (2003). *Leverage Your Libraries to Raise Test Scores: A Guide for Library Media Specialists, Principals, Teachers, and Parents*. Worthington, OH: Linworth. Explains major studies' findings and the implications for instruction, and examines elements of successful media programs.

LEADERSHIP

Langford, M. (2006). *Leadership and the School Librarian: Essays from Leaders in the Field*. Worthington, OH: Linworth. A description of the leadership roles of school library professionals and the skills and knowledge necessary to accomplish them.

Reeves, D. B. (2002). *The Daily Discipline of Leadership: How to Improve Students Achievement, Staff Motivation, and Personal Organization*. San Francisco: Jossey-Bass. Realistic advice about how to be a strategic leader. Key steps include assessment and reflection.

Author Index

Subject Index

About the Author

Jean Donham directs the library at Wartburg College in Waverly, Iowa, where she also holds an appointment as Professor of Education. Previously she directed the library at Cornell College, Mount Vernon, Iowa. Prior to her appointment there, she was a tenured member of the faculty in the School of Library and Information Science at The University of Iowa. She served as district coordinator for library media and technology in the Iowa City Community School District for 13 years. Author of numerous professional articles, Dr. Donham has been a presenter at national, regional, and state conferences. Active in the Iowa Association of School Librarians, she was the first recipient of that organization's Media Professional of the Year. In addition, she served as a member of the board for the American Association of School Librarians. She holds a master's degree in library and information studies from the University of Maryland and a PhD in educational administration from The University of Iowa.